# WINNING DECLARER PLAY

♠

♡

# WINNING

# DECLARER PLAY

*by Dorothy Hayden*          ◇

♣

HARPER & ROW, PUBLISHERS

NEW YORK, EVANSTON, AND LONDON

1817

To my parents

# Contents

# *Foreword*

IT FLATTERS THE MALE ego to consider women inferior as bridge players. The many jokes about mixed-pair bridge events bear eloquent testimony to this. But it is an attitude for which I hold but little brief.

For many years my favorite partner was a woman, Helen Sobel Smith. Helen became the first woman ever to represent her country in the Bermuda Bowl event, the world championship of bridge. Only one other woman has ever achieved this honor, and that is Dorothy Hayden.

Dorothy's record in national and international events is outstanding, and the success of her first book, *Bid Better, Play Better*, is proof of her ability to express herself on paper—no easy feat for the bridge expert.

Bridge is not really a difficult game to play well. The expert does not have some strange power that sets him apart from Mr. Smith or Mrs. Jones. He has merely learned to apply logical thinking at the bridge table. The apparently wondrous feats of the maestro—dropping a singleton king offside, a first-round finesse for the jack, etc.—are all the result of information carefully gleaned from the bidding and play to that point.

With a little bit of application, you too can learn to bring off these coups. In her easy style, highlighted by flashes of humor, Dorothy Hayden carefully dissects the characteristics of a bridge expert's game and places them before you in a concise yet thorough manner.

This book may not make you into an expert overnight, but a careful reading will certainly improve your game.

CHARLES H. GOREN

# PART I ♠ ♡ ◊ ♣ ELEMENTARY

# 1

## Card Combinations

BEFORE IT IS possible to become a good declarer, it is necessary to understand the basic card combinations. Although there are hundreds of them, ranging from elementary through intermediate to advanced, only three simple techniques are involved in their handling:

1. leading toward an honor
2. finessing
3. ducking

Before we discuss advanced combinations, look at the following elementary examples of each technique.

### Leading Toward an Honor

DUMMY
K 7

WEST                    EAST
A 10 9 5 3              Q J 6 2

DECLARER
8 4

If declarer wishes to take a trick in this suit, he naturally must

1

lead a small card from his hand toward dummy's king in the hope that West has the ace.

### The Simple Finesse

DUMMY
A Q

WEST
K J 9 5 3

EAST
10 7 6 2

DECLARER
7 6

In order to make two tricks in this suit, declarer must lead a small card from his hand, planning to play the queen from dummy. He will make two tricks any time West has been dealt the king.

### Ducking

DUMMY
A K 5 4 3 2

WEST
Q 10 9

EAST
J 8

DECLARER
7 6

The contract is no-trump, and dummy has no outside entries. Declarer can make five tricks in this suit by playing a small card from each hand on the first trick. By "ducking" this first trick to the opponents, he establishes five tricks for himself any time the opponents' cards are divided 3–2.

Here are a number of representative card combinations of varying degrees of difficulty. How many do you thoroughly understand? (Suggestion: it may help to follow some of the harder combinations if you actually use the thirteen cards of a suit and lay them out as shown.)

*Combination 1*

DUMMY

A J 10

WEST
?

EAST
?

YOU
4 3 2

You need two tricks from this combination. How do you play, and what are your chances of success?

*Answer:* The king and queen are both missing, and you must hope that West has at least one of them. Lead a small card from your hand, and if West plays small, insert the ten (or jack). East will probably take this with either the king or the queen. When you regain the lead, play another small card from your hand. If West plays small, finesse again. There are four material situations which can exist. West can have (1) the king, (2) the queen, (3) both the king and the queen, (4) neither the king nor the queen. You will succeed in making two tricks in the first three cases and you will fail in the fourth. Thus your chances are about three out of four.

*Combination 2*

DUMMY

Q 5 4

WEST
?

EAST
?

YOU
A 6 2

What is the correct way to play for two tricks with this combination?

*Answer:* Lead a small card from your hand toward the queen. You will make two tricks any time West was dealt the king. As West will have the king half the time, your chances of success are 50 per cent.

Beginners have a tendency to lead the queen from dummy with this holding. This is what is known as a "nothing" play, because it has zero chance of success against correct defense. East simply covers the queen with the king if he has it and declarer can never make more than one trick.

Notice that it would be proper to lead the queen if dummy also held the jack:

DUMMY

Q J 4

YOU

A 6 2

Now declarer is guaranteed to make two tricks in the suit whichever way he plays. If he wants to try to make two tricks without surrendering the lead he should play the queen from dummy and take a simple finesse.

*Combination 3*

DUMMY

K J 10

WEST          EAST

?                 ?

YOU

4 3 2

How do you play to make two tricks with this holding?

*Answer:* In this case it doesn't matter who has the ace. You must lose a trick to that card in any event. But you can avoid losing to the queen if it is in the West hand. Lead small from your hand and finesse the ten or the jack from dummy. If this is successful, you'll eventually return to your hand and repeat the finesse.

*Combination 4*

DUMMY

A Q 9

WEST          EAST

?                 ?

YOU

7 5 2

What is the best method of developing two tricks here?

*Answer:* The average declarer leads a small card from his hand

and finesses the queen. He is staking everything on the 50 per cent chance that West holds the king. A better play is to lead small to the nine first. If this loses to the jack or ten, you can finesse the queen next time. You still make two tricks if West holds the king, but you give yourself an additional chance of success in case West holds the jack and ten.

*Combination 5*

DUMMY
A Q 5 4

WEST
?

EAST
?

YOU
J 6 3 2

Under what conditions can you make all four tricks in this suit? How do you proceed?

*Answer:* You can only make all four tricks if West has a doubleton king. Lead small from your hand and finesse the queen. Now cash the ace. If West was dealt the doubleton king, it will drop under the ace and your jack will draw East's remaining card.

To lead the jack from your hand would be a "nothing" play. West would cover with the king if he had it, and then you could never make all the tricks, regardless of the distribution.

*Combination 6*

DUMMY
K J 5 2

WEST
?

EAST
?

YOU
Q 4 3

How do you play this suit to give yourself the maximum chance of making three tricks?

*Answer:* Most people start out correctly by leading small from their own hand to dummy's jack. If this holds, however, they get careless. Finding themselves in dummy they next lead small to their queen which loses to the ace. Now they are reduced to hoping for a 3–3 break in the suit.

The right play, after the jack holds, is to return to your hand in some other suit and lead another small card toward dummy's king. This gives you the *additional* chance that West was dealt the doubleton ace.

*Combination 7*

|  | DUMMY |  |
|---|---|---|
|  | A J 9 |  |
| WEST |  | EAST |
| ? |  | ? |
|  | YOU |  |
|  | 4 3 2 |  |

What is the best way to make two tricks with this combination?

*Answer:* Lead small from your hand and finesse the nine. If East wins this with a high honor you can now finesse the jack next time. This line of play will develop two tricks whenever West was dealt the queen-ten or the king-ten. The alternate line of finessing the jack immediately will only win if West was dealt one combination: the king-queen. Two chances are obviously better than one.

*Combination 8*

|  | DUMMY |  |
|---|---|---|
|  | A 5 4 3 |  |
| WEST |  | EAST |
| ? |  | ? |
|  | YOU |  |
|  | Q J 2 |  |

You need three tricks from this suit. What is the best way to get them?

*Answer:* Lead small from dummy to your own queen (or jack). If this holds, get back to dummy in some other suit and lead small again. You'll make three tricks in the suit any time East has the king or the suit breaks 3–3. Notice that if you start by leading the queen from your hand, correct defense will hold you to two tricks unless the suit breaks 3–3.

*Combination 9*

DUMMY
A K 7 2

WEST                           EAST
?                                 ?

YOU
J 6 3

You are hoping to make three tricks in this suit. How do you play?

*Answer:* Cash the ace and lead a small card from dummy toward your jack. You will succeed any time East has the queen or West has the singleton queen or the suit breaks 3–3.

*Combination 10*

DUMMY
K 5 4 3

WEST                           EAST
?                                 ?

YOU
Q 7 6 2

How can you make three tricks in this suit?

*Answer:* You can make three tricks with this combination only if one of the opponents has the doubleton ace. Suppose you judge from the bidding that East is more likely to hold the ace than West. Then you must start by leading a small card from dummy through East toward your own queen. East will play small (your problem would be over if he went up with the ace), and your queen will win. Now lead a small card from your hand and duck it all around. If East's ace was doubleton, he'll be forced to play it "on air," and you'll wind up with three tricks. If the ace was not doubleton, there is no way to make three tricks. This maneuver is actually a form of ducking play but is commonly called "the obligatory finesse." Once your queen holds, marking East with the ace, you are "obliged" to play small from dummy the next time you lead the suit. To go up with dummy's king would be a "nothing play."

Let's try another example of an obligatory finesse:

*Combination 11*

DUMMY
Q 4

WEST                    EAST
?                       ?

YOU
K 7 3 2

Is there any legitimate chance of developing two tricks from this motley collection?

*Answer:* Yes. You can make two tricks if West has the ace and not more than two cards with it. Lead a small card from your hand to the queen. If East has the ace, of course, he will put it on your queen and you can never win more than one trick. So if the queen holds the trick you know West must have the ace. Next lead a small card from dummy and duck in your hand. Notice that it would be futile to put up your king to be decapitated by West's ace. You are "obliged" to play low. If West started with the doubleton ace he will have to play it and your troubles are over. If West's ace doesn't fall this time lead your remaining small card next time. You will still succeed in making two tricks if West was dealt the ace and only two other cards.

*Combination 12*

DUMMY
K Q 10 5 2

WEST                    EAST
?                       ?

YOU
A 9 7 4

You need all five tricks from this suit. Does it matter which card you lead first?

*Answer:* Yes. If one opponent has all four missing cards (J 8 6 3) it will be necessary to take a finesse against the jack later. So you must play a high honor first from the hand with two high honors. Assume you lead the king and West shows out. The ace-nine now becomes a tenace over East's jack. And if East shows out on the king, dummy's queen-ten is a tenace over West's jack. Regardless of how the opponents' cards are distributed, correct play will give you five tricks. If declarer incorrectly leads the ace first, he will have to pay off if East has all four missing cards.

*Combination 13*

DUMMY
A K 8 3

WEST                                    EAST
?                                         ?

YOU
Q 9 7 3 2

Again you need all five tricks. Which honor do you play first?

*Answer:* This time you are missing the J 10 6 4, and if East has them all, it's impossible to win five tricks. The correct play is to lead the queen first. This protects you against the possibility that West holds J 10 6 4. If East fails to follow suit, you can take two finesses against West's J 10, because you still have two high honors in dummy.

*Combination 14*

DUMMY
K J 9

WEST                                      EAST
?                                         ?

YOU
A 5 3

If you need three tricks from this suit it is normal to hope that West has the queen and to finesse accordingly. But suppose you know that East has the queen. (Perhaps he has opened the bidding with one no-trump and needs the queen for his bid.) What is the best way to try for three tricks under these circumstances?

*Answer:* If you are sure that East has the queen, you must start by leading the jack from dummy. If East covers, take your ace and finesse West for the ten next round. This maneuver is known as a backward finesse.

*Combination 15*

DUMMY
Q 9 6 2

WEST                                      EAST
?                                         ?

YOU
A J 10 4

The lead is in dummy, and you need four tricks from this suit. There are no more entries to dummy. What card do you play?

*Answer:* In order to take four tricks you naturally have to assume that East has the king. The correct play of leading the nine first allows you to take all four tricks regardless of how many cards East has with the king. Suppose, for example, the East-West cards were divided like this:

DUMMY

Q 9 6 2

WEST          EAST

3              K 8 7 5

YOU

A J 10 4

Now, if you made the mistake of starting with the queen from dummy, you'd be out of luck. The queen will hold the trick, and you next lead a small card and finesse the ten. This wins but there is no way to get back to dummy for another finesse. Notice that it would do no good to drop the ten under the queen on the first trick, because then when you lead the nine to the second trick East will cover with the king, making his eight good.

Look how easy it is if you start with the nine. This wins and the lead of the queen next allows you to stay in dummy that one extra round.

*Combination 16*          DUMMY

A

WEST          EAST

?              ?

YOU

J 10 5 4 3 2

This is your trump suit, and when dummy's ace is led both opponents follow small. You return to your hand in some other suit in order to continue the process of extracting the opponents' trumps. Should you lead an honor next or a low card, and why?

*Answer:* You must lead a low card. If the opponents' trumps are divided 3–3, it doesn't matter what you do. Either way you will lose only two trump tricks. However, if one opponent was dealt K x or Q x it is vital to lead a small card. Leading the jack or the ten would result in the unnecessary loss of three trump tricks.

*Combination 17*

DUMMY
7 4 3 2

WEST          EAST
?                ?

YOU
K J 10 6 5

Again this is your trump suit, but this time there are no entries to dummy and you must lead the suit out of your own hand. You can only afford to lose one trump trick. Which card do you lead?

*Answer:* Your only chance is to lead the king and hope that some-one was dealt the singleton queen. It would be futile to lead any other card. If one opponent holds the singleton ace, his partner will have Q x x, and a second trump trick will have to be lost.

*Combination 18*

DUMMY
J 5

WEST          EAST
?                ?

YOU
A 9 7 4 3 2

How do you handle this trump suit in order to lose only one trick?

*Answer:* You must hope that West has the doubleton Q 10 or K 10. Lead small from your hand toward dummy. If West wins this, get into dummy with some other suit and lead the jack of trumps. This smothers West's ten and allows you to finesse the queen or king in East's hand.

*Combination 19*

DUMMY
Q 6 2

WEST          EAST
?                ?

YOU
A 10 8 5 4 3

You cannot afford to lose any trump trick with this holding. What is your only chance?

*Answer:* You must hope West has the singleton jack. Lead the queen from dummy. Notice that it would be futile to hope for a singleton king because you'd still have to lose one trump trick.

### To Finesse or Not to Finesse

*Combination 20*

DUMMY

A Q J 10 9

WEST                         EAST

?                          ?

YOU

8 7 6 5 4

This is your trump holding and you cannot afford to lose a trick to the king. Do you finesse, or do you play the ace hoping the king will drop?

*Answer:* With ten cards in the combined hands, it is clearly superior to finesse. Going up with the ace would win if East was dealt the singleton king. As opposed to this, the finesse wins if East was dealt the singleton two, the singleton three, or a void.

Suppose, however, that you have eleven trumps (missing the king) instead of ten. Now the correct play is almost a tossup. In the absence of any other information it is fractionally better to play for the drop. The actual odds are 52 percent for a 1–1 break and 48 percent for a 2–0 break.

The problem of when to finesse becomes a little more complicated when declarer is missing the queen. Every beginner learns the old adage "eight ever, nine never." What this means is that if you have eight cards, missing the queen, it is better to finesse, and if you have nine cards, missing the queen, it is better not to finesse. The "never" is quite an exaggeration, but it's popular because it rhymes.

Remembering a rhyme is not the same as understanding a principle, however, so if you want to think like a bridge player, you have to realize *why* it's right to finesse with eight and not with nine.

*Combination 21*

DUMMY

5 4 3 2

WEST                    EAST

?                        ?

YOU

A K J 6

You are declarer in a grand slam and this, unfortunately, is your trump holding. (Maybe your partner bid too much!) Anyway, the rest of your hand is solid and you have plenty of entries. What's the best way to play the trumps?

*Answer:* There is obviously no chance unless the opponents' trumps are divided 3–2, so you must assume this is the case. If West has three trumps it doesn't matter whether you finesse or cash the ace and king. If West's three trumps include the queen you are doomed either way, and if they don't include the queen you will succeed either way. The material cases occur when East has the three trumps. Now if East's three trumps include the queen, it is right to finesse. If they don't it is right to cash the ace and king. Who is more likely to have the queen, the opponent with three trumps or the opponent with two? Obviously the odds are three to two that the one with three trumps has the queen. Thus the finesse will succeed more often than cashing the ace and king.

The actual chances of making the grand slam are 34 percent with a finesse and only 27 percent by cashing the ace and king. (Chapter 10 will explain an easy way to figure out percentages like this.) It isn't necessary to know these exact figures, but I have included them because it is good for a player to have a general idea of how often he will succeed using either method.

Now let's improve the trump holding a little:

*Combination 22*

DUMMY

5 4 3 2

WEST                    EAST

?                        ?

YOU

A K J 10

This time, thanks to the ten spot, your chances of making the grand slam are much better. You naturally cash the ace first, just in case West holds the singleton queen. (Notice that there was no chance last time if West held the singleton queen as this would give East the 10 9 8 7 and a natural trump trick.) On the second round you finesse, and again on the third round if necessary. You can pick up East's queen even if he holds Q x x x. Your chances of making the grand slam with correct play are now 51 percent. With incorrect play (cashing the ace and king) they are about 33 percent.

The familiar adage is pretty good advice then, at least as far as "eight ever" is concerned. Let's look at the situation with nine cards.

*Combination 23*

DUMMY
5 4 3 2

WEST              EAST
?                  ?

YOU
A K J 10 6

Again you are in a grand slam. This is your trump suit, and everything else is solid. Naturally you lay down the ace first. If the queen drops, or if West shows out, everything is under control. But, if everyone follows small, what do you do next?

*Answer:* This is very close. If you have no clue at all as to the opponents' distribution, the odds slightly favor cashing the king at this point. Your chance of making the grand slam is actually 58 percent if you cash the ace and king of trumps. If you cash the ace and then get to dummy and finesse the second round your chance of success is only 56 percent.

Remember that all percentages like this only apply if you have no clue to the opponents' distribution. These particular figures are so close that any additional knowledge affects them. It would not take much to swing the odds in favor of the second-round finesse. If, for example, there was any indication that West was longer than East in some side suit, the slight odds in favor of cashing the ace and king would have already disappeared.

In conclusion, "eight ever" is sound advice. "Nine never" is an exaggeration, but in the absence of any other information, it is usually followed.

Now let's examine a few cases where declarer can finesse either way for the queen.

*Combination 24*

DUMMY

A J 8 7

WEST                EAST

?                         ?

YOU

K 10 9 5

Again the contract is a grand slam, and this is your trump holding. With only eight trumps a finesse is obviously called for. But which way do you finesse?

*Answer:* With no clue to the distribution of the opponents' cards this is mathematically a tossup. You naturally cash one high honor first to guard against a singleton queen. But whether you cash the ace first and then finesse for the queen or cash the king first and then play West for the queen is strictly a guess.

*Combination 25*

DUMMY

A J 8

WEST                EAST

?                         ?

YOU

K 10 9 7 5

With this eight-card holding it's still possible to finesse either way. Here, however, it is mathematically superior to hope that East has the queen. The reason is this: By cashing the ace first and then leading the jack and letting it ride, you protect yourself against a singleton queen in West's hand and you are still able to pick up Q x x x in East's hand. If you hope West has the queen, you can't afford to cash the king first to protect against a singleton queen with East. If you do cash the king first, it becomes impossible to pick up Q x x x in West's hand.

*Combination 26*       DUMMY
                       K 10

        WEST                   EAST
         ?                      ?

                     YOU
                   A J 4 3 2

You need five tricks from this holding and have no clues as to the distribution. Who do you hope has the queen?

*Answer:* Here it is clearly better to hope West has the queen, and you should lead a small card from your hand to the ten. You will succeed in making five tricks if West was dealt Q x or Q x x. The alternative play of leading the king first and then finessing East for the queen will only succeed if East was dealt specifically Q x x. If East has Q x, West has 9 x x x and will make a trick with the nine.

* *

Of course there are many other card combinations, and it would be impossible (as well as quite undesirable) to memorize them all. Most are variations of the representative combinations discussed here. If the reader has really grasped the thinking behind these, he will be able to work out his own solutions in the future.

It's important to realize that this chapter deals with combinations in the abstract only. That is, without reference to the rest of the hand. What is correct in the abstract may be entirely wrong in a given deal. Declarer's approach to any particular suit in actual play is usually based on his knowledge of card combinations. But it must always be tempered by the considerations of the actual hand.

# 2

# Safety Plays

DECLARER'S PRIME CONSIDERATION on any hand is naturally to make what he bids. To this end he will sometimes deviate from what is apparently the normal way to handle a particular card combination. Occasionally he will deprive himself of a possible overtrick in order to ensure the success of the contract. Such a play is appropriately called a "safety play."

*Example 1*

NORTH
♠ K 10 6 5
♡ A Q 6
◇ K J 5 2
♣ 9 2

SOUTH
♠ A 9 7 3 2
♡ K 3 2
◇ A Q 7
♣ A K

*Both vulnerable*

*The bidding:*

| SOUTH | WEST | NORTH | EAST |
|-------|------|-------|------|
| 1 ♠ | Pass | 3 ♠ | Pass |
| 6 ♠ | Pass | Pass | Pass |

*Opening lead:* Club queen

West leads the club queen against six spades. Declarer wins in

17

his hand and views the dummy with satisfaction. The small slam appears to be a cinch, and if the trumps break 2–2, he will make seven. When things look rosiest, however, one can afford to take precautions against remote disasters. South realizes that the only thing which can defeat him is a 4–0 spade split. So he decides to sacrifice any hopes of an overtrick in order to protect himself against the possibility that someone holds ♠ Q J 8 4.

At trick two he leads a low trump from his hand, and when West follows small, he makes the safety play of the ten from dummy. This will probably lose to an honor. And no matter what East returns, declarer draws the remaining trumps and chalks up 1430 for bidding and making six spades. Most of the time declarer will find he has thrown away the chance of an overtrick for nothing. About one time in twenty, however, East will show out on the first spade lead. This means that West started with Q J 8 4 and would have defeated the contract if declarer had gone up with dummy's spade king at trick two. This time the safety play was worth 1530 points (the 1430 points that North-South actually scored plus the 100 points that East-West would have scored for defeating the slam).

Thus, the premium for this insurance policy was the chance of an insignificant overtrick. The benefit was 1530 points. No intelligent declarer can afford to turn down such an investment.

*Example 2*

NORTH
♠ J 3
♡ 6 5 4
◇ A K Q 8 7 4
♣ 7 5

SOUTH
♠ A Q 7
♡ A J 8 7
◇ 6 5
♣ A J 8 2

| *The bidding:* | SOUTH | WEST | NORTH | EAST |
|---|---|---|---|---|
| | 1 NT | Pass | 3 NT | Pass |
| | Pass | Pass | | |

*Opening lead:* Spade five

West leads a spade against three no-trump, and dummy's jack wins the first trick. South sees he can make two spades, one heart, one club, and probably six diamond tricks with a normal 3–2 break. This would be a total of ten tricks. However, if declarer starts the diamonds by leading an honor and it turns out that the suit unfortunately splits 4–1, he will never make more than three diamond tricks (because there is no outside entry to dummy) and the contract will be defeated. Proper play is to lead a small diamond from dummy at trick two. Now declarer will make nine tricks whether the diamonds break 3–2 or 4–1. By sacrificing the insignificant overtrick, declarer greatly increases his chances of success.

By the way, a 4–1 break will occur about 28 times out of 100 (see table in Chapter 10), so it is well worth while to take out the insurance.

*Example 3*

NORTH
♠ 7 6
♡ A K 8 6 3
◊ Q 7 2
♣ A K J

SOUTH
♠ A K 8
♡ 10 5 2
◊ A K 6 5
♣ Q 3 2

*The bidding:*

| SOUTH | WEST | NORTH | EAST |
|-------|------|-------|------|
| 1 NT  | Pass | 6 NT  | Pass |
| Pass  | Pass |       |      |

*Opening lead:* Club ten

Declarer takes the opening lead with the ace of clubs and cashes the heart ace, on which East drops the jack. If East started with the doubleton Q J, South can make the rest of the tricks by cashing the heart king next. However, if it turns out that East had a singleton jack of hearts, this line of play will lose the contract. West will have Q 9 7 6, and after the ace and king are gone he'll be left with two natural heart tricks.

To be on the safe side, declarer leads a small heart from dummy at trick three. If East shows out, the ten forces West's queen. South wins the return in his hand and finesses West for the heart nine, making in all four hearts, two spades, three diamonds, and three clubs for a total of twelve tricks.

Again, declarer willingly gives up a chance for an overtrick to make sure of fulfilling his contract.

Now that you have an idea what is meant by insurance, the rest of the examples in this chapter will be presented in the form of problems. Try to spot the safety play before you read the answer.

*Example 4*

NORTH
♠ Q J 10
♡ 6 4 2
◇ A Q J 5
♣ K J 9

SOUTH
♠ A 6
♡ A Q 10 8 7 3
◇ 8
♣ A Q 8 7

*The bidding:*

| SOUTH | WEST | NORTH | EAST |
|-------|------|-------|------|
| 1 ♡ | Pass | 2 NT | Pass |
| 3 ♣ | Pass | 3 ♡ | Pass |
| 6 ♡ | Pass | Pass | Pass |

*Opening lead:* Spade nine

Against six hearts the spade nine is led, and dummy's queen holds the first trick. A low heart is played from the table and East follows with the five. Which heart should declarer play from his hand?

*Answer:* Thanks to the opening lead, declarer has no losers outside of the trump suit. Therefore, he can afford to lose one heart trick but not two. The proper play is the heart ace at this point, and the reason can be best appreciated by examining what may happen to declarer if he plays the queen or the ten. Suppose South plays the queen and it loses to the king. Declarer eventually leads another heart from the table, on which East plays the nine. Now what? Did West start with the singleton king? If so, East had J 9 5, and declarer must now finesse the ten. Or did West start with K J doubleton? In this case declarer must go up with the ace. If South guesses wrong, he'll go down.

Declarer could find himself in the same quandary if he finessed the heart ten the first time and it lost to the jack. Now he has to guess whether West started with the singleton jack or the K J doubleton.

This whole embarrassing predicament is avoided by the simple safety play of cashing the ace of trumps first. Now return to dummy with the diamond ace and lead another heart. Cover whatever East plays and you will automatically hold the trump losers to one any time it is possible to do so. Even if East has all four trumps, you have enough entries in dummy to hold him to one trick. Of course if West holds K J x or K J x x, the contract will fail whatever you do.

*Example 5*

NORTH
♠ K 9 2
♡ A K 9 8 2
♢ Q J 10
♣ 4 3

SOUTH
♠ A J 5 4 3
♡ 4 3
♢ 8 6 5
♣ A K Q

*The bidding:*

| SOUTH | WEST | NORTH | EAST |
|---|---|---|---|
| 1 ♠ | Pass | 2 ♡ | Pass |
| 2 ♠ | Pass | 4 ♠ | Pass |
| Pass | Pass | | |

*Opening lead:* Diamond seven

West leads a diamond against four spades and East takes the first two tricks with the king and ace. He then returns a third diamond. You breath a sigh of relief as West follows suit and the queen wins in dummy. It's obviously time to draw the trumps. How do you proceed?

*Answer:* With this spade holding, players have a tendency to want to cash the king first and then finesse the jack. This would be all right if declarer could not afford to lose a trump trick. But on this actual hand it would be wrong, because it would risk defeat if West started with Q 10 x x of spades.

The fact that declarer can afford to lose one spade trick here means that he can afford the luxury of a safety play to ensure himself against the loss of two spade tricks.

If the trumps break 3–2, the contract is always safe. And if they break 5–0, the contract is always doomed. So what the situation declarer must protect against is a 4–1 split.

Cash the spade ace first. Assume everyone follows small. Now lead a small spade from your hand toward dummy. If West plays low, put on the nine. You don't mind if East wins this trick because in this case it will mean the suit has broken 3–2 and the rest of the tricks are yours. Of course if West shows out on the second spade lead, you go up with dummy's king and return a spade toward your own jack. Whatever happens, you are guaranteed to lose no more than one trump trick whether the suit breaks 4–1 or 3–2. (If you don't believe it, get out some cards and try it yourself.)

*Example 6*

NORTH
♠ 8 7 4
♡ A J 9 3
◇ 9 2
♣ J 6 4 2

SOUTH
♠ A Q J
♡ 8 7
◇ A K Q 10 4
♣ A 9 5

*The bidding:*

| SOUTH | WEST | NORTH | EAST |
|-------|------|-------|------|
| 1 ◇ | Pass | 1 ♡ | Pass |
| 3 NT | Pass | Pass | Pass |

*Opening lead:* Spade five

West leads the five of spades, East plays the king, and South wins with the ace. How should declarer play to be sure of making three no-trump?

*Answer:* The contract is foolproof provided declarer doesn't get greedy and try for an overtrick. At trick two, cash one high diamond just in case the singleton jack falls. Then lead the diamond four to dummy's nine. This will probably lose to the jack, and declarer now has four diamond tricks, three spades, one heart, and one club for a total of nine certain tricks.

If declarer is greedy and tries to make all five diamond tricks, he could go down if the suit breaks 5–1.

*Example 7*

NORTH
♠ 7 6 4
♡ 6 2
◇ 3
♣ A K J 6 4 3 2

SOUTH
♠ A K Q 9
♡ A Q 9 5
◇ A Q 4
♣ 7 5

*North-South vulnerable East deals*

*The bidding:*

| EAST | SOUTH | WEST | NORTH |
|------|--------|------|-------|
| 3 ◇ | Double | Pass | 5 ♣ |
| Pass | 6 NT | Pass | Pass |
| Pass | | | |

*Opening lead:* Diamond nine

East opens the bidding with a pre-emptive bid of three diamonds, and South doubles for take-out. North jumps to five clubs, and South becomes declarer at the excellent contract of six no-trump. The opening lead is the diamond nine. East plays the ten, and South wins with the queen. At trick two declarer leads the club seven, and West plays the eight. What should declarer play from dummy in order to guarantee his contract?

*Answer:* If declarer plays the jack from dummy and East fails to follow suit, the slam will be defeated. West's Q 10 9 8 will prevent declarer from running the clubs. To guard against this, declarer should duck the first club lead entirely. Now nothing can prevent him from making six club tricks and the contract.

*Example 8*

NORTH
♠ 8 5 4
♡ A K 7
◇ 4 3 2
♣ K J 7 4

SOUTH
♠ A 9 3 2
♡ Q 10 8
◇ A K 5
♣ A 6 2

*The bidding:*

| SOUTH | WEST | NORTH | EAST |
|-------|------|-------|------|
| 1 NT | Pass | 3 NT | Pass |
| Pass | Pass | | |

*Opening lead:* Diamond jack

West leads the diamond jack against three no-trump, and declarer sees eight tricks: three hearts, one spade, two diamonds, and two clubs. The best chance for a ninth trick lies in the club suit. How should he handle the clubs to give himself the maximum chance of making three tricks in this suit?

*Answer:* Cash the king and ace of clubs. Then lead a small club toward dummy's jack. You will succeed in making three club tricks any time:

1. The suit breaks 3–3.
2. West has the queen.
3. East has the singleton queen.
4. East has the doubleton queen.

Notice that it would be a mistake to cash the club ace and then finesse the jack. While this would be the proper way to play if you needed four club tricks, it would be economically unsound when you actually need only three. If East held a doubleton queen of clubs, you would have thrown a perfectly good contract right out the window.

✻ ✻

The safety plays discussed here are relatively common ones. Obviously there are hundreds of others, and the reader who tries to remember the solutions is bound to get lost sooner or later.

The thing to acquire is a certain state of mind. When you're faced with a situation where you can afford to lose one trick in a suit but can't afford to lose two, it's time to look for a safety play. Don't strain to remember what you've learned. That's usually fatal because you are just as likely to remember something that isn't applicable. Instead, just relax. Now, mentally juggle the opponents' cards around in your mind and consider the different lines of play available to you.

Here's a tip: To finesse or not to finesse is often the big question. Finesses generally involve risk, and a man who is wealthy enough to be able to afford to lose a trick is usually better off not taking a risk.

*Example 9*

NORTH
♡ 6 5 2

SOUTH
♡ A Q J 4 3

The contract is six hearts, and this is your trump holding. The rest of the hand is solid, and there are plenty of entries. You can afford one trump loser but not two. How do you analyze the situation?

First you juggle the opponents' cards around mentally. You realize that if they're divided 3–2 any line of play will succeed. If they break 5–0, any line will fail. Now examine the 4–1 cases and you'll see that the only time it matters what you do is when West has the singleton king. Here the finesse would be fatal. West would make his king and East would still get a trick from his 10 9 8 7.

So, the safety play with this combination is to cash the ace first. If the king doesn't fall, get to dummy in some other suit, and you'll be able to lead toward the Q J *twice* if necessary.

On some hands declarer will not know when he sees the dummy whether or not he can afford a safety play. Look at the heart suit in the following example:

*Example 10*

NORTH
♠ A 3 2
♡ A 9 5 4
◇ K J 2
♣ K Q 6

SOUTH
♠ Q J 10
♡ K J 3 2
◇ A Q 9
♣ A 10 8

*The bidding:*

| SOUTH | WEST | NORTH | EAST |
|-------|------|-------|------|
| 1 NT  | Pass | 6 NT  | Pass |
| Pass  | Pass |       |      |

*Opening lead:* Club two

West leads a club, and declarer can count three diamond tricks, three club tricks, either two or three spade tricks depending on who has the king and an indeterminate number of heart tricks. If the spade finesse loses, he will need four heart tricks for his slam. And if the spade finesse wins, three heart tricks are sufficient. So declarer postpones the heart situation until he has tested the spades.

He wins the club lead in his hand and plays the spade queen for a finesse. Suppose this loses to East's king. Now South must go all out to make four heart tricks. The proper play is a low heart from dummy to the jack. This will succeed if East started with Q x x, Q x, or the singleton queen. (Notice that it would be an error to cash the ace first. Four heart tricks can never be made if West has the singleton queen. And North's A 9 is needed as a tenace over West's ten in case East has the singleton queen.)

Now, suppose West shows up with the spade king. This means the contract is in the bag because declarer can afford the 100 percent safety play for three heart tricks. He cashes the heart king first, and then leads a low heart toward dummy with the intention of playing the nine if West plays small. Whatever happens, declarer makes three heart tricks and his contract.

This last hand forcefully points out the important fact that the *same* card combination in the *same* hand is treated in entirely different ways depending upon the circumstances.

*In the abstract,* without reference to a given hand, there is an ideal method of handling any particular card combination. (See Chapter 1.)

*In real life,* there's more than one way to skin a cat!

# 3

## *"Let Me Play the No-Trumps, Dear"*

IN MIXED-PAIR TOURNAMENTS, there is a standing joke that the female partner is not allowed to bid no-trump. The idea is that the "superior male intelligence" is better able to cope with the greater difficulties encountered by the no-trump declarer.

There is no evidence that members of the fair sex ever heed this advice. And, as any woman will be glad to tell you, the "superior intelligence" angle is strictly a figment of the male imagination.

However, it's true that no-trump contracts are apt to be the trickiest to handle, because declarer doesn't have the protection offered by a long trump suit. To play no-trump well requires an organized mind. This chapter organizes the basic problems which beset the no-trump declarer, and presents them as far as possible in order of difficulty. Let's look at some hands.

28

## The Problem of Developing Tricks

NORTH
♠ A K J 10
♡ A 10 6
◇ J 9 4
♣ A K 8

SOUTH
♠ 7 5 2
♡ K 8
◇ Q 10 3 2
♣ Q 6 5 2

| *The bidding:* | NORTH | EAST | SOUTH | WEST |
|---|---|---|---|---|
| | 1 ♠ | Pass | 1 NT | Pass |
| | 3 NT | Pass | Pass | Pass |

*Opening lead:* Club jack

West leads the club jack against your contract of three no-trump, and it is important to stop now and review the whole hand. Inexperienced players are often embarrassed to delay the game. They even may be under the impression that it looks more intelligent to proceed quickly. In a good game of bridge the declarer automatically stops to plan before playing to trick one. Get into the habit of deciding on your entire campaign before you touch a card and you will eliminate many costly mistakes.

In a no-trump contract, the first thing to do is to count the tricks that are ready to cash. There are seven here, two spades, two hearts, and three clubs. Now check each suit as a possible source for developing the two additional tricks needed for the contract.

One might consider finessing spades. If West has the queen, this would produce two extra spade tricks. Even if the finesse loses, there would be one extra spade trick, and a 3–3 club break could produce the ninth trick.

However, the spade finesse would be the wrong play. The right play is to work on the diamond suit. Knocking out the ace and king of diamonds automatically sets up two diamond tricks and guarantees the contract.

Notice that if declarer tries the spade finesse first it may be too late to set up diamonds. East may switch to hearts when he wins the spade queen and the opponents may get their hearts established before declarer can get his diamonds going.

Don't stop analyzing as soon as you see a play that gives you a good chance of success. Look at *all* the possibilities, and you may find one that gives you 100 percent chance of success.

### Selecting the Best Play

NORTH
♠ A Q 8 7 6 5
♡ J 2
◊ 6 4 2
♣ 6 5

SOUTH
♠ 4
♡ A K Q 10 9
◊ A J 10
♣ A K Q J

| *The bidding:* | SOUTH | WEST | NORTH | EAST |
|---|---|---|---|---|
| | 2 ♡ | Pass | 2 ♠ | Pass |
| | 3 ♣ | Pass | 3 ♠ | Pass |
| | 6 NT | Pass | Pass | Pass |

*Opening lead:* Club ten

It's not always possible to find a line of play that gives you 100 percent chance of success. Look at this hand where West leads the club ten against your contract of six no-trump. You count eleven tricks—five hearts, four clubs, and the other two aces. There are two prospects of a twelfth trick. You can finesse the spade queen, or you can take two finesses in diamonds. Which should you try?

The right play is to take two diamond finesses. There are four material diamond situations that can exist. West can have: (1) the diamond king, (2) the diamond queen, (3) both, or (4) neither. In only one of these situations, number 3, will you be defeated by taking two diamond finesses. In the other three situations you'll wind up taking two diamond tricks and making your contract. Thus, the chances of success are about three out of four.

The chance of the spade finesse working is, of course, only even money, or 50 percent. A play that succeeds about three times out of four is much better than one that succeeds only half the time, so the diamond suit is clearly the one to tackle. Win the club lead in your hand and enter dummy with the heart jack to take one diamond finesse. If this loses, you will eventually return to dummy with the spade ace to take another diamond finesse.

### Combining Your Chances

NORTH
♠ A Q 8 6
♡ 8 6
◇ A Q 8
♣ 5 4 3 2

SOUTH
♠ 9 3 2
♡ A 10
◇ K J 7 6
♣ A K J 8

| *The bidding:* | SOUTH | WEST | NORTH | EAST |
|---|---|---|---|---|
| | 1 NT | Pass | 2 ♣ | Pass |
| | 2 ◇ | Pass | 3 NT | Pass |
| | Pass | Pass | | |

*Opening lead:* Heart four

You become declarer at three no-trump with no bidding by the opposition. West leads the heart four, and East plays the queen, which you duck. East continues with the heart two, which you win with the ace as West contributes the three spot. How do you proceed to give yourself the maximum chance of making nine tricks?

You have eight tricks on top, with the possibility of developing a ninth in either spades or clubs. The problem is that the minute the enemy gets the lead, they will cash enough hearts to set you. Thus if you decide to rely on a spade finesse, you are giving yourself a 50 percent play for the contract. Likewise, if you decide to finesse in clubs, you are depending on the 50 percent chance that East has the club queen. How do you know which one to try? You don't know. But there's a way to combine your chances.

First cash the ace and king of clubs. With five clubs outstanding the queen probably won't drop, but it may. If the queen doesn't drop, you now fall back on the spade finesse. This line of play gives you a distinctly greater than 50 percent chance of making the contract. You now have the chance of dropping the club queen in two rounds *in addition* to the 50 percent spade finesse.

Notice that if your only prospect of a ninth trick lay in the club suit, it would be correct to cash one high club only and then finesse for the queen (see Chapter 1). In this hand, however, you have two strings to your bow. You deliberately choose the inferior club play of cashing the ace and king, because if it doesn't work you are still alive and can try the spade finesse next.

Inexperienced players tend to think in terms of one suit at a time. Strive always to combine all your possibilities to give yourself the greatest *total* chance of success.

### Preserving Entries

NORTH
♠ A K J 6 3
♡ A Q 2
◇ K 10
♣ A 5 4

WEST
♠ 2
♡ J 10 9 8
◇ A Q 8 5
♣ 9 7 6 2

EAST
♠ Q 10 9 8 5
♡ 6 4 3
◇ 7 3
♣ Q J 10

SOUTH
♠ 7 4
♡ K 7 5
◇ J 9 6 4 2
♣ K 8 3

| *The bidding:* | NORTH | EAST | SOUTH | WEST |
|---|---|---|---|---|
| | 1 ♠ | Pass | 1 NT | Pass |
| | 3 NT | Pass | Pass | Pass |

*Opening lead:* Heart jack

West leads the heart jack, and declarer can see only seven tricks—two spades, three hearts, and two clubs. It's tempting to try for the extra two tricks from that very attractive spade suit. Establishing spades is not a sure thing, however, so declarer curbs the instinct to start on that suit and looks a little further. When he gets to the diamond suit, he realizes his search is over. By giving the enemy two diamond tricks, he will have at least two and maybe three good diamonds left in his hand.

Declarer isn't out of the woods yet, however. Suppose, for instance, he wins the first trick in his hand with the king of hearts and leads a diamond to the ten, which holds. Then he leads the diamond king, which loses to West's ace. Now declarer has only one more entry to his hand, the club king, and West still has the diamond queen to stop the suit. Declarer can set up his diamonds but can never get back to cash them.

The solution, of course, is to win the heart lead in dummy and lead the diamond king at trick two. Now declarer still has two entries in his hand, and nothing can stop him from taking at least two diamond tricks and making his contract.

Moral: Don't relax when you find the necessary number of tricks. Check the entry situation before you play or you may find it is too late.

## Hidden Entries

NORTH
♠ J 10 2
♡ Q 3
◇ 9 5 4 3
♣ K Q 4 2

WEST
♠ A 7 6
♡ J 10 9 8 7 6
◇ 2
♣ J 9 6

EAST
♠ K 8 4 3
♡ K 5 2
◇ K 8 7 6
♣ 10 5

SOUTH
♠ Q 9 5
♡ A 4
◇ A Q J 10
♣ A 8 7 3

*The bidding:*

| SOUTH | WEST | NORTH | EAST |
|-------|------|-------|------|
| 1 NT | Pass | 2 NT | Pass |
| 3 NT | Pass | Pass | Pass |

*Opening lead:* Heart jack

Some entries aren't easy to spot. Take this hand, for example, where West leads the heart jack against three no-trump. Declarer hopefully covers with the queen and East wins the trick with the king as south ducks. Declarer wins the heart continuation with the ace and sees that he's going to need four diamond tricks and four club tricks to make his contract.

He leads the club seven to dummy's king and takes a diamond finesse. Fortunately this wins, and he leads the club eight to dummy's queen and takes another diamond finesse. This time West shows out, and it becomes apparent that a third diamond finesse is necessary. Declarer cashes the ace of clubs and enters dummy by leading his carefully preserved club three to dummy's four spot. He takes one more diamond finesse, and the contract is home.

Notice that a short-sighted declarer would probably have led the club three to dummy the first time. Now he would have only two entries to dummy and the contract would fail.

An insufficient number of entries will often spell the difference between victory and defeat. Don't squander your entries!

\* \*

While you are industriously planning your campaign and setting up tricks for yourself, the opponents naturally don't just sit there twiddling their thumbs. They are busy setting up the tricks necessary to set you. Furthermore, they have a head start because the defense always has the opening lead. Against a three no-trump contract, for example, an opponent will usually lead fourth best from his longest and strongest suit. By the time you have established your nine tricks, he will often have established this long suit. And if he can do so, he will grab his five tricks before you can cash the nine you were planning on.

So, declarer not only has to worry about setting up tricks for himself. He also has to worry about preventing the enemy from cashing their tricks first. Here are some weapons you can use to impede the defense:

## The Holdup Play

NORTH
♠ 7 6 4 2
♡ 9 6
◇ K J 10 9
♣ K Q 7

WEST
♠ J 10 8 5
♡ K J 8 4 3
◇ 5 4
♣ 3 2

EAST
♠ Q 3
♡ Q 10 2
◇ A 7 3
♣ J 9 8 6 4

SOUTH
♠ A K 9
♡ A 7 5
◇ Q 8 6 2
♣ A 10 5

| *The bidding:* | SOUTH | WEST | NORTH | EAST |
|---|---|---|---|---|
| | 1 NT | Pass | 3 NT | Pass |
| | Pass | Pass | | |

*Opening lead:* Heart four

Against three no-trump, West leads his fourth-best heart, East plays the queen and declarer pauses to take stock. He sees that in order to take nine tricks he will have to knock out the ace of diamonds. The danger is that when the opponents take the diamond ace, they may run enough hearts to set the contract.

Declarer can reduce this danger by refusing to win the first trick. East will lead a second heart and declarer should hold up again. Now declarer wins the third heart, crosses his fingers, and leads a diamond. If the opponent with the length in hearts has the diamond ace, the contract is doomed. But if the opponent who is short in hearts has the diamond ace, he won't be able to return a heart, and declarer makes three no-trump.

Of course, if the hearts were divided 4–4, it wouldn't matter who had the diamond ace, because neither opponent would have enough hearts to set the contract.

### When Not to Hold Up

NORTH
♠ A
♡ 7 5 2
◊ 6 3 2
♣ K Q J 10 6 5

WEST
♠ K 9 8 7
♡ Q J 9 7
◊ Q 10 9 7
♣ 3

EAST
♠ J 6 5 3 2
♡ K 5 4
◊ 8
♣ A 8 7 4

SOUTH
♠ Q 10 4
♡ A 10 8
◊ A K J 5 4
♣ 9 2

*The bidding:*

| SOUTH | WEST | NORTH | EAST |
|-------|------|-------|------|
| 1 ◊   | Pass | 2 ♣   | Pass |
| 2 NT  | Pass | 3 NT  | Pass |
| Pass  | Pass |       |      |

*Opening lead:* Heart queen

As a general rule one should not hold up winning a trick in a particular suit when a shift by opponents to another suit would be worse.

For example, West opens the queen of hearts against three no-trump. When dummy appears, declarer should thank his lucky stars that West didn't get his thumb on a spade lead. If the spade ace were removed before the clubs were established, East would duck the first club lead, dummy would be dead, and the whole hand would collapse.

With this particular heart combination, it would be normal to hold up at least once as a precaution against a 5–2 heart break. However, it would be foolish to hold up here. West might shift to a spade, which would be fatal. This is a case where the cure is worse than the disease.

Your best bet is to grab the first trick, knock out the club ace, and pray for a 4–3 heart split.

## How Long Should You Hold Up?

```
                    NORTH
                ♠ 10 9 4
                ♡ Q 10 4 2
                ◇ A 9 8 5
                ♣ 10 2
   WEST                          EAST
♠ K J 8 7 5                   ♠ Q 6
♡ 9 6 3                       ♡ 8 7 5
◇ J 10 7                      ◇ K Q 6
♣ 8 7                         ♣ A 6 5 4 3
                    SOUTH
                ♠ A 3 2
                ♡ A K J
                ◇ 4 3 2
                ♣ K Q J 9
```

*The bidding:*

| SOUTH | WEST | NORTH | EAST |
|-------|------|-------|------|
| 1 ♣   | Pass | 1 ◇   | Pass |
| 2 NT  | Pass | 3 NT  | Pass |
| Pass  | Pass |       |      |

*Opening lead:* Spade seven

West leads his fourth-best spade and declarer counts his tricks. The spade ace, the diamond ace, and four heart tricks make six. And the club suit can easily be established for three more to bring the total to nine. The obvious danger here is that when the opponents gain the lead with the club ace they may be able to take five tricks before declarer can cash his nine winners.

The correct play is to let East win the first trick with the spade queen. East continues with another spade and declarer wins the second trick. Now he establishes the clubs by knocking out the ace.

If West had the club ace, declarer's goose would be cooked, because of the 5–2 spade split. But fortunately East has the club ace and can't return a spade, so declarer makes three no-trump.

This seems elementary, doesn't it? But there were two pitfalls, which declarer had to avoid. A beginner might have fallen into the first trap and won the opening lead with the spade ace. Now, when East wins the club ace, he would have a spade left to return. West would cash four spade tricks and set the contract.

More-experienced players have learned to hold up their ace in a situation like this in order to cut the opponent's communications. They are now sufficiently advanced to fall into the second trap, which is the temptation to hold up too long. On this hand, a player who wasn't thinking might hold up his ace twice, just to be doubly sure that East had no more spades. Sometimes it is necessary to hold up twice, but not on this hand. If East has a third spade, it would mean that West started with only four and wouldn't have enough spades to defeat the contract.

If declarer holds up twice with the spade ace, West may abandon the suit when he wins the second trick. He knows there is no point in continuing to establish spades, because he has no entry to cash them once they're set up. Consequently he may shift to the diamond jack at trick three in an effort to set up some tricks for his partner. If that happens, declarer is going to lose two diamonds and one club in addition to the two spades he has already given to the enemy.

In this situation, the declarer who holds up too long pays the same penalty as the beginner who doesn't hold up at all. They both go down.

### The Bath Coup

NORTH
♠ A 6 4
♡ 5
♦ A J 10 9 5
♣ 10 8 4 2

WEST
♠ J 10 7 3
♡ K Q 10 8 4
♦ 3 2
♣ Q 5

EAST
♠ Q 9
♡ 9 7 6 3
♦ K 7 6
♣ J 9 6 3

SOUTH
♠ K 8 5 2
♡ A J 2
♦ Q 8 4
♣ A K 7

| *The Bidding:* | SOUTH | WEST | NORTH | EAST |
|---|---|---|---|---|
| | 1 NT | Pass | 3 NT | Pass |
| | Pass | Pass | | |

*Opening lead:* Heart king

West opens the heart king, on which South should play the two. Now if West chooses to continue the suit, he has to lead into the ace-jack giving declarer two heart tricks instead of one. So West will undoubtedly shift to some other suit. This gives declarer time to knock out the diamond king and make his contract.

Notice that if declarer takes the first trick with the heart ace, the defense will get four heart tricks in addition to the diamond king, and the contract is down.

This particular form of holdup play—when the king is led, and declarer holds the ace, jack, and another—has been known since the days of whist as the Bath Coup. The elegant title derives no doubt from Bath, England, where the fashionable Bath Whist Club was located.

The Bath Coup is a particularly efficient form of holdup play. The purpose of the normal holdup play is to exhaust one opponent of cards in the suit led, thereby possibly interfering with the enemy's communications. The Bath Coup is even better, because it actually stops the opponent on lead from continuing the suit profitably.

Here is a similar situation:

NORTH

A x x

SOUTH

J x x

If West leads the king, he can be presumed to have the queen also, and declarer does best by ducking. Now West can't continue the suit without sacrificing a trick.

Declarer must be careful not to hold up in cases where winning the first trick will guarantee a second stopper. For example:

NORTH
10 x

SOUTH
A J x

West leads the king and declarer must win with the ace. The presence of the ten spot ensures him of two tricks this way. If he holds up, West may not continue the suit, and declarer will make only his ace.

## Holding Up with Other Combinations

NORTH
♠ K 4 2
♡ 8 7 2
◇ A 9 8 5
♣ A 10 2

WEST
♠ 10 8 5
♡ A 10 6 5 4
◇ 7 4
♣ Q 8 7

EAST
♠ J 9 7 6
♡ J 9
◇ K 3 2
♣ J 6 5 4

SOUTH
♠ A Q 3
♡ K Q 3
◇ Q J 10 6
♣ K 9 3

*The bidding:*

| SOUTH | WEST | NORTH | EAST |
|-------|------|-------|------|
| 1 NT  | Pass | 3 NT  | Pass |
| Pass  | Pass |       |      |

*Opening lead:* Heart five.

West leads what appears to be his fourth-best heart, and East plays the jack. Should South take this trick or not? Clearly he should not.

The situation declarer fears is that West has a five-card heart suit and East has the diamond king. (If West has only four hearts the opponents won't be able to take enough tricks to set the contract. And if West has the diamond king, declarer can take ten tricks without ever losing the lead.) But if the unfavorable situation exists, and declarer takes the first trick, East will return a heart when he wins the diamond king and the contract will be set.

If declarer refuses the first trick, he avoids this unpleasant result. East will lead another heart at trick two. But when he wins the diamond king, he won't have any hearts left to return. (If West has five hearts, East can only have two.)

Now let's exchange the diamond holdings in the North and South hands:

NORTH
♠ K 4 2
♡ 8 7 2
◊ Q J 10 6
♣ A 10 2

SOUTH
♠ A Q 3
♡ K Q 3
◊ A 9 8 5
♣ K 9 3

Again West leads the heart five against three no-trump, and East plays the jack. This time declarer naturally wins the first trick, because by doing so he guarantees the contract. East cannot possibly get the lead, and if West wins the diamond king he can't lead another heart from his side of the table without giving declarer two heart tricks.

Here are two more situations that are similar

| (1) NORTH | (2) NORTH |
| --- | --- |
| 5 4 3 | 5 4 3 |
| SOUTH | SOUTH |
| K J 7 | A J 7 |

In both cases West leads what appears to be a fourth-best card, and East plays the queen. Again it's a case of which opponent is going to get the lead. If the only finesse you have to take is into the West hand, you should win the first trick. If the only finesse you have to take is into the East hand, you should duck the first trick to protect yourself against the possibility that West is leading from a five-card suit.

### Holding Up with Two Stoppers

NORTH
♠ 8 6 3
♡ K 10 5
◇ K J
♣ Q J 10 5 2

WEST
♠ Q 10 7 5 2
♡ 4 3 2
◇ 7 5
♣ A 7 4

EAST
♠ J 9
♡ Q 8 7 6
◇ Q 10 9 6 3
♣ K 3

SOUTH
♠ A K 4
♡ A J 9
◇ A 8 4 2
♣ 9 8 6

| The bidding: | SOUTH | WEST | NORTH | EAST |
|---|---|---|---|---|
| | 1 NT | Pass | 3 NT | Pass |
| | Pass | Pass | | |

*Opening lead:* Spade five

It's frequently necessary for declarer to refuse the first trick even when he holds two stoppers. For example, on this hand West leads the spade five, East plays the jack, and South realizes he'll have to establish the club suit to make his contract. In order to do this he'll have to relinquish the lead twice, once to the ace and once to the king. If south takes the first spade trick, East will win the first club lead and return his remaining spade. Now when West takes the ace of clubs, he'll cash three spade tricks to defeat the contract.

As the cards lie, declarer can make his contract by ducking the first trick. East will continue spades, but when he takes the club king he won't have any more spades and will have to lead some other suit. Now when West wins the club ace, declarer will still have a spade stopper, and the contract is safe.

Notice that the holdup play was necessary here even with *two* spade stoppers, because declarer needs to knock out *two* of the opponent's cards.

It goes without saying that declarer should not hold up with the ace and king if there is some other suit that he fears more.

### The Avoidance Play

```
                        NORTH
                    ♠ Q 4
                    ♡ K Q 9 5 3
                    ◇ A K 3
                    ♣ 8 5 2

   WEST                                      EAST
 ♠ A J 9 6 3                               ♠ 10 8 5
 ♡ 10 2                                    ♡ J 7 6 4
 ◇ 7 6 5                                   ◇ Q J 9
 ♣ J 7 4                                   ♣ Q 10 9

                        SOUTH
                    ♠ K 7 2
                    ♡ A 8
                    ◇ 10 8 4 2
                    ♣ A K 6 3
```

*The bidding:*

| | SOUTH | WEST | NORTH | EAST |
|---|---|---|---|---|
| | 1 ♣ | Pass | 1 ♡ | Pass |
| | 1 NT | Pass | 3 NT | Pass |
| | Pass | Pass | | |

*Opening lead:* Spade six

West leads the spade six and dummy's queen holds the first trick. It's clear that if East gets the lead and returns a spade, the contract will be in jeopardy. If West gets the lead, however, he cannot attack spades profitably and declarer is in no danger.

Consequently South plans his play so that East will not get the lead. Declarer has eight tricks on top—the spade he has already won, two clubs, two diamonds, and three hearts. The obvious place to find a ninth trick is in the long heart suit. Therefore, at trick two he leads a small heart from dummy, and when East plays low, declarer puts in the eight. West wins with the ten, but the defense is now helpless. Dummy's fifth heart provides the ninth trick, and the contract is home.

It's true that if the hearts had broken 3–3, declarer could have taken all five heart tricks by playing out the ace, king, and queen instead of finessing the eight spot. But South only needed four heart tricks, not five. He was willing to lose one, provided he could lose it to West and not to East. As the cards lie, declarer would be set if he cashed the ace, king, and queen of hearts first. East would win the fourth round and return a spade.

Any maneuver aimed at keeping a particular opponent from gaining the lead is called an avoidance play. In this case, by deliberately giving West a heart trick, declarer made sure that East, the dangerous opponent, was never able to get the lead.

On this hand it's worth considering what would have happened if East had played the ace of spades on dummy's queen at trick one. Suppose the opponent's cards had actually been divided like this:

NORTH
♠ Q 4
♡ K Q 9 5 3
◇ A K 3
♣ 8 5 2

WEST
♠ J 9 8 6 3
♡ 10 6 4 2
◇ 7 6
♣ J 7

EAST
♠ A 10 5
♡ J 7
◇ Q J 9 5
♣ Q 10 9 4

SOUTH
♠ K 7 2
♡ A 8
◇ 10 8 4 2
♣ A K 6 3

West would still lead the six of spades, dummy would play the Queen and East would win with the ace and return the spade ten. This time declarer falls back on the holdup play. He lets East hold the ten and wins the spade continuation with the king. Now West's spades are established and ready to be cashed, so declarer arranges to develop his fifth heart without letting West have the lead. This time, therefore, he leads the ace of hearts and then passes the eight of hearts to East, who has no more spades, and contract is home.

Notice the flexibility of playing the queen from dummy's doubleton at trick one. If the queen holds, declarer is immediately in a position where he can afford to lose a trick to West. And if the queen loses, he holds up his king until the third round and then is in a position where he can afford to lose a trick to East.

### Blocking a Suit

NORTH
♠ K Q J 3
♡ K Q 7 5
◇ 7 6 2
♣ A 4

WEST
♠ 7 4
♡ A 10 9
◇ Q 9 4
♣ K J 8 6 5

EAST
♠ 10 9 8 5 2
♡ 8 6 4 2
◇ J 5
♣ Q 7

SOUTH
♠ A 6
♡ J 3
◇ A K 10 8 3
♣ 10 9 3 2

*The bidding:*

| SOUTH | WEST | NORTH | EAST |
|-------|------|-------|------|
| 1 ◇ | Pass | 1 ♠ | Pass |
| 2 ◇ | Pass | 2 ♡ | Pass |
| 2 NT | Pass | 3 NT | Pass |
| Pass | Pass | | |

*Opening lead:* Club six

Against three no-trump West leads the six of clubs, and declarer examines the situation. He has four spade winners, two diamonds, and one club, for a total of seven immediate tricks. And by simply knocking out the heart ace he can develop two heart tricks to bring the total to nine.

Of course, the trouble is that when the opponents take the heart ace, they may run enough club tricks to defeat the conract.

Suppose that declarer holds up his ace on the first trick. East wins with the queen and returns a club to dummy's ace. Now when West wins the heart ace, he cashes the rest of his clubs, and the contract is down.

Declarer can prevent West from running his club suit by going up with dummy's ace at trick one. He knows East must have at least one of the club honors. (West wouldn't lead a small club from a holding which included the K Q J. He would lead the king.) If East has three clubs, there's no danger whatever declarer does at trick one, because the opponents can't have enough club tricks to set the contract. But if East has only two clubs, the play of the ace at trick one blocks the suit. At trick two declarer knocks out the heart ace, and West is stuck. If he leads a small club, East wins with the queen but has no clubs left to return, and South makes at least three no-trump. And if West leads the king of clubs, dropping his partner's queen, declarer's 10 9 3 2 produces a second club trick, and declarer makes four no-trump. (Note that it doesn't help East to throw his queen under dummy's ace at trick one, as in this case declarer automatically has a second club stopper.)

### Summary

In a no-trump contract the main problem is finding and developing the required number of tricks. Get in the habit of selecting a 100 percent play for the contract if there is one. If not, choose the play or combination of plays that offers the best total chance of success. In all cases, check the entry situation before proceeding.

Remember also that no-trump is usually a race between declarer and the defense. Thus, if the contract is three no-trump, declarer's aim is to develop and cash nine tricks. At the same time the defenders are trying to develop and cash five tricks of their own.

By judicious use of the various holdup, avoidance, and blocking plays, declarer can frequently slow down the defense and win the race.

# 4

# *How to Handle a Suit Contract*

PLAYING A SUIT CONTRACT is less hazardous than playing no-trump. The presence of the trump suit is a protection to declarer and hinders the opponents in their efforts to win tricks in other suits.

Although safer to play, suit contracts are much more complicated than no-trump. Many additional techniques become possible because of that extra factor, the trump suit.

Naturally, any play available to declarer at no-trump is also available in a suit contract. Thus, everything in Chapter 3 applies here as well. This chapter will deal with situations that pertain only to suit play.

### *Drawing Trumps*

On most hands, trumps need to be drawn sooner or later. Frequently declarer's *first* job is to tackle the trump suit.

NORTH
♠ 8 7 6 5
♡ 4 3
◇ A J 10 9
♣ A K Q

WEST
♠ A J 10
♡ Q J 10 9 6 2
◇ 4 2
♣ 6 5

EAST
♠ K Q
♡ 8 7
◇ 8 7 6 5
♣ J 10 9 8 7

SOUTH
♠ 9 4 3 2
♡ A K 5
◇ K Q 3
♣ 4 3 2

| *The bidding:* | NORTH | EAST | SOUTH | WEST |
|---|---|---|---|---|
| | 1 ◇ | Pass | 1 ♠ | Pass |
| | 2 ♠ | Pass | 3 ◇ | Pass |
| | 4 ♠ | Pass | Pass | Pass |

*Opening lead:* Heart queen

Although three no-trump would be the easiest game with these cards, South becomes declarer at the very reasonable contract of four spades. There are no problems outside of the trump suit, and success obviously depends on finding the opponents' spades divided 3–2. South takes the heart lead in his hand and promptly leads a trump. East wins this and probably returns another heart. South wins and leads a second trump, which East wins, and the hand is now over. West will eventually get his spade ace, making a total of three tricks for East-West.

If declarer fools around on this hand, the opponents may make their spades separately and set the contract. Suppose South tries to trump a heart in dummy before leading two rounds of spades. East overruffs, and West still gets three trump tricks for down one. Trying to ruff a heart first is pointless. The heart loser can be thrown on dummy's fourth diamond later, or it can be ruffed after two rounds of spades are led.

The important thing here is to lead spades twice, as fast as possible. Now the opponents' five spade honors fall together and East-West make only three spade tricks.

### *Drawing Trumps Sooner*

Sometimes it's necessary to ignore an apparently normal finesse in order to extract trumps with the utmost speed.

NORTH
♠ J 10 6
♡ A Q J 10
♢ 6 3
♣ A K Q J

WEST
♠ A Q 9 8 7
♡ 5 4
♢ K Q J 2
♣ 3 2

EAST
♠ 3 2
♡ K 7
♢ 10 9 8 7 5 4
♣ 10 7 4

SOUTH
♠ K 5 4
♡ 9 8 6 3 2
♢ A
♣ 9 8 6 5

*The bidding:*

| NORTH | EAST | SOUTH | WEST |
|-------|------|-------|------|
| 1 ♣ | Pass | 1 ♡ | 1 ♠ |
| 3 ♡ | Pass | 4 ♡ | Pass |
| Pass | Pass | | |

*Open lead:* Diamond king

South buys the contract at four hearts after West has made an overcall of one spade. Declarer wins the first trick with the diamond ace and sees that game is a lay-down provided none of his winners gets ruffed. At trick two he leads a heart to the ace and continues with the heart queen. East wins with the king, but the opponents' trumps are now gone, and West can score only the ace and queen of spades. If declarer had taken the heart finesse, East would have returned a spade. West would take his two winners and defeat the contract by giving East a ruff.

### *Drawing Trumps Later*

On many hands declarer will have business that needs to be taken care of before trumps are drawn.

NORTH
♠ K
♡ 7 6 5
♢ A 10 5 3
♣ A 9 6 5 4

WEST
♠ A 10 4 2
♡ 9 8 3
♢ K Q J 8
♣ 3 2

EAST
♠ Q J 6 5 3
♡ 4 2
♢ 9 7
♣ Q J 10 7

SOUTH
♠ 9 8 7
♡ A K Q J 10
♢ 6 4 2
♣ K 8

*The bidding:*

| SOUTH | WEST | NORTH | EAST |
|-------|------|-------|------|
| 1 ♡ | Pass | 2 ♣ | Pass |
| 2 ♡ | Pass | 4 ♡ | Pass |
| Pass | Pass | | |

*Opening lead:* Diamond king

West leads the diamond king against four hearts, and dummy's ace wins the first trick. If declarer draws all the trumps it's obvious he'll be left with five losers in his hand—three spades and two diamonds. Rather than concede a two-trick defeat, South arranges to ruff two of his losers in dummy. At trick two he leads the spade king. West takes the ace and will probably return a trump. Declarer wins in his hand and ruffs one spade loser. He then returns to his hand with the club king and ruffs his other spade loser. Now that the ruffs have been attended to, it's time to draw trumps. Declarer must first get to his hand so he cashes the club ace and breathes a sigh of relief when this holds. Now he ruffs a club and draws the outstanding trumps. In the end he concedes two diamond tricks, but the contract is made.

It will pay the reader to give a little extra attention to this hand. Here are a couple of points to consider:

1. If declarer had led one round of trumps before starting on spades, he would have been defeated. West would have led a second trump when he took the spade ace, and dummy would not have been able to ruff both spade losers.

2. By not drawing trumps immediately, declarer ran the risk that his ace or king of clubs would get ruffed. However—and this is the crux of the whole matter—if declarer does draw trumps immediately, it's impossible to make the hand. A risky existence is better than certain death!

### Ruffing a Loser

Here's another hand where declarer must ruff a loser before drawing trumps:

NORTH
♠ Q J 4
♡ 7 6 4
◇ A 8 5 2
♣ A Q 4

WEST
♠ 5
♡ K J 8 5
◇ K Q J 9
♣ J 9 8 3

EAST
♠ 9 8 3
♡ Q 10
◇ 10 6 4 3
♣ K 10 7 2

SOUTH
♠ A K 10 7 6 2
♡ A 9 3 2
◇ 7
♣ 6 5

*The bidding:*

| SOUTH | WEST | NORTH | EAST |
|-------|------|-------|------|
| 1 ♠   | Pass | 2 ◇   | Pass |
| 2 ♡   | Pass | 3 ♠   | Pass |
| 4 ♠   | Pass | Pass  | Pass |

*Opening lead:* Diamond king

West leads the diamond king against the four-spade contract, and declarer can see four possible losers—one club and three hearts. He sees that he can avoid the club loser if West has the club king and that he can avoid one of the heart losers if the suit breaks 3–3. This is all the planning the average player can stomach before the irresistible urge to draw trumps gets the better of him. So he wins the first trick with the diamond ace and leads three rounds of spades. Unfortunately the club king is wrong, the hearts don't split, and declarer is down one.

Why did he go down? Because he forgot to ruff his fourth heart in dummy.

Any time the hearts *do not* split 3–3, the fourth round will need to be ruffed. Only if the hearts *do* split 3–3 can declarer afford to draw the trumps first.

Therefore the correct play is to test the hearts immediately. Win the opening lead with the diamond ace, cash the heart ace, and give away two heart tricks as fast as possible. Now, if the suit has divided 3–3, all is well and you draw trumps as soon as you regain the lead. If the suit does not divide 3–3, you ruff your fourth heart in dummy with the spade jack if necessary and then draw trumps. Eventually you can take a club finesse in the hope of an overtrick.

### *Suit Establishment*

```
                      NORTH
                   ♠ A K 7 6 2
                   ♡ 10
                   ◇ A 6 4 2
                   ♣ J 5 4

      WEST                           EAST
   ♠ J 3                          ♠ Q 10 9 4
   ♡ 6 5 3                        ♡ 4 2
   ◇ Q J 10 9                     ◇ 5 3
   ♣ Q 10 3 2                     ♣ K 9 8 7 6

                      SOUTH
                   ♠ 8 5
                   ♡ A K Q J 9 8 7
                   ◇ K 8 7
                   ♣ A
```

The bidding:

| NORTH | EAST | SOUTH | WEST |
|-------|------|-------|------|
| 1 ♠ | Pass | 3 ♡ | Pass |
| 3 ♠ | Pass | 4 NT | Pass |
| 5 ♡ | Pass | 5 NT | Pass |
| 6 ◇ | Pass | 7 ♡ | Pass |
| Pass | Pass | | |

*Opening lead:* Diamond queen

This time you are declarer at seven hearts and you have one loser, a diamond. In other words you have twelve tricks and have to find a thirteenth.

Clearly the way to get this extra trick is to establish dummy's long spade suit. Accordingly you win the first trick with the diamond king, cash the ace and king of spades, and ruff a spade. If the spades had broken 3–3, your work would be over. But they don't, so you return to dummy with the heart ten and ruff another spade. Now you draw all the trumps and get to dummy with the diamond ace to pitch your losing diamond on the fifth spade, which is now good.

This isn't difficult, but there are two points worth noting. *First,* you must win the opening lead in your hand, *not* in dummy. Entries to dummy are scarce, and the diamond ace must be preserved as a means of getting to the fifth spade once it is established.

*Second,* you must start to establish the spades before you draw the trumps, because the heart ten is needed as an entry to ruff the fourth spade. The inexperienced declarer tends to go wrong here. He has a compulsion to draw all the trumps first. Then he tries to establish the spades. If they break 4–2, which is normal, he winds up one entry short and goes down. If you ask him why he drew trumps before starting on the spades, he tells you he was afraid his ace or king of spades would get ruffed. Of course this is a completely unreasonable fear. If one opponent could ruff the first or second round of spades, it would mean the other opponent had started with five or six spades, and it would be impossible ever to establish dummy's fifth spade anyhow.

This obsession to draw trumps immediately, without thinking, has to be overcome. Most players have heard the sad tale of the men who walk the streets of London barefoot because they forgot to draw trumps. Believe me, there are just as many who walk the streets of London barefoot because they drew trumps when they shouldn't have.

About half the time it's right to draw trumps first and half the time it isn't. There is no general rule. Declarer simply has to ask himself, "Is there anything that needs to be done before I draw trumps?" On this hand the answer is apparent. The spade suit must be started before trumps are drawn, because dummy's heart ten is needed as an entry.

### Playing the Two-Suited Hand

NORTH
♠ 8 7
♡ K 5
♢ Q 10 7 3 2
♣ K 7 6 3

WEST
♠ 6 4 2
♡ 10 4
♢ K 9 6 5
♣ Q J 10 9

EAST
♠ 10 5 3
♡ J 9 7 6
♢ A J
♣ A 8 5 4

SOUTH
♠ A K Q J 9
♡ A Q 8 3 2
♢ 8 4
♣ 2

The bidding:

| SOUTH | WEST | NORTH | EAST |
|-------|------|-------|------|
| 1 ♠ | Pass | 1 NT | Pass |
| 3 ♡ | Pass | 3 NT | Pass |
| 4 ♡ | Pass | 4 ♠ | Pass |
| Pass | Pass | | |

Opening lead: Club queen

Here is another situation where declarer should not draw trumps until he has taken care of another matter. In this case, the "other matter" is the establishment of declarer's second suit.

Notice that if declarer does draw trumps first he will lose a heart trick in addition to three tricks in the minor suits.

West leads the club queen, which holds the trick, and continues with a second club, which declarer ruffs. Declarer doesn't know at this point that the missing hearts are not divided 3–3. However, he should immediately cash the king and ace of hearts, then lead a small heart and ruff it in dummy. If it turns out that the hearts were divided 3–3 all the time, no harm has been done. He simply draws trumps and makes ten tricks. If the hearts were 4–2, he has to hope that the fellow with only two hearts doesn't have the spade ten. Fortunately this is the case, and once declarer has ruffed the low heart in dummy, he can draw trumps, cash the rest of his hearts, and make four spades.

Yes, it's true that if the opponent with the doubleton heart happened to have the spade ten, declarer would have been down. But in that case nothing could have saved him. He would be down however he played. It is also true that if one opponent had a singleton or void in hearts, he would ruff the ace or king, sinking declarer's ship immediately. But again it wouldn't matter. If the hearts break 5–1 or 6–0, declarer is doomed whatever he does.

### Loser on Loser Play

NORTH
♠ 9 6 5
♡ 8 5
♢ 9 5 2
♣ K J 6 5 2

WEST
♠ 4
♡ A K Q J 10 3
♢ 10 8 6
♣ Q 4 3

EAST
♠ 10 8
♡ 7 6
♢ Q J 7 3
♣ A 10 9 8 7

SOUTH
♠ A K Q J 7 3 2
♡ 9 4 2
♢ A K 4
♣ —

*The bidding:*

| WEST | NORTH | EAST | SOUTH |
|------|-------|------|-------|
| 3 ♡ | Pass | Pass | 4 ♠ |
| Pass | Pass | Pass | |

*Opening lead:* Heart king

West cashes the king and ace of hearts, on which East follows first with the seven and then with the six. West continues with the heart queen, and declarer pauses to take stock. It's apparent both from the bidding and the play so far that East has no more hearts. An inexperienced player would ruff with the spade nine at this point in the hope that East would be unable to overruff. But, as the cards lie, East would overruff with the ten and the defense would eventually get a diamond trick for down one.

The correct play is to throw a diamond loser from dummy on the heart queen, deliberately giving the opponents a heart trick instead of a diamond trick. After drawing two rounds of trumps, declarer cashes the ace and king of diamonds, and ruffs his small one in dummy.

In effect, declarer simply exchanges a heart loser for a diamond loser. But in so doing he avoids the overruff and makes his contract.

### The Ruffing Finesse

NORTH
♠ Q 9 6 5
♡ A Q J
◇ 8 4 2
♣ 7 6 5

SOUTH
♠ A K J 10 4 3 2
♡ 7
◇ A 9
♣ J 9 8

*The bidding:*

| EAST | SOUTH | WEST | NORTH |
|------|-------|------|-------|
| 1 ◇  | 4 ♠   | Pass | Pass  |
| Pass |       |      |       |

*Opening lead:* Diamond queen

South becomes declarer at four spades after East has opened the bidding with one diamond. The diamond queen is led, and South sees four losers. A parking place for one of these must obviously be found in the heart suit. Declarer wins the opening lead, draws the trumps, and then has two options:

1. If he thinks *West* has the heart king, he should lead a small heart from his hand and finesse the queen. If this works, the heart ace takes care of one of his losers and the contract is home.

2. If declarer thinks *East* has the heart king, he should cash the heart ace and lead the queen from dummy for a ruffing finesse. East will probably play a small heart on the queen, and South must throw away a loser. Of course, if East makes things easy for declarer by covering the queen with the king, South trumps and later throws his loser on the good heart jack.

Thus, declarer can make his contract if he can just guess who has the king of hearts. On this particular hand, South should resort to the ruffing finesse. The fact that East opened the bidding makes it more likely that he holds the heart king.

Even when there is no clue to the location of the missing king, it is usually better to prefer a ruffing finesse over a straight finesse. The reason is that if you are wrong, the ruffing finesse will lose one less trick. For example, on this hand if South takes a straight finesse and is wrong, he will lose five tricks—three clubs, one diamond and one heart. If he takes a ruffing finesse and is wrong, he will lose only four tricks.

## The Ruffing Finesse Continued

Sometimes the ruffing finesse will guarantee the contract regardless of the location of the missing king. Look at this next hand:

NORTH
♠ A 9 5 4
♡ 10 6
◇ A Q J 10 9
♣ J 8

WEST
♠ 8
♡ K Q J 9
◇ 7 5 2
♣ K 7 4 3 2

EAST
♠ J 7
♡ 8 7 5 3 2
◇ K 8 6 4
♣ 6 5

SOUTH
♠ K Q 10 6 3 2
♡ A 4
◇ 3
♣ A Q 10 9

*The bidding:*

| NORTH | EAST | SOUTH | WEST |
|-------|------|-------|------|
| 1 ◇ | Pass | 1 ♠ | Pass |
| 2 ♠ | Pass | 4 NT | Pass |
| 5 ♡ | Pass | 6 ♠ | Pass |
| Pass | Pass | | |

*Opening lead:* Heart king

West leads the heart king against six spades. South wins the first trick and cashes the king and queen of trumps. West discards a club on the second spade. How should declarer proceed?

The correct play is to lead a diamond to the ace and continue with the diamond queen. If East produces the king, South is on easy street. He simply ruffs the king, gets back to dummy with a trump, and throws the heart loser on a good diamond.

If East plays a small diamond when the queen is led from dummy, South just throws away his losing heart. He doesn't particularly mind if West wins this trick with the diamond king, because in this case the defense will never get a club trick. South's three losing clubs will be discarded on the jack, ten, and nine of diamonds.

Thus, if declarer takes a ruffing finesse on this hand, the contract is assured. However, if he takes a straight finesse and loses, the defense will cash a heart trick, and the contract will fail.

### The Long-Hand-Short-Hand Principle

The most important general concept of suit play is the long-hand-short-hand principle. This must be thoroughly understood before any progress can be made. Let's start with an elementary example:

NORTH
♠ 10 9 8 7
♡ 9
◊ A Q 10 5
♣ 7 6 4 2

WEST
♠ —
♡ 10 7 6 5 3 2
◊ K 4 3 2
♣ A K Q

EAST
♠ 5 4 3 2
♡ K Q J
◊ J 9 7 6
♣ 5 3

SOUTH
♠ A K Q J 6
♡ A 8 4
◊ 8
♣ J 10 9 8

The bidding:

| | SOUTH | WEST | NORTH | EAST |
|---|---|---|---|---|
| | 1 ♠ | 2 ♡ | 2 ♠ | 3 ♡ |
| | 4 ♠ | Pass | Pass | Pass |

Opening lead: Club king

West cashes three rounds of clubs and then leads a heart. Declarer wins with the ace and reviews the situation. The only possible losers remaining in his hand are the two little hearts, and both of these can be trumped in dummy. So he ruffs a heart, leads a spade to his hand, ruffs a second heart, draws all the trumps, and claims the balance.

This is not difficult, and most declarers would play it correctly. However, it is worth taking a close look at the principles involved here so they may be applied properly to hands that are more complicated.

First notice that South has more trumps than North. In bridge terminology, the hand with the greater trump length is called the long hand and the hand with the fewer trumps is called the short hand.

The long hand is generally used for drawing the opponents' trumps. Extra tricks are created by ruffing losers in the short hand. Count declarer's tricks on this deal. He starts with five spades in his hand, the two red aces, and the club jack. By ruffing the two heart losers in the short hand, he adds two extra tricks bringing the total to ten.

An inexperienced player might think he could get an extra trick by ruffing one of dummy's diamonds in his hand. Of course, this is not an extra trick at all. It's one of the same five spade tricks already counted. Extra tricks come from ruffing in the short hand, not the long hand. Ruffing losers in the long hand usually leads nowhere and can be dangerous. Notice that a declarer who carelessly ruffs a couple of diamonds in his hand will wind up with fewer trumps than East. Now he won't be able to draw all the trumps, and East will get the last trick for down one.

In this relatively elementary hand can be seen three important principles, which apply to the majority of suit contracts.

1. Ruff losers in the short hand.
2. Draw trumps with the long hand.
3. Avoid ruffing in the long hand (unless you have plenty of trumps).

Now try applying these principles to a more complicated hand!

NORTH
♠ —
♡ A Q 10 5
◇ K Q 9 8 5
♣ 9 8 4 3

WEST
♠ J 10 4 3 2
♡ 9 6 2
◇ 7 4 2
♣ A 2

EAST
♠ A 7 6 5
♡ K J 7 4 3
◇ 3
♣ 7 6 5

SOUTH
♠ K Q 9 8
♡ 8
◇ A J 10 6
♣ K Q J 10

*The bidding:*

| SOUTH | WEST | NORTH | EAST |
|-------|------|-------|------|
| 1 ◇ | Pass | 1 ♡ | Pass |
| 1 ♠ | Pass | 3 ◇ | Pass |
| 4 ♣ | Pass | 6 ◇ | Pass |
| Pass | Pass | | |

*Opening lead:* Club ace

West leads the ace of clubs and continues with a club, which South wins. The inexperienced player is accustomed to looking at the cards from the point of view of his own hand. He sees four spade losers which need to be disposed of. So, at trick three he promptly leads a spade and ruffs it in dummy. Now, however, he squirms, he eventually loses control, and he goes down. To ruff four spades in dummy, get back to the South hand each time, and eventually draw the opponents' trumps so the good clubs can be cashed is a hopeless task.

Notice that North is the long hand this time, not South. When the inexperienced declarer ruffed a spade in dummy at trick three he was ruffing in the long hand, which is usually the best way to get nowhere fast.

Look how much simpler life is if declarer considers the hand from the point of view of drawing trumps with the long hand. North has only three losers that need to be trumped—the queen, ten, and five of hearts. At trick three, declarer leads a heart to the ace and ruffs one heart loser. He then leads a diamond to dummy and ruffs the second heart loser. A spade ruff puts him back in dummy to ruff the third heart loser. Another spade ruff gets him back to dummy to draw the remaining trumps and the contract is home.

Declarer has to get to dummy four times, three times to ruff hearts and once to draw trumps. He makes every effort to do this without ruffing in the long hand. The heart ace is his first entry, and one round of trumps is the second entry. Two spade ruffs have to be used for the final two entries. Fortunately, North started with two more diamonds than West and is able to draw all the trumps, making the slam. One more spade ruff would have been fatal.

### The 4–3 Fit

The warning, "Don't ruff in the *long* hand!" is especially important when the "long" hand happens to have only four trumps.

```
                        NORTH
                    ♠ Q 10 6
                    ♡ 5 3 2
                    ◇ A K 8 3
                    ♣ A J 10
       WEST                             EAST
   ♠ 5 4 3 2                         ♠ 8 7
   ♡ A K J 9 7                       ♡ Q 10 8
   ◇ 4 2                             ◇ Q 10 9 5
   ♣ 5 2                             ♣ 9 7 4 3
                        SOUTH
                    ♠ A K J 9
                    ♡ 6 4
                    ◇ J 7 6
                    ♣ K Q 8 6
```

| *The bidding:* | SOUTH | WEST | NORTH | EAST |
|---|---|---|---|---|
| | 1 ♣ | Pass | 1 ◇ | Pass |
| | 1 ♠ | Pass | 3 ♣ | Pass |
| | 3 ◇ | Pass | 3 ♠ | Pass |
| | 4 ♠ | Pass | Pass | Pass |

*Opening lead:* Heart king

North-South did well to avoid game in no-trump, where declarer would have to lose the first five heart tricks. Against the four-spade contract, West starts out with three rounds of hearts. South is the long hand, and he must *not* ruff the third heart. If he does he will go down unless the spades break 3–3, which is unlikely. Declarer should simply throw away a diamond on the third heart. Now dummy (the short hand) can handle any further heart leads, and the contract is safe against the normal 4–2 trump division.

### The 4–4 Fit

What about the hands where dummy and declarer both have four trumps?

NORTH
♠ K Q 10 7 4 2
♡ 5
◇ J 6
♣ Q J 10 9

| WEST | EAST |
|---|---|
| ♠ A 3 | ♠ J 9 8 5 |
| ♡ 8 7 6 4 2 | ♡ K Q 10 3 |
| ◇ 7 2 | ◇ K Q 10 9 |
| ♣ 8 7 5 4 | ♣ 6 |

SOUTH
♠ 6
♡ A J 9
◇ A 8 5 4 3
♣ A K 3 2

| The bidding: | SOUTH | WEST | NORTH | EAST |
|---|---|---|---|---|
| | 1 ◇ | Pass | 1 ♠ | Pass |
| | 2 ♣ | Pass | 3 ♣ | Pass |
| | 3 NT | Pass | 4 ♠ | Pass |
| | 5 ♣ | Pass | Pass | Pass |

*Opening lead:* Heart eight

Both the North and South hands have four trumps, and declarer must choose which hand to make the "long" hand.

West leads the heart eight, and declarer takes East's queen with the ace and leads his singleton spade. West takes the spade ace and continues with another heart. Dummy must *not* ruff. North's spades are nearly established, while the South hand is full of losers. Thus it's sensible to make dummy the master hand. It will probably be necessary to ruff one more spade in the South hand. As soon as spades are completely established, declarer plans to draw trumps ending in dummy. Dummy, in effect, becomes the long hand and must not be shortened. Discard a diamond from dummy on the heart. East wins the heart king, but declarer's jack can now take care of another heart lead. East will probably return a diamond, on which declarer plays the ace and leads a trump to dummy. A small spade is now ruffed with the club ace. When both opponents follow, declarer simply draws the remaining trumps, starting with the king in his hand and ending up in dummy, which is now high.

### Maintaining Control

Here is another example of the extent to which declarer should go to avoid ruffing in the long hand.

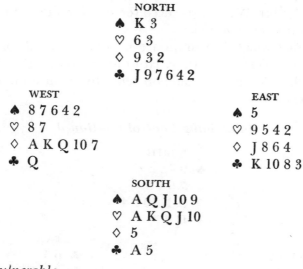

NORTH
♠ K 3
♡ 6 3
◇ 9 3 2
♣ J 9 7 6 4 2

WEST
♠ 8 7 6 4 2
♡ 8 7
◇ A K Q 10 7
♣ Q

EAST
♠ 5
♡ 9 5 4 2
◇ J 8 6 4
♣ K 10 8 3

SOUTH
♠ A Q J 10 9
♡ A K Q J 10
◇ 5
♣ A 5

*Both vulnerable*

*The bidding:*

| SOUTH | WEST | NORTH | EAST |
|-------|------|-------|------|
| 2 ♠   | Pass | 2 NT  | Pass |
| 3 ♡   | Pass | 3 ♠   | Pass |
| 4 ♠   | Pass | Pass  | Pass |

*Opening lead:* Diamond king

This deal comes from a rubber bridge game, and declarer apparently starts with eleven winners, five spades, five hearts, and the ace of clubs.

West leads the diamond king and continues with the ace. Declarer has no way to avoid a club loser, so he throws the club five on the second diamond. West persists with another diamond, and declarer has no more losers to throw away. The inexperienced declarer hates to discard one of his obvious winners, so he ruffs the third diamond and starts to draw the trumps. Unfortunately, East shows out on the second round of spades. This means West has one more trump left than South, and whatever he does, declarer goes down two. He can never take more than five spades, two hearts, and one club. Because of the bad trump break, he lost control of the hand and wound up with eight tricks instead of the eleven he had anticipated. Embarrassing, isn't it?

A more careful declarer would make this hand. At trick three, instead of ruffing in the long hand he would discard one of his good hearts on the third diamond. If West continues the diamond assault, dummy's spade king can take care of the next round. And, regardless of what West leads, declarer quickly draws five rounds of trumps and makes ten tricks.

It's true that when six trumps are missing, they will only break 5–1 about 15 percent of the time. However, an overtrick means very little at rubber bridge. It's common sense to sacrifice the overtrick to ensure the contract.

### Maintaining Control Continued

NORTH
♠ 9
♡ 7 6 4 3
♢ A K 10 9 4
♣ Q 4 3

WEST
♠ Q 4 3 2
♡ K Q J 10 9 2
♢ 6 5
♣ A

EAST
♠ 6 5
♡ A 8 5
♢ Q J 8 7
♣ 7 6 5 2

SOUTH
♠ A K J 10 8 7
♡ —
♢ 3 2
♣ K J 10 9 8

*The bidding:*

| WEST | NORTH | EAST | SOUTH |
|------|-------|------|-------|
| 1 ♡ | Pass | 2 ♡ | 4 ♠ |
| Pass | Pass | Pass | |

*Opening lead:* Heart king

Let's take another look at the very important problem of maintaining control of the trump suit.

Here's a case where there are apparently only two losers, the club ace and the trump queen. Suppose South ruffs the opening lead and plays out the ace, king, and jack of spades. West wins this with the queen and forces declarer with another heart. The hand has now collapsed because South and West each have one trump left and the club ace is still at large. Whether declarer draws the last trump or whether he starts on clubs is immaterial. He will wind up losing a total of six tricks. (If you don't believe it, play it out yourself.)

Declarer could have avoided this debacle. After both opponents follow to the ace and king of trumps, the hand is cold if he just doesn't draw any more trumps. Declarer must resign himself to losing two trump tricks. At trick four he should knock out the club ace. West will probably lead another heart, and South ruffs. At this point, South has the jack and ten of spades left, and West has the queen and two. South now leads out all his winners. West can ruff any time he chooses and will make tricks with both the queen and two of spades. But declarer makes ten tricks and his contract.

## *The Crossruff*

NORTH
♠ A J 10 3
♡ A J 6 4 2
◇ 4
♣ K 8 7

WEST
♠ 7 5 4 2
♡ K Q 10 9 8
◇ Q 3
♣ J 6

EAST
♠ 6
♡ 5 3
◇ K 10 9 5 2
♣ Q 10 9 5 2

SOUTH
♠ K Q 9 8
♡ 7
◇ A J 8 7 6
♣ A 4 3

*The bidding:*

| SOUTH | WEST | NORTH | EAST |
|-------|------|-------|------|
| 1 ◇ | Pass | 1 ♡ | Pass |
| 1 ♠ | Pass | 3 ♠ | Pass |
| 4 ♣ | Pass | 6 ♠ | Pass |
| Pass | Pass | | |

*Opening lead:* Heart king

With singletons in both the North and South hands, this is the ideal setup for the technique known as crossruff. You can take eight trump tricks if you take them all separately. Adding the four winners in the side suits gives a total of twelve tricks.

So, you win the first trick with the heart ace, cash the ace and king of clubs and the diamond ace, then proceed to ruff diamonds and hearts alternately until you have twelve tricks in all.

You never draw trumps, so even a 5–0 spade split won't bother you. Bad breaks in the side suits are no worry either, because you're not trying to establish any side suit.

Of course, you have to ruff the first diamond with the spade three, and there's a remote chance that East may overruff if he also has a singleton diamond. Once you get over this hurdle, however, the opponents can no longer defeat you, because you'll be crossruffing with all high trumps.

*Warning:* When you plan to crossruff a hand, it's important to cash all the winners in the side suits first. Look what would happen on this hand to a careless declarer who started his crossruff before cashing the ace and king of clubs. West would throw a club at his first opportunity. Now, when declarer belatedly tried to cash his club honors, West would ruff in and then lead a trump, and the roof would cave in.

Yes, West could have defeated this hand with an original spade lead. Then declarer could not have made eight separate trump tricks by crossruffing and would be forced to try to establish either hearts or diamonds. As neither suit breaks favorably, the hand would be set.

The crossruff is an exception to the general principle governing the long and short hand. Normally it's dangerous to ruff in the long hand, thereby weakening the holding that eventually is going to draw the trumps. Here, however, declarer never draws the trumps, so the principle does not apply.

There are two other major exceptions to the general rule that it's dangerous to ruff in the long hand. These are the dummy reversal and the trump coup. They are both advanced techniques and will be dealt with in Chapter 7.

### Summary

Almost the first lesson a bridge player learns is the importance of extracting the opponents' trumps. Sometimes it's right to draw them immediately, and sometimes one has to take care of other business first. Drawing trumps should often be postponed when the trumps in the short hand are needed for ruffing purposes or as entries. There is no general rule. Declarer must plan ahead to determine whether he can afford to pull the trumps first or whether he will need them later for some purpose.

In the vast majority of suit contracts, trumps are drawn with the long hand, and additional tricks are created by ruffing in the short hand if necessary. Declarer should beware of ruffing in the long hand unless he has plenty of extra trumps. Otherwise he is apt to lose control of the trump suit, and the whole hand may collapse.

PART II ♠♡◇♣ ADVANCED

# 5

# *End Play*

A FAMOUS PLAYER once summed up the difference between an average declarer and an expert as follows:

The average declarer knows how to finesse.
The expert knows how *not* to finesse.

Naturally this is an oversimplification, but there is a great deal of truth in the remark. Take this situation for example:

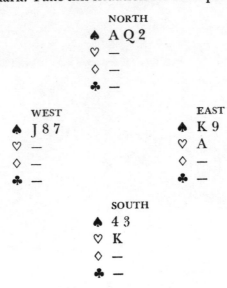

NORTH
♠ A Q 2
♡ —
◇ —
♣ —

WEST
♠ J 8 7
♡ —
◇ —
♣ —

EAST
♠ K 9
♡ A
◇ —
♣ —

SOUTH
♠ 4 3
♡ K
◇ —
♣ —

South has to lead at a no-trump contract and needs two of the three remaining tricks. The average declarer leads a spade to dummy's queen and goes down if the finesse loses. The expert leads the heart king to East's ace and makes the hand without resorting to a finesse when East is forced to return a spade into the ace-queen.

The expert's method in this situation is known as an end play. Of course, it's not difficult when you see all four hands exposed. The trick is to be able to do this without seeing the opponents' cards.

Naturally you would not try to teach a beginner this play. It's important that a player understands how to finesse before he can understand how *not* to finesse. Similarly it would be poor tactics to teach a dummy reversal, or a trump coup to a player who has not already digested the long-hand-short-hand principle. It would just mix him up. In fact, most of the techniques discussed in Part II will only benefit players who are thoroughly familiar with the straightforward techniques discussed in Part I. If you are hazy about anything in Chapters 1 through 4, now is the time to stop and review. It doesn't pay to try to run before you learn how to walk.

\* \*

Many advanced plays belong to a general class known as end play. A player is said to be end played when he has to lead at a moment when any card he returns will cost his side a trick. In the three-card ending above, East was end-played when he won the heart ace. This situation usually occurs toward the end of a hand, hence the term, end play.

In some books the term is used to refer to any of the various advanced techniques (including trump coup and squeeze) that occur toward the end of a hand. This book will follow the more common usage and limit the term end play to the throwing of the lead to an opponent in order to force a favorable return.

The simplest form of end play takes place in a suit contract where both dummy and declarer have adequate trump length. The procedure here can be called, descriptively, an elimination and throw in.

## Elimination and Throw In

NORTH
♠ A 9 8
♡ K 10 9 8
◇ K 6 2
♣ K J 3

WEST
♠ Q J 10
♡ 6 3 2
◇ J 9 5 3
♣ Q 6 2

EAST
♠ 7 4 3 2
♡ 7
◇ Q 10 8 7
♣ 9 8 5 4

SOUTH
♠ K 6 5
♡ A Q J 5 4
◇ A 4
♣ A 10 7

*The bidding:*

| SOUTH | WEST | NORTH | EAST |
|-------|------|-------|------|
| 1 ♡ | Pass | 3 ♡ | Pass |
| 6 ♡ | Pass | Pass | Pass |

*Opening lead:* Spade queen

West leads the spade queen against six hearts, and declarer examines the situation. There is an obvious spade loser so the problem is to avoid losing a club trick. Declarer can finesse either way for the club queen, but if he guesses wrong the contract will fail.

To remove the guesswork, South plans to force an opponent to lead clubs for him. He wins the spade lead in either hand and draws all the opponents' trumps. Next he takes the ace and king of diamonds and ruffs dummy's third diamond. This eliminates all the diamonds from the North and South hands. Declarer cashes the other spade honor reaching the following position:

NORTH
♠ 8
♡ 10
♢ —
♣ K J 3

WEST
♠ J
♡ —
♢ J
♣ Q 6 2

EAST
♠ —
♡ —
♢ Q
♣ 9 8 5 4

SOUTH
♠ 5
♡ J
♢ —
♣ A 10 7

The stage is now set and declarer throws the opponents into the lead with a spade. West wins and must return a club or concede a ruff and a discard. In either case South automatically makes the rest of the tricks.

There are many awkward card combinations, like the North and South club holding in the above hand, which are easy to play if an opponent leads the suit. For example:

DUMMY
Q x x

DECLARER
J x x

If declarer has to lead this suit himself, he is apt to lose all three tricks. However, if an opponent leads the suit for him, declarer is guaranteed to win one trick.

DUMMY
K 10 x

DECLARER
Q 9 x

If declarer leads this suit, he may misguess the jack and win only one trick. If an opponent leads the suit, declarer must make two tricks.

Be on the lookout for combinations like these. In a trump contract you may be able to avoid the guesswork by elimination and throw in.

### Elimination Play Continued

Here's another example in which declarer improves his chances with an elimination play. ("Elimination and throw in play" is quite a mouthful. The term "elimination play" is more commonly used although it is not quite as descriptive. The term "strip" is occasionally used for elimination.)

```
                        NORTH
                     ♠ A 9 5
                     ♡ J 9
                     ◇ K Q
                     ♣ A J 10 7 5 2

        WEST                            EAST
     ♠ Q 8 7                         ♠ 10 3 2
     ♡ K 8 7 6 3                     ♡ A Q 10 5
     ◇ 10 9 8 7                      ◇ 6 5 4 3 2
     ♣ 6                            ♣ 4

                        SOUTH
                     ♠ K J 6 4
                     ♡ 4 2
                     ◇ A J
                     ♣ K Q 9 8 3
```

| The bidding: | SOUTH | WEST | NORTH | EAST |
|---|---|---|---|---|
| | 1 ♣ | Pass | 3 ♣ | Pass |
| | 3 ♠ | Pass | 4 ♣ | Pass |
| | 5 ♣ | Pass | Pass | Pass |

*Opening lead:* Diamond ten

Against five clubs West leads the diamond ten, and declarer sees two heart losers and a possible spade loser. To improve his chances of avoiding a spade loser, declarer plans an elimination play. He wins the opening lead, draws the outstanding trumps, and cashes the other diamond. Now he gives the opponents their heart tricks. East does best to win the second heart trick, but if he leads a third heart or a diamond, declarer automatically makes his contract by ruffing in the South hand and discarding a spade from dummy. So

East returns a small spade, and South ducks. As it happens, West has to play the queen, and declarer's problems are over. If West had played the ten of spades instead of the queen, declarer would still have the opportunity to finesse East for the queen next time.

Thus, by compelling the opponents to lead a spade, declarer makes his contract if East has *either* the queen or the ten. If he plays spades himself, he is entirely dependent on the favorable location of the queen.

## Elimination Play Continued

```
                    NORTH
                  ♠ 10 6 4 2
                  ♡ J 8 6 5 4
                  ◇ A 2
                  ♣ A 2

    WEST                              EAST
  ♠ 7                               ♠ J 9
  ♡ Q 10 9                          ♡ K 3
  ◇ J 10 9 8 7                      ◇ 6 5 4 3
  ♣ J 7 6 3                         ♣ 10 9 8 5 4

                    SOUTH
                  ♠ A K Q 8 5 3
                  ♡ A 7 2
                  ◇ K Q
                  ♣ K Q
```

*The bidding:*

| SOUTH | WEST | NORTH | EAST |
|-------|------|-------|------|
| 2 ♠   | Pass | 3 ♠   | Pass |
| 4 ♠   | Pass | 6 ♠   | Pass |
| Pass  | Pass |       |      |

*Opening lead:* Diamond jack

In the previous examples declarer used the elimination play to force the opponents to lead a certain suit. Here is a hand in which declarer is not interested in having a particular suit led. He uses the elimination play purely to get the advantage of a ruff and a discard.

West leads the diamond jack against the small slam in spades, and South sees two heart losers. His best bet is to hope for a "ruff and a sluff." Accordingly he wins the first trick with the diamond ace and immediately leads a heart to his ace. Next he draws the trumps and cashes his remaining winners in the minor suits. Now a heart lead puts East in with the king. East has no more hearts or spades left, so he has to return a club or a diamond. Declarer happily sluffs the losing heart from his hand as he ruffs in dummy and the contract is home.

The reader may ask, "Why in the world didn't South draw the trumps before cashing his heart ace?" Well, there's method in this madness. Suppose the East-West heart and spade holdings had been reversed:

NORTH
♠ 10 6 4 2
♡ J 8 6 5 4
◇ A 2
♣ A 2

WEST
♠ J 9
♡ K 3
◇ J 10 9 8 7
♣ J 7 6 3

EAST
♠ 7
♡ Q 10 9
◇ 6 5 4 3
♣ 10 9 8 5 4

SOUTH
♠ A K Q 8 5 3
♡ A 7 2
◇ K Q
♣ K Q

Now the contract can always be defeated with proper defense. All West has to do is throw his heart king under South's ace. East will win the second heart lead and cash his other heart for down one.

West *should* throw his king under the ace. And if declarer draws the trumps and eliminates the side suits before cashing the heart ace, West undoubtedly *will* jettison his king. He can see he's about to be thrown in and forced to give declarer a ruff and a discard. But if declarer cashes the heart ace at trick two, West may not be alert to the impending danger. If he makes a mistake and fails to throw away his king, he is a dead duck.

In a situation like this, your chances of catching someone napping are better than if you cash the ace as soon as possible.

### Partial Elimination

**NORTH**
♠ A 6 3
♡ A K 10
◇ J 10 9 8 7
♣ 10 9

| WEST | EAST |
|------|------|
| ♠ J 8 4 2 | ♠ Q 10 7 5 |
| ♡ 3 2 | ♡ 7 6 4 |
| ◇ Q 4 3 | ◇ 6 5 |
| ♣ K Q 7 6 | ♣ 8 5 4 3 2 |

**SOUTH**
♠ K 9
♡ Q J 9 8 5
◇ A K 2
♣ A J

*The bidding:*

| NORTH | EAST | SOUTH | WEST |
|-------|------|-------|------|
| 1 ◇ | Pass | 1 ♡ | Pass |
| 2 ♡ | Pass | 4 NT | Pass |
| 5 ♡ | Pass | 6 ♡ | Pass |
| Pass | Pass | | |

*Opening lead:* Club king

West leads the club king against six hearts, and declarer must find some way to avoid a diamond loser. Rather than stake everything on the favorable location of the diamond queen he decides to try a partial elimination first. He wins the opening lead with the club ace and draws two rounds of trumps. Next he cashes the king and ace of spades and ruffs dummy's last spade. Now he throws West in with the club queen. If West had the remaining heart he would lead it, and the partial elimination would fail. As the cards lie, however, West is stuck. He must either return a diamond or concede a ruff and a discard, and declarer makes twelve tricks despite the unfavorable location of the diamond queen.

This procedure is called a partial elemination because declarer wasn't able to extract all of the opponents' hearts before the throw in. In order to leave one trump in dummy it was only possible to draw two rounds.

Note that on this hand the partial elimination is far superior to the ordinary play of drawing trumps and then tackling diamonds. Even if West has the missing trump to get out with (which means the partial elimination has failed), declarer is still able to fall back on the diamond finesse as a last resort.

### Repeated Throw In

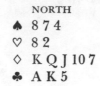

NORTH
♠ 8 7 4
♡ 8 2
◇ K Q J 10 7
♣ A K 5

WEST
♠ 2
♡ K J 10 9 7 6 5 4
◇ 4 3
♣ Q 7

EAST
♠ K Q J 10 6 5
♡ 3
◇ 2
♣ J 10 9 8 6

SOUTH
♠ A 9 3
♡ A Q
◇ A 9 8 6 5
♣ 4 3 2

*North-South vulnerable*

*The bidding:*

| SOUTH | WEST | NORTH | EAST |
|-------|------|-------|------|
| 1 ◇ | 4 ♡ | 5 ◇ | Pass |
| Pass | Pass | | |

*Opening lead:* Spade two

Sometimes it's possible to get *two* extra tricks by end-playing an opponent twice. In this example South reaches the rather precarious contract of five diamonds after West has made a pre-emptive overcall of four hearts. West leads the singleton spade, and declarer can see four losers: two spades, one club, and one heart.

South wins the first trick with the spade ace, draws the trumps in two rounds, and cashes the ace and king of clubs. The heart finesse appears hopeless, so declarer leads a small heart to his ace and throws West in with the heart queen.

West is forced to return a heart (because he has nothing else left), and declarer happily throws away a club from dummy and a spade from his own hand. This gives West a heart trick, which he apparently doesn't deserve. But it also saddles him with the lead again.

Naturally he has to play another heart, and this time dummy ruffs as declarer throws his last spade. The South hand is now good except for one club, which is ruffed in dummy. So, declarer makes the rest of the tricks and his contract.

Because West was forced to make *two* losing heart leads, declarer made *two* extra tricks.

### Pseudo Elimination

```
                     NORTH
                  ♠ A 9 8 5
                  ♡ 5 2
                  ◊ A 9 2
                  ♣ K 9 3 2

        WEST                      EAST
     ♠ 4 2                     ♠ 10 7 6
     ♡ K Q 10 9                ♡ 8 7 6 4 3
     ◊ Q 10 7 4                ◊ K 8 3
     ♣ J 6 4                   ♣ Q 5

                     SOUTH
                  ♠ K Q J 3
                  ♡ A J
                  ◊ J 6 5
                  ♣ A 10 8 7
```

*The bidding:*

| SOUTH | WEST | NORTH | EAST |
|-------|------|-------|------|
| 1 NT  | Pass | 2 ♣   | Pass |
| 2 ♠   | Pass | 4 ♠   | Pass |
| Pass  | Pass |       |      |

*Opening lead:* Heart king

Sometimes an inexpert defender will think he is end-played when actually he is not. In such a case declarer is likely to benefit.

West leads the heart king against four spades, and declarer is in danger of losing two diamonds, one heart, and one club. He wins the first trick with the heart ace, draws three rounds of trumps, and throws West in with the heart jack. West takes his queen and exits safely with a diamond. Dummy ducks, and East wins with the king and returns a diamond. South plays low, and the ten forces the ace. Now declarer throws West in again with the third round of diamonds.

When this hand actually occurred, West thought he was end-played at this point. He feared that South was out of red cards, and he knew it is almost always a losing proposition to give declarer a ruff and a discard. In desperation he switched to a club. This enabled declarer to avoid a club loser and make his contract.

West wasn't really end-played when he won the third diamond. He should have exited with a heart. In the first place declarer might actually have another heart, in which case a heart return couldn't hurt the defense. In the second place, declarer is known to have started with four spades and three diamonds. If he only has two hearts, he has to have *four* clubs. In this case one club sluff will do him no good. This is the unusual situation where a ruff and discard doesn't benefit the declarer. With a heart return he will eventually lose a club trick for down one.

West was the victim of a pseudo elimination. His fear of conceding a ruff and a discard (which in this case would have proved harmless) drove him to the fatal club shift.

### The End Play at No-Trump

An end play at no-trump requires a little more care than an elimination play in a suit contract, because declarer doesn't have the protection of a trump suit. Nevertheless, the basic principle is the same.

```
                      NORTH
                    ♠ K 5 4
                    ♡ 4 3 2
                    ◇ 8 4 3
                    ♣ A K Q J

        WEST                          EAST
      ♠ Q 10 2                      ♠ 9 8 7 3
      ♡ K 9 8                       ♡ J 10 6 5
      ◇ K Q 10 2                    ◇ 9 7 6
      ♣ 5 4 3                       ♣ 10 6

                      SOUTH
                    ♠ A J 6
                    ♡ A Q 7
                    ◇ A J 5
                    ♣ 9 8 7 2
```

| The bidding: | SOUTH | WEST | NORTH | EAST |
|---|---|---|---|---|
| | 1 NT | Pass | 3 NT | Pass |
| | Pass | Pass | | |

*Opening lead:* Diamond king

West leads the diamond king against three no-trump, and declarer can see eight tricks: four clubs, two spades, and the two red aces. He lets West hold the diamond king in hopes he will continue the suit or perhaps shift to a heart or a spade, in which case declarer's problems would be over. Unfortunately West is uncooperative and shifts to a club. South now cashes three rounds of clubs, thereby removing all the clubs from West's hand, and leads a diamond to the ace. When East follows suit, it means West started with, at most, five diamonds, not enough to set the contract. So declarer throws him in with the diamond jack. West is end-played. He can cash his diamonds, but then must return a heart or a spade. Either lead gives declarer his ninth trick.

### The Throw-In Card

To bring off an end play, declarer must have a card with which to throw the lead to an opponent. For this reason he will often reject an ordinary holdup play.

NORTH
♠ A 7 6
♡ 5 4 3
◇ Q J 10
♣ K Q J 2

WEST
♠ J 3 2
♡ Q J 8 6 2
◇ K 3 2
♣ A 3

EAST
♠ Q 10 9 5
♡ 10 9
◇ 9 7 6 4
♣ 6 5 4

SOUTH
♠ K 8 4
♡ A K 7
◇ A 8 5
♣ 10 9 8 7

| *The bidding:* | SOUTH | WEST | NORTH | EAST |
|---|---|---|---|---|
| | 1 ♣ | 1 ♡ | 3 ♣ | Pass |
| | 3 NT | Pass | Pass | Pass |

*Opening lead:* Heart six

South becomes declarer at three no-trump after West has made an overcall of one heart. The heart six is led, and South wins with the ace and knocks out the ace of clubs. West continues with the heart queen, and declarer must not hold up, because he may need his small heart later as a throw-in card. So, he wins the second heart and cashes all his clubs. West discards one diamond and one spade, and the position has become this:

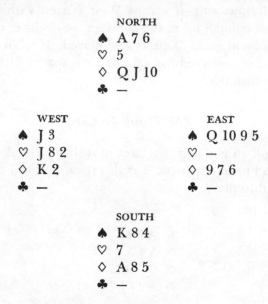

NORTH
♠ A 7 6
♡ 5
◇ Q J 10
♣ —

WEST
♠ J 3
♡ J 8 2
◇ K 2
♣ —

EAST
♠ Q 10 9 5
♡ —
◇ 9 7 6
♣ —

SOUTH
♠ K 8 4
♡ 7
◇ A 8 5
♣ —

South has already taken five tricks at this point, and if East has the diamond king, declarer can easily make a total of ten tricks by finessing. If the finesse loses, however, West will cash his three good hearts and the contract will fail.

In view of West's overcall, South decides he probably holds the diamond king. So he cashes the ace and king of spades and throws West in with the seven of hearts. West takes his three heart tricks and then has to lead a diamond away from his king, and declarer makes three no-trump.

Notice that the contract would fail if South ducked the first or second heart lead. Without his small heart, declarer has no throw-in card and can make only eight tricks. Notice also that no defense will beat the contract if declarer plays properly and is able to *read the opponents' cards correctly.*

This necessity to read the position is the factor which makes the end play at no-trump tougher than an elimination play in a suit contract. With trumps in both hands, declarer can often strip the hand and throw the lead without really caring who has what. If the opponent who is thrown in pulls some surprise card out of a hat, instead of making the expected return, it doesn't matter. Declarer gets a ruff and discard, which usually is just as good.

At no-trump, however, declarer has to keep his eye on the ball every minute. For example, on this hand West's last two cards must be diamonds or the end play won't work. Thus, in the seven-card end position shown above, when South makes the decision to try an end play instead of a finesse, he has to be pretty sure of West's distribution. He reasons as follows:

1. West needs the diamond king for his overcall. He's unlikely to leave the king unguarded. Therefore, he has the king and at least one other diamond left.

2. West wouldn't overcall on a flimsy four-card suit. Yet he can't have started with six hearts, since East has already shown up with two. Therefore West started with five hearts and must have exactly three remaining.

3. If West's last seven cards include exactly three hearts and at least two diamonds, he can have *at most* two spades left. Therefore, after the ace and king of spades are cashed, the stage must be set for an end play.

It's worth noting that West's only chance to avoid this trap is to save three spades. Naturally he can't throw a heart, because in that case declarer can afford to lose a diamond trick and still make the hand. But he can probably fool declarer by throwing two diamonds on the clubs if he has the nerve. Now declarer *can* cash the diamond ace, felling the king for an overtrick. However, if West blanks the king smoothly, declarer is almost certain to misread the position. Whether he tries the finesse or the end play, he has to pay off.

Fortunately declarer seldom has to worry about such Machiavellian tactics. There just aren't many defenders who are that good.

### Repeated Throw-In at No-Trump

```
                    NORTH
                    ♠ 10 8 6
                    ♡ 10 3 2
                    ◇ Q 6 5 4
                    ♣ 4 3 2

     WEST                        EAST
     ♠ A Q J                     ♠ 9 4 3 2
     ♡ K J 8 7                   ♡ 9 6 4
     ◇ J 10 9 8                  ◇ 3 2
     ♣ 6 5                       ♣ J 10 9 7

                    SOUTH
                    ♠ K 7 5
                    ♡ A Q 5
                    ◇ A K 7
                    ♣ A K Q 8
```

| *The bidding:* | SOUTH | WEST | NORTH | EAST |
|---|---|---|---|---|
| | 3 NT | Pass | Pass | Pass |

*Opening lead:* Diamond jack

Occasionally a player can benefit from two end plays in a no-trump contract. Here's a case where declarer starts with only seven winners. Prospects for extra tricks include:

1. The clubs may break 3–3.
2. The diamonds may break 3–3.
3. East may have the heart king.
4. East may have the spade ace.
5. West may be subject to an end play.

South wins the first trick with the diamond ace and cashes the ace, king, and queen of clubs. West throws a heart on the third round which puts an end to prospect number one. Declarer next cashes the king and queen of diamonds, and when East shows out, prospect number two goes down the drain.

The lead is now in dummy for the one and only time. Naturally, declarer rejects the spade or heart plays (which are only 50 percent shots) for the guaranteed end play against West. So he leads dummy's fourth diamond and throws the small club from his own hand. West wins the diamond and has to make a losing return. Let's suppose he exits with the queen of spades. Declarer takes this with the king and returns a spade. If East had a spade entry, he would cash his black winners and return a heart at the twelfth trick through the ace-queen. Since West has the heart king, the contract would fail.

However, as the cards lie, West must win the spade. After cashing the other spade he has to lead a heart into the ace-queen, and declarer makes nine tricks.

The result would be the same if West chose to exit with a heart when he won the fourth diamond. Declarer simply cashes two heart tricks and leads his third heart. In either case, correct technique brings in nine tricks in spite of the fact that prospects numbers one, two, three, and four all fail.

Although end plays usually occur late in the hand, they may occasionally come up at the beginning. Here's an example in which West suffered the rare indignity of being end-played on the opening lead. To make matters worse, both East and West were subsequently endplayed by declarer in the process of fulfilling his doubled contract.

```
                    NORTH
                ♠ K 8 7 6 5 4
                ♡ 7
                ◊ A Q 7
                ♣ 9 6 2

    WEST                            EAST
♠ —                             ♠ A Q J 10 9
♡ K J 9 8 6 2                   ♡ 5 3
◊ K 5 3                         ◊ 10 9 6
♣ Q 10 5 3                      ♣ 8 7 4

                    SOUTH
                ♠ 3 2
                ♡ A Q 10 4
                ◊ J 8 4 2
                ♣ A K J
```

| *The bidding:* | SOUTH | WEST | NORTH | EAST |
|---|---|---|---|---|
| | 1 ♡ | Pass | 1 ♠ | Pass |
| | 1 NT | Pass | 3 ♠ | Pass |
| | 3 NT | Pass | Pass | Double |
| | Pass | Pass | Pass | |

*Opening lead:* Club three

When this deal occurred in a tournament, most North-South pairs were doubled in four spades and the contract was badly wrecked on the rocks of distribution. One South succeeded in making three no-trump doubled, and the bidding at his table went as shown in the diagram. Over three no-trump North hesitated, apparently considering whether to correct to four spades. East was rooting for him to do so, and when North decided to pass, East doubled in annoyance.

Oddly enough, West was end-played before he began. A diamond lead allows declarer to make four diamond tricks instead of three. A heart or a club lead into South's tenaces costs a trick. And the poor man has no spades.

West chose to lead the club three, and South won with the jack and surveyed the situation. A double of three no-trump when no suits have been bid by the defense generally calls for a lead of dummy's suit. It was clear from West's choice of a club that he had no spades. Armed with this information, declarer set about the task of obtaining a few more favorable leads. He led a diamond to the queen and cashed the ace. Next he played the ace and king of clubs and threw West in with the third round of diamonds. West took his long club but then had to lead a heart into declarer's tenace. South won the heart and cashed the heart ace and the fourth diamond. At this point everyone was reduced to three cards, and both North and East had only spades left. So declarer led a spade and ducked in dummy. East won and cashed his ace but dummy won the last trick with the king. In all, declarer took three clubs, three diamonds, two hearts, and one spade for a well-earned top.

### To Sum Up

When the inexperienced player has to handle a card combination, he generally considers the problem from the point of view of leading the suit himself. Subconsciously he may be aware that life would be simpler if the enemy led the suit. But it's only the relatively advanced player who carries his reasoning a little further and asks himself, "How can I force my opponent to lead this suit for me?"

Once a declarer opens his mind to this idea of compelling an opponent to do the job for him, he's over the hump, at least as far as the elimination play in a suit is concerned. The actual strip and throw in is really downhill work.

End play at no-trump is much tougher, however, because declarer has to have a pretty good idea of who has what before he throws the lead. It's safe to say that any player who has thoroughly mastered end play at no-trump is already an expert declarer.

# 6

# *Reading the Cards*

PERHAPS THE GREATEST advantage enjoyed by the first-class declarer is his ability to "read" the opponents' cards. After two or three tricks have been played, he will sometimes know the exact distribution of all four hands as well as the location of every important honor. Black magic? Not at all. It is simply the art of putting information together and reading the answer.

Much of what is called card reading is really a matter of counting. A bridge player's life is full of counting. He counts tricks and he counts trumps. He counts points and he counts losers. But if he wants to become an expert declarer, he must get into the habit of counting the hand.

Counting the hand refers to the process of working out the opponents' original distribution. Situations where a declarer has to locate a queen are often solved in this manner.

NORTH
♠ K 10 7
♡ A K 5 3
◊ K J 6 3
♣ 5 4

WEST
♠ 6
♡ 10 8 7 2
◊ 4 2
♣ K 10 8 6 3 2

EAST
♠ Q 9 5 3 2
♡ Q J 9 4
◊ 8 7
♣ A Q

SOUTH
♠ A J 8 4
♡ 6
◊ A Q 10 9 5
♣ J 9 7

*The bidding:*

| SOUTH | WEST | NORTH | EAST |
|-------|------|-------|------|
| 1 ◊ | Pass | 1 ♡ | Pass |
| 1 ♠ | Pass | 3 ◊ | Pass |
| 4 ◊ | Pass | 5 ◊ | Pass |
| Pass | Pass | | |

*Opening lead:* Club six

East wins the first two tricks with the ace and queen of clubs and shifts to the heart queen. Declarer takes the ace and pulls trump in two rounds. He throws a spade on the king of hearts, and the only problem left is to locate the queen of spades.

Instead of simply guessing who has the queen, declarer sets out to determine the opponents' exact original distribution. He ruffs a heart in his hand, ruffs a club in dummy, and ruffs the last heart. The count is now complete. East is known to have started with two clubs (he failed to follow suit when South ruffed a club) and he has shown up with precisely two diamonds and four hearts. Therefore, by subtraction, he must have been dealt five spades, and West must have a singleton.

Declarer cashes the king of spades, and when both of the opponents follow small, he finesses the jack with complete confidence.

Suppose the East-West cards were divided differently, and the count revealed that West started with two spades and East had four. Now the contract would no longer be a sure thing. However, the odds would be four to two that East had the queen, and declarer should follow the odds and finesse through East. (If you don't see why the odds should be four to two that East has the queen, try this experiment. Take the missing Q 9 6 5 3 2 of spades, shuffle them up, and deal four to East and two to West. Now guess who has the queen. Obviously East is twice as likely to have the queen because he has twice as many cards.)

Of course the count of the hand might have shown that the suit was divided 3–3. In this case you'd be no better off than you were to begin with. But you'd be no worse off either. In fact you'd be back to a straight 50 percent guess.

\* \*

On this next example, the importance of counting the hand is less obvious, and most declarers would muff it.

```
                      NORTH
                   ♠ K 8
                   ♡ Q 10 8 7
                   ◊ A 10 5
                   ♣ A 6 3 2

   WEST                                    EAST
♠ Q J 9 6 4 3 2                          ♠ 10
♡ 5 4                                     ♡ 3 2
◊ J 9 7                                   ◊ K Q 6 4 3 2
♣ 4                                       ♣ J 10 8 5

                      SOUTH
                   ♠ A 7 5
                   ♡ A K J 9 6
                   ◊ 8
                   ♣ K Q 9 7
```

*The bidding:*

| SOUTH | WEST | NORTH | EAST |
|-------|------|-------|------|
| 1 ♡ | Pass | 3 ♡ | Pass |
| 4 NT | Pass | 5 ♡ | Pass |
| 5 NT | Pass | 6 ◊ | Pass |
| 7 ♡ | Pass | Pass | Pass |

*Opening lead:* Heart five

South wins the opening lead and draws the trumps in two rounds. The contract is a lay-down, with a normal 3–2 club break, and it can also succeed as the cards lie *provided declarer is aware of the distribution.* Obviously the thing to do is to count the opponents' hands before tackling the club suit. After drawing trumps, declarer cashes the diamond ace and ruffs a diamond. Now he cashes the king and ace of spades, ruffs a spade in dummy, and another diamond in his hand. East discards two diamonds on the second and third round of spades, and declarer has all the information he needs. West is known to have started with seven spades, two hearts, and at least three diamonds. Therefore, he can have at most one club.

South leads a club to the ace and returns a small club. If East follows with a low one, declarer finesses the nine and makes the rest of the tricks. And if East splits his honors, declarer covers and returns to dummy with a trump to take a club finesse next time.

Nothing that declarer did in this hand could be described as difficult, yet 99 percent of all bridge players would go down in the grand slam. And they would blame the disaster on the unlucky club break.

Acquire a habit of counting your opponents' cards and you won't need so much luck.

* *

Declarer is rarely able to get a perfect count early in the play, so it is usually advantageous to postpone any vital decision as long as possible. This may require delicate handling, as in the following example:

NORTH
♠ K 7 2
♡ A Q 9 3
◊ A 9 5
♣ 4 3 2

WEST
♠ 9 6
♡ J 8 7 5
◊ 8 2
♣ K Q J 9 6

EAST
♠ Q J 10 5 4
♡ 6 4
◊ Q J 10 3
♣ 10 5

SOUTH
♠ A 8 3
♡ K 10 2
◊ K 7 6 4
♣ A 8 7

*The bidding:*

| SOUTH | WEST | NORTH | EAST |
|-------|------|-------|------|
| 1 ◊ | Pass | 1 ♡ | Pass |
| 1 NT | Pass | 3 NT | Pass |
| Pass | Pass | | |

*Opening lead:* Club king

West leads the club king against three no-trump, and declarer sees eight tricks on top: two spades, three hearts, two diamonds, and one club. There's a possibility of making an extra diamond trick if the suit breaks 3–3. And there's an even better chance of making an extra heart trick. In fact, declarer can be certain of four heart tricks if he knows where the jack is.

South ducks the opening lead and ducks again when West continues with the club queen. He takes the third club with the ace as East discards a spade. Now it is safe to lose a trick to East, so declarer plays a diamond to dummy's nine. East wins and returns the spade queen, and declarer ducks again.

The defense has four tricks and South must make the rest. He wins the spade continuation and cashes the other spade as well as the ace and king of diamonds. West throws a club on the third round of spades and on the third round of diamonds. At this point the distribution is an open book. West started with five clubs and only two diamonds and two spades. Therefore, he has four hearts, and East has a doubleton. South plays the heart ten to the ace and then returns dummy's small heart to the king. At trick twelve declarer leads the carefully preserved heart deuce. When West follows with a small heart, he finesses the nine and claims the contract.

It's worth taking a closer look at several points here:

1. Ducking the first two club leads is a normal holdup play, which is actually designed to break the opponents' communications. In this case it also reveals the 5–2 club break, giving declarer a good start on his count of the hand.

2. Ducking a diamond to East puts declarer in position to run three diamond tricks if the suit breaks 3–3. It also allows him to count the diamond suit without West's obtaining the lead.

3. Ducking the spade queen is another good move. If declarer takes the first spade, he can't lead more than two rounds of the suit, and he won't learn that West started with a doubleton.

4. South's play of the heart ten under dummy's ace is an essential unblock. If he carelessly leads the two originally, he will have to lead the ten at trick twelve. Now he can't cash dummy's long heart, and all his counting will have been in vain.

* *

In addition to counting distribution, declarer must not forget to count his opponents' points. Try this one:

NORTH
♠ K 5 3
♡ K Q 2
◇ A Q J 10 6 3
♣ 6

WEST
♠ 8 7 6
♡ 9 8 4
◇ 7 5 4
♣ A 10 8 4

EAST
♠ 10 4
♡ A J 10 3
◇ K
♣ K Q 9 7 3 2

SOUTH
♠ A Q J 9 2
♡ 7 6 5
◇ 9 8 3
♣ J 5

*East deals*

*Both vulnerable*

*The bidding:*

| EAST | SOUTH | WEST | NORTH |
|------|-------|------|-------|
| 1 ♣ | Pass | Pass | Double |
| Pass | 1 ♠ | Pass | 2 ◇ |
| Pass | 2 ♠ | Pass | 3 ♠ |
| Pass | 4 ♠ | Pass | Pass |
| Pass | | | |

*Opening lead:* Club ace

East opens the bidding with one club, and South eventually becomes declarer at four spades. West leads the club ace and switches to the nine of hearts. Dummy covers with the king, East takes his ace and returns the jack to dummy's queen.

Declarer draws the trumps in three rounds, leads a diamond to the ace dropping the singleton king, and claims the rest of the tricks.

Does South have eyes in the back of his head? Of course not! He simply knows that West cannot have the diamond king in addition to the club ace, because he passed his partner's opening bid. It's true that the chances of the diamond king being a singleton are poor. But the chances of the diamond finesse working are zero. And a poor chance is obviously better than no chance at all.

\* \*

Even a lowly jack can sometimes be found by counting points:

NORTH
♠ K 6 5 3
♡ J 5 4
♢ Q 8 7 3
♣ Q 5

WEST
♠ A J 8
♡ A K 9
♢ 9 5 4
♣ A 6 3 2

EAST
♠ 9 7 4
♡ Q 8 7 3
♢ 10
♣ 10 9 8 7 4

SOUTH
♠ Q 10 2
♡ 10 6 2
♢ A K J 6 2
♣ K J

*The bidding:*

| WEST | NORTH | EAST | SOUTH |
|------|-------|------|-------|
| 1 NT | Pass | Pass | 2 ◊ |
| Pass | Pass | Pass | |

*Opening lead:* Heart king

South becomes declarer at two diamonds after West has opened the bidding with one no-trump. The defense take the first three tricks with the king, ace, and queen of hearts, and East returns the club ten to partner's ace. West exits with the club two, and South wins and draws three rounds of trumps.

Declarer has already lost four tricks and must obviously lose the spade ace, so he can't afford to lose a trick to the spade jack. The normal way to handle this spade combination is to lead the two to dummy's king and then return a small spade to South's ten. The contract will succeed if East has the spade jack.

Before making this "normal" play, however, declarer counts West's points. Without the spade jack he wouldn't have the sixteen points required for a standard one no-trump opening. Of course this is not a sure thing. West could have miscounted. Or, he could have decided to fudge a bit and bid one no-trump with only fifteen points. But the chances are that with ♠ A x x, ♡ A K x, ♢ x x x, ♣ A x x x, West would have opened one club and not one no-trump. Thus the odds are against East having the spade jack, and the normal play will probably fail.

So, declarer decides to end-play West, and he leads the spade queen out of his hand. West has no choice but to win this and return the spade eight. (A club return would be conceding a ruff and discard.) Declarer wins with the ten, and the contract is home.

* *

Reading the cards is much more than just counting distribution and points. Every card played tells a story. Don't just look at the cards. Read the story!

Many inferences are based on declarer's knowledge of standard defensive conventions. For example:

NORTH<br>6 5 2

SOUTH<br>A 8 4

South has bid one no-trump, North has raised to three no-trump, and West leads the queen of this suit, on which East plays the nine. Declarer immediately pictures the entire suit as being distributed like this:

NORTH<br>6 5 2

| WEST | | EAST |
|---|---|---|
| Q J 10 x | | K 9 x |

SOUTH<br>A 8 4

Although this picture seems to pop into his head without any conscious effort, it's really a matter of reading the cards. If one could see the thought processes, they would run something like this:

1. The queen is apparently top of a sequence. Therefore, the jack is in the West hand and the king is with East.

2. East can't have the doubleton K 9. With this holding he would play the king to avoid blocking the suit.

3. West must hold the ten, because East would prefer to signal with the ten rather than the nine if he held both.

4. There's a possibility that West started with the Q J 10 alone. This is not likely, however, as with K 9 7 3 East would probably play the seven.

The reader may say, "But suppose East is a poor player. For example, lots of my friends don't know enough to play the king on the queen holding K 9 doubleton."

Don't worry. A good declarer is rarely at a disadvantage because his opponents are inexperienced. A bad player holding K 9 doubleton isn't sure which card to play. The indecision in his manner is easier to read than the card itself.

It may not be important to know the exact distribution of this particular suit at trick one. Nevertheless, declarer should get into the habit of reading the cards as he goes along. Then when a problem does arise, the information will be at his fingertips.

Suppose the bidding is the same and the North-South cards are the same, but this time West leads the three and East plays the king. How do you read this lead?

NORTH<br>
6 5 2

WEST                  EAST<br>
3                    K

SOUTH<br>
A 8 4

From a long suit it is standard to lead fourth best. Thus the fact that the three is the smallest possible spot means that West can have no more than four cards. (He could be leading from a three-card suit, but on this auction it's more normal to expect four.)

West must hold the queen, because with both the king and the queen East would try to win the trick with the lower of equal honors.

West wouldn't lead the three with Q J 10 3 or Q J 9 3. However, it's not possible to be sure of the exact cards, so for the time being declarer pictures the situation something like this:

NORTH<br>
6 5 2

WEST                  EAST<br>
Q 10 x x            K J 9

SOUTH<br>
A 8 4<br>
* *

The rule of eleven is just as helpful to declarer as it is to the defenders. Suppose this is the actual layout:

DUMMY
Q 8 2

WEST              EAST
K J 9 7 3          10 6

DECLARER
A 5 4

Against three no-trump West leads the seven, which is assumed to be his fourth best. Although declarer can see only the North-South cards, he knows immediately that East has only one card higher than the seven. It is rather tedious to work this out from scratch each time, so most players use a short cut called the "rule of eleven." Here are both methods:

1. (Tedious method) There are seven cards in the deck which are higher than the seven spot (eight, nine, ten, jack, queen, king, and ace). Three of these must be in the West hand, since the seven is his fourth-best card. Thus four of them are elsewhere. North and South have three of these four—the ace, queen, and eight. Therefore there is one remaining, and that must be in the East hand.

2. (Short cut) Subtract the card led from eleven. This gives the total number of higher cards in the other three hands. In this case it would take declarer one second to say to himself, "Seven from eleven equals four. I can see three of those four. Thus East must have the one that is left."

A little further thought will tell declarer that East's one higher card cannot be the king. With a suit headed by J 10 9 7, West surely would have elected to lead the jack, not the seven. Thus even before playing to trick one, declarer is in position to know that dummy's queen is an entry.

So far we have dealt with only one suit and what the opening lead reveals about this suit. In many cases, the opening lead will give much more valuable information about some other suit.

NORTH
♠ J 10 7
♡ K J 10 9
◇ 7 5 2
♣ 8 7 3

SOUTH
♠ A K Q 9 8 2
♡ 7 4
◇ Q 9 6
♣ A J

| *The bidding:* | WEST | NORTH | EAST | SOUTH |
|---|---|---|---|---|
| | 1 ◇ | Pass | 1 NT | 2 ♠ |
| | Pass | Pass | Pass | |

*Opening lead:* Club two

West opens one diamond, East responds one no-trump, and South becomes declarer at two spades. The opening lead is the club two, and south sees six possible losers: three diamonds, one club and two hearts. Before proceeding he naturally analyzes this two of clubs carefully. West cannot have the king and queen of clubs or he would have led the king. He may have something like Q 10 x x, or possibly he led from the king.

The most striking thing about the club lead, however, is that it means West cannot have both the ace and king of diamonds. The A K of a side suit is an ideal lead against a trump contract. West's failure to make such an automatic lead marks East with one of the high diamond honors. This gives West, at the most, the A J 10 of diamonds and the K 10 of clubs. In order to have an opening bid he *must* have the ace of hearts. All of declarer's problems are now solved. He can easily avoid one of the heart losers, and the contract is safe.

Here is a case where declarer is able to read the location of the vitally important heart ace after seeing only one of his opponents' cards, the lowly two of clubs!

* *

In some situations declarer can improve his chances of reading a suit by choosing his own card with care. Suppose this is the trump holding:

NORTH
A 5 4

WEST                     EAST
K                        9 8 6 2

SOUTH
Q J 10 7 3

If South cannot afford to lose a trump trick, he must naturally assume that West has the king. To start by leading the queen for a finesse may seem normal, but look what happens. The queen is covered by the king and ace, and East follows with the two. Now a small trump is led from dummy, on which East plays the six. South could finesse the seven and make the contract if he were aware of the distribution. But he doesn't know the king was singleton, so he plays the jack and East's 9 8 becomes a natural trick.

South's proper play is the ten originally. West would hardly cover the ten with the king if he could help it. Therefore, when the king does appear, declarer can assume it is a singleton. He can now afford to play East for 9 8 6 2 and avoid a trump loser.

Now let's try some actual deals and see how well you can read the cards.

*Problem 1*            NORTH
                       ♠ A K 8 7
                       ♡ 7 5 4
                       ◇ 3
                       ♣ 9 8 6 3 2
                       SOUTH
                       ♠ 4 2
                       ♡ A K 6
                       ◇ A K Q J 10 9
                       ♣ A 10

*The bidding:*

| SOUTH | WEST | NORTH | EAST |
|-------|------|-------|------|
| 2 ◇   | Pass | 2 ♠   | Pass |
| 4 NT  | Pass | 5 ◇   | Pass |
| 5 NT  | Pass | 6 ◇   | Pass |
| Pass  | Pass |       |      |

*Opening lead:* Heart three

Against six diamonds, West leads the heart three, East plays the queen, and South wins with the ace. Both opponents follow to three rounds of trumps, and dummy discards a heart and a spade. Declarer now cashes the club ace, on which West drops the jack and continues with the ten, which is won by West's queen. West returns the spade queen to dummy's king, and the nine of clubs is led. East follows with a small club, and the crucial moment has arrived.

Who has the king of clubs? If East has the king, declarer must discard his losing heart on this trick. But if West has the king, declarer must ruff. If he guesses wrong, he will lose the slam. Read the clues carefully and make up your mind what you would do.

*Answer:* Declarer must discard the heart on this trick. He knows West doesn't have the club king from the opening lead. West would not have led from a relatively meager heart suit with the king, queen, and jack of clubs in his hand. The entire deal was:

NORTH
♠ A K 8 7
♡ 7 5 4
◇ 3
♣ 9 8 6 3 2

WEST
♠ Q J 9
♡ J 9 8 3 2
◇ 7 6 2
♣ Q J

EAST
♠ 10 6 5 3
♡ Q 10
◇ 8 5 4
♣ K 7 5 4

SOUTH
♠ 4 2
♡ A K 6
◇ A K Q J 10 9
♣ A 10

Problem 2

NORTH
♠ K 7 2
♡ Q J
◇ 7 4 2
♣ K 10 9 3 2

SOUTH
♠ A 10 8
♡ 9 5 3
◇ A K
♣ A J 8 7 5

The bidding:

| SOUTH | WEST | NORTH | EAST |
|-------|------|-------|------|
| 1 NT | Pass | 3 NT | Pass |
| Pass | Pass | | |

*Opening lead:* Diamond three

West leads the three of diamonds, dummy plays the two, East plays the jack, and declarer wins with the ace. It looks as though nine tricks are a cinch (five clubs, two spades, and two diamonds). However, there's a small fly in the ointment. One opponent *might* have all three missing clubs. In this case, if declarer guesses wrong, he will have to lose a trick to the queen, and the contract will fail.

Should declarer lead a club to the king immediately? This will be fatal if *West* has all three clubs. Or, should he start by cashing the club ace? This will be fatal if *East* has all three clubs.

Stop now and read all the clues before making your decision.

*Answer:* The solution lies in West's opening lead. Since there are no cards missing smaller than the three, he has apparently led from a four-card suit. It's reasonable to assume that he would not have led from a four-card diamond suit if he had five or more cards in some other suit.

Thus West has no suit longer than four cards in his hand, and it's impossible for him to be void in clubs. If anyone is void in clubs, it must be East, and the proper play at trick two is the ace.

The actual cards were:

|  | NORTH |  |
|---|---|---|
|  | ♠ K 7 2 |  |
|  | ♡ Q J |  |
|  | ◊ 7 4 2 |  |
|  | ♣ K 10 9 3 2 |  |

| WEST | | EAST |
|---|---|---|
| ♠ 9 5 4 | | ♠ Q J 6 3 |
| ♡ K 4 2 | | ♡ A 10 8 7 6 |
| ◊ Q 10 8 3 | | ◊ J 9 6 5 |
| ♣ Q 6 4 | | ♣ — |

|  | SOUTH |  |
|---|---|---|
|  | ♠ A 10 8 |  |
|  | ♡ 9 5 3 |  |
|  | ◊ A K |  |
|  | ♣ A J 8 7 5 |  |

By this time the reader may begin to wonder why the defenders have any lead conventions at all. Perhaps he thinks they should just pull out cards at random in order to confuse declarer, instead of sticking to fourth best, top of a sequence, and so on.

Fortunately for declarer, defense is much more difficult than dummy play. Declarer sees all twenty-six of his side's cards. A defender sees only thirteen of his and must rely upon partner's cooperation to judge his team's total assets. Thus, conventional leads that are mildly helpful to declarer are absolutely essential to the defenders.

Of course the defenders could agree to use some *nonstandard* methods. For example, they could decide to always lead third best, instead of fourth best. Or, they could agree to play the second-highest honor instead of the top of a sequence (jack from Q J and queen from K Q, etc.) . But they are ethically bound to explain this fully to their opponents. Naturally, declarer can read just as much information from the *nonstandard* leads once he is informed of their meaning. So, for simplicity's sake, most players stick to standard defense.

Signaling is another important defense weapon. For a full discussion of defensive signals and lead conventions see *Bid Better, Play Better* by Dorothy Hayden (Harper & Row) , pp. 121–162.

Here again the signaler's partner generally stands to gain much more than declarer. However, a good declarer automatically tunes in on his opponents' signals and once in a while will come up with some vital information.

NORTH

♠ 9 3
♡ K 3 2
◇ Q 10 2
♣ K Q 8 6 5

SOUTH

♠ K 8 2
♡ A Q 9
◇ K J 9 4 3
♣ A 3

| *The bidding:* | SOUTH | WEST | NORTH | EAST |
|---|---|---|---|---|
| | 1 NT | Pass | 3 NT | Pass |
| | Pass | Pass | | |

*Opening lead:* Spade five

West leads the five of spades, East plays the queen, and South wins the king. If West has led from a four-card suit, declarer can simply knock out the ace of diamonds. The defenders will cash three spades and fold up their tents. However, the four of spades is missing, which means West may well have started with a five-card suit. In this case, the defenders will promptly defeat the contract when they win the diamond ace.

Alternatively, declarer can hope for a 3–3 club break. This would give him nine tricks without losing the lead. However, if he takes the A K Q of clubs and finds the suit has broken 4–2, he's dead. Now it's too late to make the contract even if the spades split 4–4 because the defenders will be able to cash a club in addition to the diamond ace and three spades.

Should South hope for a 4–4 spade break or a 3–3 club break? A pure mathematician might play out the A K Q of clubs first because he knows that a 3–3 break will occur about 36 percent of the time as opposed to a 33 percent chance of a 4–4 break (see table in Chapter 10). But this only proves that pure mathematicians don't necessarily make the best bridge players.

A first-class declarer sees that a little wire tapping is called for, and at trick two he leads his small club toward dummy's king. Remember, the opponents don't know who has the club ace, and if they are good players they will almost surely signal length. In this situation, a player with an even number of clubs should play high-low. If he holds an odd number, he should follow from the bottom up. Now, declarer leads a club from dummy back to his ace and reads the cards. If the spots indicate that the clubs are going to break, declarer returns to dummy with the heart king, expecting to run three more club tricks. If they indicate that the clubs will not break, he switches his attention to diamonds and prays for an even spade division.

Naturally, this wire tapping isn't foolproof, especially against weak opponents. But it is a lot more reliable than the slight mathematical difference between a 4–4 and a 3–3 break.

*Problem 3*

NORTH
♠ A K Q 3
♡ K 6
◇ A 5 3
♣ 8 6 5 4

SOUTH
♠ 7
♡ A J 9 8 7 4 2
◇ 9 7
♣ 7 3 2

*The bidding:*

| WEST | NORTH | EAST | SOUTH |
|------|-------|------|-------|
| 1 ♣ | 1 ♠ | Pass | 2 ♡ |
| Pass | 3 ♡ | Pass | 4 ♡ |
| Pass | Pass | Pass | |

*Opening lead:* Club king

West opens the bidding with one club, and South eventually becomes declarer at four hearts. West cashes the club king and ace, with East dropping the ten and queen. West continues with the club jack, on which East discards the spade two, and the club nine, on which East discards the diamond two, and South ruffs.

Declarer leads a trump to dummy's king, and West follows with the three and East the five. Dummy's small trump is led, and East produces the ten. Should South finesse or play for the drop? If you have read the cards carefully, you will know the exact distribution of both hands by this time.

*Answer:* The most important clue here is East's discard of a small spade at trick three. No player in his right mind would throw a spade from a four-card suit with dummy's A K Q 3 staring him in the face. Thus East can have *more* than four spades or *less* than four spades, but he cannot have exactly four.

Now let's consider West's hand for a moment. He is known to have started with four clubs. It is standard to bid one's longest suit first, so it can be assumed that he has no suit of five or more cards. This means that if West has a singleton heart, his distribution must be precisely 4–1–4–4. But West cannot have four spades, because that would give East four spades, which is impossible. Thus West cannot have a singleton heart, and there is only one distribution that fits all the facts:

NORTH
♠ A K Q 3
♡ K 6
♢ A 5 3
♣ 8 6 5 4

WEST
♠ J 9 5
♡ Q 3
♢ K J 8 6
♣ A K J 9

EAST
♠ 10 8 6 4 2
♡ 10 5
♢ Q 10 4 2
♣ Q 10

SOUTH
♠ 7
♡ A J 9 8 7 4 2
♢ 9 7
♣ 7 3 2

### Summary

Declarer must strive to build up a complete picture of his opponents' hands. Before playing to trick one, he makes a tentative estimate of the distribution and the point count based on the bidding (or lack of bidding) and the opening lead.

Each card played adds to the story and either corroborates the original estimate or causes a slight revision. After several tricks, declarer generally is able to play as though he were looking at all fifty-two cards.

It's much easier to play like an expert when you are looking at all fifty-two cards!

# 7

# *Hocus-Pocus with the Trump Suit*

THERE ARE SEVERAL advanced techniques that are available only in a suit contract. To the uninitiated these often look impossible. Even to the initiated they can resemble sleight of hand.

Try this one:

```
              NORTH
              ♠ J 9 8
              ♡ Q 4 3
              ◊ A J 7 6
              ♣ Q 8 5

WEST                          EAST
♠ 7 6 2                       ♠ 4 3
♡ 9 8 7 5                     ♡ K J 10 2
◊ K Q 10 8 5                  ◊ 4 3 2
♣ 3                           ♣ 9 7 6 4

              SOUTH
              ♠ A K Q 10 5
              ♡ A 6
              ◊ 9
              ♣ A K J 10 2
```

*The bidding:*

| SOUTH | WEST | NORTH | EAST |
|-------|------|-------|------|
| 2 ♠ | Pass | 3 NT | Pass |
| 4 ♣ | Pass | 4 ♠ | Pass |
| 4 NT | Pass | 5 ◇ | Pass |
| 7 ♠ | Pass | Pass | Pass |

*Opening lead:* Diamond king

South reaches seven spades, and there is apparently an inescapable heart loser. Before reading any further, see if you can figure out a way to make the grand slam. (Yes, you may look at all four hands.)

Most declarers give up on this hand. They go down one because they assume the contract is impossible. Actually seven spades is quite a good contract, as it will probably succeed with a normal 3–2 trump break. But it does require a little mental gymnastics.

Imagine that you get up from your South chair, walk around the table, and sit in the North seat. Now, pretend the North hand is yours and that South is the dummy. You will be pleasantly surprised at how much brighter things look from this angle.

Although your trump holding (the J 9 8) is not pretentious, it's good enough to draw the five outstanding trumps, provided they break 3–2. Your three diamond losers can all be ruffed in "dummy." And best of all, your two heart losers can eventually be thrown on "dummy's" magnificent club suit.

Win the opening lead with the diamond ace, and ruff a diamond with the spade ace. Lead the spade five to North's eight, and ruff another diamond with the king. Lead the spade ten to North's jack, and ruff the last diamond with South's last spade, the queen. Now return to the North hand with the club queen, and lead the spade nine. This draws the opponents' last trump, and as South has no spades left, he discards the heart six. The South hand is now high and the grand slam is home!

### Dummy Reversal

The above technique is known as a "dummy reversal." What you have done, in effect, is to make the "short" hand, North, into the master hand.

For an explanation of why this works, consider just the trump holding for a moment.

NORTH
♠ J 9 8

SOUTH
♠ A K Q 10 5

You have five trump tricks. The normal way to get an extra trick here is to ruff once in the North hand and then draw trumps with the South hand $(5 + 1 = 6)$.

The *unusual* way to get an extra trump trick is to ruff three times in the South hand and then draw trumps with the North hand $(3 + 3 = 6)$.

On the actual hand, declarer has twelve tricks and needs to find a thirteenth. The normal procedure of ruffing a loser in dummy is impossible. But the unusual technique of reversing the dummy brings home the bacon.

How does declarer diagnose that the conditions for a dummy reversal are present?

*First,* the trump holding in the short hand must be strong enough to draw the opponents' trumps. In this case the J 9 8 of spades are all high and can easily take care of a normal 3–2 spade break.

*Second,* the short side suit must be in the hand with the long trumps. Here declarer has the singleton diamond and the spade length.

*Warning:* A dummy reversal will not work unless there are sufficient entries to dummy. In this case, three entries are needed to ruff dummy's three diamonds and one extra entry is needed to draw the last trump. Before embarking on a dummy reversal, declarer must count his entries. The diamond ace and the two trump entries are used to ruff the three diamonds, and the club queen is the extra entry to draw the last trump. Incidentally, declarer doesn't trump those diamonds with the A K Q of spades just to be flamboyant. He *has* to ruff high because the ten and the five spot are his entries to dummy.

Frequently declarer will have a choice between a dummy reversal and other lines of play. Naturally he should select the method that offers the best chance of success.

NORTH
♠ 10 6 5
♡ Q 10 9
◊ Q 3 2
♣ A 7 4 2

WEST
♠ K Q 9 4
♡ 5 4
◊ J 10 7 4
♣ 9 6 3

EAST
♠ A 8 7
♡ 8 7 6
◊ 9 8
♣ K Q 10 8 5

SOUTH
♠ J 3 2
♡ A K J 3 2
◊ A K 6 5
♣ J

*The bidding:*

| | SOUTH | WEST | NORTH | EAST |
|---|---|---|---|---|
| | 1 ♡ | Pass | 1 NT | Pass |
| | 2 ◊ | Pass | 2 ♡ | Pass |
| | 3 ♡ | Pass | 4 ♡ | Pass |
| | Pass | Pass | | |

*Opening lead:* Spade king

The opponents cash the first three spade tricks and shift to a club, which is won by the ace. There are now three different ways to try to make the contract:

1. Declarer can draw all the trumps and hope that the opponents' diamonds are divided 3–3. When six cards are outstanding, they probably will not break 3–3 (see table in Chapter 10), and this method of play will succeed only about one-third of the time.

2. Declarer can considerably improve his chances by drawing only two rounds of trumps before playing three rounds of diamonds. He is still all right if the diamonds are 3–3, and he gives himself the extra chance that the opponent who is short in diamonds does not have more than two trumps. This method will succeed a little more than half the time.

3. There is also the option of reversing the dummy. After winning the club ace, ruff a club with a high trump. Lead a small trump to dummy, and ruff another club high. Lead the other small trump to dummy, and ruff dummy's last club with South's last trump. Now

enter dummy with the diamond queen and play dummy's last trump, discarding a diamond from the South hand. The ace and king of diamonds win the last two tricks, and the contract is home. This method can be expected to succeed any time the outstanding trumps break 3–2. As a 3–2 break occurs about two-thirds of the time, the dummy reversal is clearly the superior line of play.

Sometimes the dummy will have such an abundance of entries that declarer is able to test the trump suit before committing himself to a dummy reversal.

NORTH
♠ Q J 9
♡ K 7 5 2
◊ 8 7 4 2
♣ Q J

SOUTH
♠ A K 10 7 5
♡ 4
◊ A K 6
♣ A K 10 3

| *The bidding:* | SOUTH | WEST | NORTH | EAST |
|---|---|---|---|---|
| | 2 ♠ | Pass | 3 ♠ | Pass |
| | 6 ♠ | Pass | Pass | Pass |

*Opening lead:* Heart queen

West leads the heart queen against six spades and everybody ducks. West continues with the jack, which is ruffed by declarer, and the problem is what to do with South's little diamond.

As North's three trumps are all high, it may be possible to make dummy the master hand. In this case the two remaining hearts must be ruffed, and dummy's two losing diamonds will eventually be thrown on South's good clubs.

Fortunately, dummy has plenty of entries, and declarer is able to cash the J 9 of trumps before making up his mind to reverse the dummy. If both opponents follow to two rounds of spades, he ruffs a heart, returns to dummy with the club queen, and ruffs the last heart with South's last trump. Now back to the club jack to draw the opponents' last spade with the queen. The six of diamonds is discarded on this trick, and the South hand is high.

Suppose after cashing the J 9 of spades declarer learns that the trumps break 4–1. Now he abandons the idea of a dummy reversal, because the North trumps are not long enough. His only chance is to attempt to cash four rounds of clubs and discard two diamonds from dummy. If the opponent with four trumps also has at least four clubs all will be well.

\* \*

Sometimes the dummy will be one entry short for a dummy reversal. In this case it may be possible to enlist the cooperation of an unwary opponent.

```
                          NORTH
                        ♠ J 7 3 2
                        ♡ K J 9
                        ◇ Q 9 2
                        ♣ K 8 3
        WEST                              EAST
      ♠ K Q 6 5                         ♠ A 10 9 8 4
      ♡ 6                               ♡ 5 3 2
      ◇ K 5 4 3                         ◇ A J 10
      ♣ J 9 5 4                         ♣ 10 7
                          SOUTH
                        ♠ —
                        ♡ A Q 10 8 7 4
                        ◇ 8 7 6
                        ♣ A Q 6 2
```

*The bidding:*   SOUTH   WEST   NORTH   EAST
                  1 ♡     Pass    2 ♡    Pass
                  4 ♡     Pass    Pass   Pass

*Opening lead:* Spade king

South ruffs the opening spade and sees three obvious diamond losers. If the trumps are 3–1 and the clubs do not break, declarer may wind up with a club loser as well. So he examines the idea of making dummy the master hand. Dummy has no club loser to worry about, and the K J 9 of hearts can take care of the opponents' trumps. However, four entries to the dummy are needed, three to ruff the remaining three spades and one to draw the last trump.

Unfortunately, if declarer is going to ruff all of North's spades, he will have only two trumps that can be used as entries. These, together with the club king, make a total of only three entries, and the dummy reversal will fail.

Instead of abandoning the idea, however, declarer decides to give the opponents a chance to help. At trick two he exits with a diamond. The enemy may view this Trojan horse with suspicion, but looking at dummy they are unlikely to return a heart or a club. They may cash three rounds of diamonds, and then the chances are an opponent will make the "safe" lead of a spade. Declarer ruffs happily in his hand, and now he only needs *three* entries to dummy instead of four. A heart to the nine lets him ruff the third spade, and another heart to the jack lets him ruff the last spade with South's last trump. The club king is the final entry to draw the outstanding trump, and the A Q of clubs take the last two tricks.

It's true that East-West can defeat the contract by exiting with a club or a heart after cashing their three diamond tricks. But how many players can defend perfectly against a dummy reversal this early in the hand?

The dummy reversal is the major exception to the general policy of avoiding ruffs in the "long" hand. Another exception is the trump coup.

## *Trump Coup*

NORTH
♠ A K 8 6 5 2
♡ K 8
◇ A 7 6
♣ A K

WEST
♠ Q J 4
♡ 5
◇ J 10 9 8
♣ J 10 9 3 2

EAST
♠ 10 9
♡ J 9 3 2
◇ 5 4 3
♣ Q 8 7 6

SOUTH
♠ 7 3
♡ A Q 10 7 6 4
◇ K Q 2
♣ 5 4

| The bidding: | SOUTH | WEST | NORTH | EAST |
|---|---|---|---|---|
| | 1 ♡ | Pass | 2 ♠ | Pass |
| | 3 ♡ | Pass | 5 NT | Pass |
| | 7 ♡ | Pass | Pass | Pass |

*Opening lead:* Diamond jack

North's bid of five no-trump in this sequence is the grand-slam force, asking partner to bid seven if he has two of the top three trump honors. South obediently bids the grand slam, and when dummy appears he is well pleased with the contract. Declarer wins the opening lead in his hand and cashes the king and ace of trumps, revealing the bad news. East apparently has a sure trump trick because there are no more hearts in dummy with which to finesse. An inexperienced player might give up at this point and settle for down one. However, an experienced declarer knows that East will very likely be subject to a trump coup, which is just as effective as a finesse and much more elegant.

He cashes the A K of spades and ruffs a spade. He returns to dummy with a club and ruffs another spade. Now back to dummy with the other club to run the spades. If East ruffs at any time, declarer overruffs and claims the balance. If East doesn't ruff, declarer throws away his diamonds. With only two cards left the situation is:

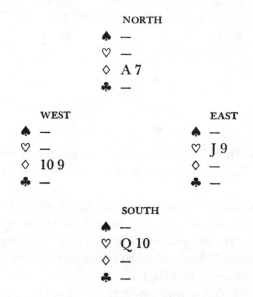

NORTH
♠ —
♡ —
◇ A 7
♣ —

WEST
♠ —
♡ —
◇ 10 9
♣ —

EAST
♠ —
♡ J 9
◇ —
♣ —

SOUTH
♠ —
♡ Q 10
◇ —
♣ —

Dummy leads a diamond, and East's natural trump trick vanishes into thin air.

Isn't that artistic? And, it's not actually difficult if declarer keeps in mind one essential detail: *A trump coup will not work unless declarer has the same number of trumps remaining as his opponent.* In this case, South starts with six trumps and East starts with four.

Therefore, to get down to East's length, South has to shorten himself *twice* by ruffing two spades.

On this hand many declarers would fall into the trap of ruffing only one spade. The spades are established after one ruff, and it does seem extravagant to ruff dummy's winners. Furthermore, it goes against the grain to trump unnecessarily in the long hand. So, they would discard on the spades and leave themselves with three trumps instead of two. The last three cards would be:

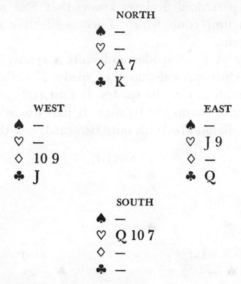

NORTH
♠ —
♡ —
◇ A 7
♣ K

WEST
♠ —
♡ —
◇ 10 9
♣ J

EAST
♠ —
♡ J 9
◇ —
♣ Q

SOUTH
♠ —
♡ Q 10 7
◇ —
♣ —

Whatever dummy leads, East discards the club and declarer is forced to ruff. This puts the lead in the South hand and spoils the whole project.

So, even if dummy's spades on this hand were A K Q J 10 9, declarer must grit his teeth and ruff two of them. (By the way, a coup which involves the ruffing of high cards is sometimes referred to as a "grand coup." A grand coup is not any harder than a regular coup. It's just more spectacular.)

This process of shortening one's trump holding often requires a good many entries to dummy. Declarer must learn to look ahead in order to make full use of these entries when there is the possibility of a coup in the offing.

NORTH
♠ A 5
♡ A K Q 10 8
◊ A 7 6 3 2
♣ 9

WEST
♠ 3
♡ 7 5 4 2
◊ J 10 8 5
♣ A 8 5 4

EAST
♠ Q 6 4 2
♡ 6 3
◊ K 9 4
♣ 10 6 3 2

SOUTH
♠ K J 10 9 8 7
♡ J 9
◊ Q
♣ K Q J 7

*The bidding:*

| SOUTH | WEST | NORTH | EAST |
|-------|------|-------|------|
| 1 ♠ | Pass | 3 ♡ | Pass |
| 3 ♠ | Pass | 4 ◊ | Pass |
| 4 ♠ | Pass | 6 ♠ | Pass |
| Pass | Pass | | |

*Opening lead:* Club ace

West cashes the club ace and switches to the jack of diamonds. Declarer wins with the ace in dummy and sees that the slam depends upon finding the trump queen. With eight trumps he naturally plans to finesse East for the queen. Before starting on spades, however, it is good technique to shorten himself once by ruffing a diamond. Now he leads a spade to the ace and finesses the jack on the way back. When West shows out, this forethought pays off. A heart to dummy and another diamond ruff brings declarer down to the same trump length as East. Now another heart puts the lead in dummy, and the contract can no longer be defeated. Three more hearts are led, and if East doesn't ruff, declarer discards the K Q J of clubs. This leaves South with only two cards, the king and ten of spades. As the lead is in dummy, he must make them both.

Notice what happens to declarer if he doesn't ruff a diamond at trick three. Suppose after winning the diamond ace he cashes the ace of spades and finesses the jack. When West shows out, declarer wakes up to the need for a coup, but it's too late. He has *two* more trumps than East, which means he needs *three* more entries to dummy. (Two entries are needed to shorten himself twice, and one more entry is required in order to get back to dummy for the coup position.) Unfortunately, there are only the two heart entries left at this point, so the coup must fail, and the slam is defeated.

Of course declarer doesn't know at trick three that a coup is going to be necessary. But he *can* see that he has superfluous trump length and limited access to dummy. The diamond ace is a precious entry that shouldn't be squandered. It is good technique to use this entry to reduce his trump length in preparation for a possible coup.

### Trump End Play

```
                         NORTH
                    ♠  K 9 5 2
                    ♡  A K Q
                    ◇  K Q 8 4
                    ♣  5 2

    WEST                                      EAST
♠  J 8 3                                  ♠  10 6 4
♡  J 10 9                                 ♡  8 7 6 5 4 3 2
◇  J 3 2                                  ◇  10 9 5
♣  Q 10 9 8                               ♣  —

                         SOUTH
                    ♠  A Q 7
                    ♡  —
                    ◇  A 7 6
                    ♣  A K J 7 6 4 3
```

| The bidding: | SOUTH | WEST | NORTH | EAST |
|---|---|---|---|---|
| | 1 ♣ | Pass | 3 NT | Pass |
| | 6 ♣ | Pass | Pass | Pass |

*Opening lead:* Heart jack

Six no-trump would be easy, but South, not unnaturally, chooses to play six clubs, and the opening lead is the heart jack. Declarer has no losers to discard, so he ruffs dummy's high heart to reduce his own unwieldy trump length. At trick two he lays down the club ace and receives a shock when East shows out!

It looks as though West has two ironclad trump tricks. There is a chance that declarer may be able to effect a trump end play, however, if West's distribution is 3–3–3–4. To do this he must shorten himself until he has the same number of trumps as West. A diamond to the king, a second heart ruff, another diamond to the queen, and a third heart ruff leave South and West both holding three trumps. Fortunately West has to follow suit as declarer cashes three rounds of spades and one more diamond. The position is:

NORTH
♠ 9
♡ —
♢ 8
♣ 5

WEST
♠ —
♡ —
♢ —
♣ Q 10 9

EAST
♠ —
♡ 8 7 6
♢ —
♣ —

SOUTH
♠ —
♡ —
♢ —
♣ K J 7

Declarer leads the club seven and West's two ironclad trump tricks have been welded into one.

By the way, South could never have achieved this feat of legerdemain if he had discarded his low spade or a small diamond at trick one. (Try it!) Fortunately he had no use for a discard, and as a matter of good technique he ruffed to reduce his superfluous trump length.

### Coup en Passant

```
                    NORTH
                  ♠ 7 5 2
                  ♡ 9 7 6 2
                  ◇ K Q 6
                  ♣ K 3 2

      WEST                              EAST
    ♠ —                              ♠ Q J 10 9
    ♡ A K J 10 3                     ♡ 8 5 4
    ◇ 10 9 5 4                       ◇ J 3 2
    ♣ 9 8 7 4                        ♣ Q J 10

                    SOUTH
                  ♠ A K 8 6 4 3
                  ♡ Q
                  ◇ A 8 7
                  ♣ A 6 5
```

*The bidding:*

| SOUTH | WEST | NORTH | EAST |
|-------|------|-------|------|
| 1 ♠ | Pass | 1 NT | Pass |
| 3 ♠ | Pass | 4 ♠ | Pass |
| Pass | Pass | | |

*Opening lead:* Heart king

West leads the king of hearts and continues with the ace, which South ruffs. Declarer cashes the ace of trumps and gets the bad news. It certainly looks as though he has two trump losers and one club loser as well as the heart trick already lost. Nevertheless he proceeds to make his contract with ease. At trick three he leads a diamond to the queen and ruffs another heart. Next he cashes the ace and king of diamonds and the ace and king of clubs, winding up in dummy. The position is now this:

NORTH
♠ 7 5
♡ 9
♢ —
♣ 3

WEST
♠ —
♡ J
♢ 10
♣ 9 8

EAST
♠ Q J 10
♡ —
♢ —
♣ Q

SOUTH
♠ K 8 6
♡ —
♢ —
♣ 6

Declarer already has eight tricks, and he leads the heart nine from dummy. If East discards the club queen, South ruffs. And if East ruffs, South discards his club. In either case he can't be prevented from making two more tricks and his contract.

This maneuver is known as a coup en passant, an analogy to the pawn capture "en passant" at chess.

Note that South does not have a tenace position in the trump suit here as he does in a trump coup or a trump end play. In this case the defender's trump holding is solid. By leading a plain suit from the North hand, declarer forces East to play first, thereby promoting a trump loser into a winner.

### Smother Play

One of the most remarkable examples of prestidigitation with cards is surely the smother play. The occasion for its use is rare, but when it does arise it is guaranteed to leave the defenders dizzy.

NORTH
♠ A 6 5
♡ 5 4 3 2
◊ J 10 7
♣ K 9 4

WEST
♠ K 7 4 3
♡ 9 8 7
◊ 9 3 2
♣ Q 7 5

EAST
♠ 2
♡ Q J 10
◊ 8 6 5 4
♣ J 8 6 3 2

SOUTH
♠ Q J 10 9 8
♡ A K 6
◊ A K Q
♣ A 10

*The bidding:*

| SOUTH | WEST | NORTH | EAST |
|-------|------|-------|------|
| 2 ♠ | Pass | 3 ♠ | Pass |
| 6 ♠ | Pass | Pass | Pass |

*Open lead:* Heart nine

Declarer wins the heart lead with the ace and realizes he will eventually have to lose a heart trick. Therefore, the slam depends on trapping the trump king. South leads the queen of spades and relaxes slightly when this holds. He continues with the jack and catches a triumphant glint in West's eye as East discards a club.

At this point West has the K 7 of spades left and dummy's ace is alone. There is apparently no way for declarer to avoid a trump loser, but look what happens! South plays the ace and king of clubs and ruffs a club. He then cashes the ace, king, and queen of diamonds and the king of hearts. This leaves:

NORTH
♠ A
♡ 5 4
◇ —
♣ —

WEST
♠ K 7
♡ 7
◇ —
♣ —

EAST
♠ —
♡ Q
◇ 8
♣ J

SOUTH
♠ 10 9
♡ 6
◇ —
♣ —

Declarer leads his losing heart, which is won by East with the queen. It doesn't matter what East returns. The king of trumps is smothered, and South scores up his slam amidst a round of applause from the kibitzers.

### Devil's Coup

NORTH
♠ K J
♡ A 7 6 3
◇ K 9 4
♣ Q 6 4 2

WEST
♠ 8 3 2
♡ 10 4 2
◇ Q 7 6
♣ J 10 9 8

EAST
♠ Q 10 9 5
♡ J 8 5
◇ J 8
♣ K 7 5 3

SOUTH
♠ A 7 6 4
♡ K Q 9
◇ A 10 5 3 2
♣ A

For our final hat trick let's watch declarer make a grand slam with the opponents holding a "sure" trump trick.

South becomes declarer at seven diamonds, and for once no bidding diagram will be printed. (This book might fall into the hands of young children.)

West leads the club jack and looking at all fifty-two cards finds it is apparently impossible to avoid a trump loser. Nevertheless, declarer makes his contract by means of what is known as a "devil's coup." He wins the first trick with the club ace and cashes three rounds of hearts ending in the dummy. Then he ruffs a club, leads a spade to the king, and ruffs another club. The ace of spades, a spade ruff in dummy, and still another club ruff brings the hand down to this position:

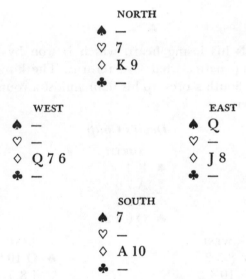

NORTH
♠ —
♡ 7
◇ K 9
♣ —

WEST
♠ —
♡ —
◇ Q 7 6
♣ —

EAST
♠ Q
♡ —
◇ J 8
♣ —

SOUTH
♠ 7
♡ —
◇ A 10
♣ —

South leads his last spade and the defenders' "sure" trump trick goes up in smoke.

The devil's coup is an astonishing accomplishment, but as a technique it is not too useful. In order for it to succeed, the East-West distribution must be precisely as in the diagram. Looking at the North-South hands only, declarer may well decide, for practical purposes, to play one opponent to hold a doubleton Q J of trumps. In this case thirteen tricks can be taken in a variety of ways. (It's much less dramatic, but a lot simpler!)

The last two examples are rare curiosities, and the reader is advised not to lose any sleep learning how to execute a smother play or a devil's coup. The essence of this chapter is the concept that it may be good technique at an advanced level to take ruffs in the long hand. One reason involves making the short hand into the master hand or, in bridge terminology, reversing the dummy. Another reason is to reduce declarer's trump length in preparation for a trump coup, or a trump end play. Still another is to promote an extra trump trick by leading a plain suit through an opponent's apparently impregnable trump holding (coup en passant).

Once again, a word of caution: In the meat-and-potato variety of suit contracts it is usually poor technique to ruff unnecessarily in the long hand (see Chapter 4). If the reader has not completely mastered the meat and potatoes, he should forget about the crêpe suzettes. In other words, if you are at all hazy about Chapter 4, don't concentrate on Chapter 7 or you'll wind up with indigestion.

# 8

# *Squeeze Play*

THE SQUEEZE IS OFTEN considered the hallmark of the expert. As a result, the average player assumes the whole subject must be exceedingly difficult. It isn't. In fact the majority of squeezes are fun to execute and require almost no serious thought.

Some squeezes are so easy a beginner "falls into" the correct play without having any idea what he is doing.

*Hand 1*

NORTH
♠ A J 6
♡ A K Q J
♢ A K Q J
♣ 3 2

WEST
♠ K Q 10 9
♡ 7 6
♢ 8 6 5
♣ J 9 7 6

EAST
♠ 8 7 5
♡ 10 9 8 5
♢ 10 9 7
♣ 10 8 5

SOUTH
♠ 4 3 2
♡ 4 3 2
♢ 4 3 2
♣ A K Q 4

122

Let's assume that East-West are good players and that North-South are just beginners. In some manner, South stumbles into a contract of seven no-trump and West leads the king of spades.

Declarer wins the ace of spades and counts his tricks. One spade, four hearts, four diamonds, and three clubs bring the total to twelve. South knows his little club is not a trick, because one defender must have at least four cards in the suit. However, he hopes that if he saves the clubs until last, this defender will get mixed up and discard one. Accordingly he clutches the A K Q 4 of clubs tightly to his breast as he cashes the eight red winners. Lo and behold, when the last red winner is led, West discards a club and the grand slam rolls home!

West didn't get "mixed up." He got squeezed.

With five cards left the position was:

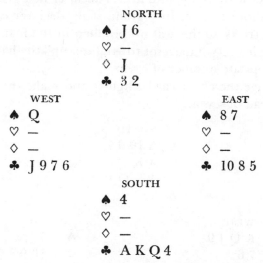

```
                        NORTH
                      ♠ J 6
                      ♡ —
                      ◇ J
                      ♣ 3 2
        WEST                            EAST
      ♠ Q                             ♠ 8 7
      ♡ —                             ♡ —
      ◇ —                             ◇ —
      ♣ J 9 7 6                       ♣ 10 8 5
                        SOUTH
                      ♠ 4
                      ♡ —
                      ◇ —
                      ♣ A K Q 4
```

When declarer cashed his last red winner, the jack of diamonds, both East and South threw spades. West couldn't throw the spade queen, as this would establish dummy's jack. So, he gnashed his teeth and threw a club. (Imagine how ignominious it is for a good player to be squeezed by a beginner!)

Although this squeeze was very easy, it's a good idea to take a close look at the principles involved. Obviously, declarer can never make more than four heart tricks or four diamond tricks, because he has no extra cards in those suits. However, he does have an extra club, which *could* become a trick. And, he has the jack of spades, which *could* become a trick. These cards are called threat cards, or menaces. The four of clubs is a threat against the defender who must hold on to four clubs, and the jack of spades is a threat against the defender who must keep the queen.

On this hand, West is the only one who can guard the clubs and the only one who can beat the jack of spades. When the diamond jack is cashed, the burden of guarding both suits becomes too much for him. Everyone has to come down to four cards and there is no room in West's hand for the spade queen as well as the four clubs. He is squeezed.

### Giving Up Losers

Most squeezes will not operate unless declarer first gives up all the tricks he can afford to lose. In a grand slam, declarer cannot afford to give up any tricks, so this was no problem in the first deal. But in other contracts it's very important to "tighten up" the hand by giving away the appropriate number of losers.

Let's rearrange the above cards slightly and make the contract six no-trump instead of seven.

*Hand 2*

NORTH
♠ A 10 6 5
♡ A K Q
♢ A K Q J
♣ 3 2

WEST
♠ K Q J 9
♡ 7 6
♢ 8 6 5
♣ J 9 7 6

EAST
♠ 8 7
♡ J 10 9 8 5
♢ 10 9 7
♣ 10 8 5

SOUTH
♠ 4 3 2
♡ 4 3 2
♢ 4 3 2
♣ A K Q 4

Again West leads the king of spades, but this time declarer can count only eleven tricks. The ten of spades and the four of clubs are threat cards and will result in a squeeze if one defender is obliged to guard them both.

South needs twelve tricks, so he can afford to give one away. If he is an experienced player, he ducks the opening lead. West continues with the spade queen, and declarer takes the ace and runs the hearts and diamonds. Before the last winner is cashed, the situation is:

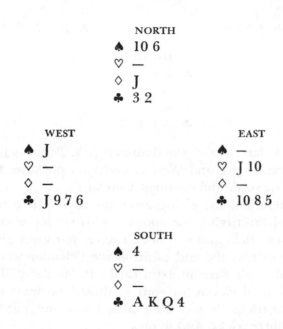

NORTH
♠ 10 6
♡ —
◇ J
♣ 3 2

WEST
♠ J
♡ —
◇ —
♣ J 9 7 6

EAST
♠ —
♡ J 10
◇ —
♣ 10 8 5

SOUTH
♠ 4
♡ —
◇ —
♣ A K Q 4

Now declarer leads the diamond jack. This last winner is often referred to as the "squeeze card," because it turns the screw on the defender, who is trying valiantly to protect both menaces. Poor West has to hang on to his spade jack (dummy's ten is staring him in the face), so he is forced to throw a club, and South makes the last four tricks with the A K Q 4 of clubs.

Now let's see what happens if declarer neglects to lose a trick first. Suppose he takes the opening lead with the spade ace. Just before the last red winner is cashed, the position becomes:

NORTH
♠ 10 6 5
♡ —
◇ J
♣ 3 2

WEST
♠ Q J
♡ —
◇ —
♣ J 9 7 6

EAST
♠ 8
♡ J 10
◇ —
♣ 10 8 5

SOUTH
♠ 4 3
♡ —
◇ —
♣ A K Q 4

As before, declarer cashes the diamond jack. But this time everyone has one extra card, and West is under no pressure. He simply discards his extra spade and the small slam fails.

In bridge terminology, giving away the appropriate number of losers is called "rectifying the count." This simply means that if you have eleven tricks and you need twelve, you must give up one trick early so that in the end position the defender who is about to be squeezed won't have an extra card left. Similarly, if you have ten tricks and need eleven for your contract, you must arrange to give away two tricks. If you have nine tricks and need ten, you must give up three tricks. And so on.

It's generally wise to give up these losers as soon as possible. On the last hand it was essential to give the opponents the first trick. If declarer wins the first trick, he can never afford to lose the lead, because he will be wide open in spades.

### Getting into the Mood

A player who is not accustomed to squeezes will miss many of them simply because he is not used to this idea of giving up losers.

*Hand 3*

NORTH
♠ A Q 7 4
♡ 7 2
◊ Q 5 2
♣ A Q 5 4

WEST
♠ J 8
♡ K J 8 5 3
◊ 10 8
♣ 9 8 7 6

EAST
♠ 10 9 6 5
♡ Q 10 6 4
◊ J 9 6 4
♣ 2

SOUTH
♠ K 3 2
♡ A 9
◊ A K 7 3
♣ K J 10 3

| The bidding: | SOUTH | WEST | NORTH | EAST |
|---|---|---|---|---|
| | 1 ◊ | Pass | 1 ♠ | Pass |
| | 2 NT | Pass | 6 NT | Pass |
| | Pass | Pass | | |

*Opening lead:* Club nine

West leads the club nine against six no-trump, and declarer can count eleven tricks: four clubs, three spades, three diamonds, and one heart. If either the spades or the diamonds break 3–3, the slam will be home. And if neither suit breaks 3–3, there is still a chance of a squeeze if one opponent has to guard both suits.

Declarer can afford to lose one trick and knows that a squeeze cannot operate until he does lose that one trick. Accordingly he wins the first trick with dummy's queen of clubs and leads a heart to his nine. West wins with the jack and continues with the eight of clubs. East throws a heart on this trick and discards two more hearts on the next two clubs. This leaves the following position:

NORTH
♠ A Q 7 4
♡ 7
◇ Q 5 2
♣ —

WEST
♠ J 8
♡ K 8 5 3
◇ 10 8
♣ —

EAST
♠ 10 9 6 5
♡ —
◇ J 9 6 4
♣ —

SOUTH
♠ K 3 2
♡ A
◇ A K 7 3
♣ —

South leads the ace of hearts, and East is helpless. He has to unguard the spades or the diamonds, and in either case declarer makes twelve tricks.

If declarer hadn't given away that heart trick, East would be under no pressure. He would still have a heart to play on the ace and the squeeze would fail.

\* \*

Thus far we have been discussing what is called the "simple squeeze." A simple squeeze is one that operates against one opponent in two suits. On Hands 1 and 2, West was squeezed in spades and clubs. On Hand 3 East was squeezed in spades and diamonds.

It is worth noting that all simple squeezes do not work. The question of entries is very important. The threat card that is in the hand opposite the squeeze card must be accompanied by a winner. What good is a threat card if there is no entry to it at the appropriate moment?

The matter of position is also important. For example, a simple squeeze where both threat cards are in the North hand may work against West but not against East.

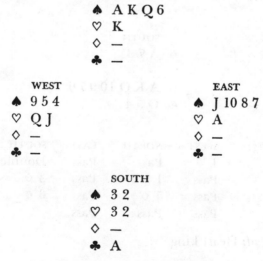

NORTH
♠ A K Q 6
♡ K
◇ —
♣ —

WEST
♠ J 10 8 7
♡ A
◇ —
♣ —

EAST
♠ 9 5 4
♡ Q J
◇ —
♣ —

SOUTH
♠ 3 2
♡ 3 2
◇ —
♣ A

South leads the ace of clubs, and West is squeezed because he has to discard before dummy.

Let's exchange the East and West cards:

NORTH
♠ A K Q 6
♡ K
◇ —
♣ —

WEST
♠ 9 5 4
♡ Q J
◇ —
♣ —

EAST
♠ J 10 8 7
♡ A
◇ —
♣ —

SOUTH
♠ 3 2
♡ 3 2
◇ —
♣ A

This time when South cashes the club ace, the squeeze is ruined because dummy has to discard before East.

Now for an encouraging word to the reader who is beginning to bog down under all these complications. Cheer up! Squeezes are not nearly as complicated to execute as they are to discuss. Just remember to give away the appropriate number of losers as soon as you can. If a squeeze is possible you will probably succeed even if you don't understand why.

Try this one:

*Hand 4*

NORTH
♠ K 6
♡ Q 7 6 4
◊ 5 4 3 2
♣ A 7 6

WEST
♠ Q 9 4 2
♡ A K 10 8 3
◊ J
♣ K 10 9

EAST
♠ J 10 8 5
♡ J 9 5 2
◊ 8
♣ J 8 3 2

SOUTH
♠ A 7 3
♡ —
◊ A K Q 10 9 7 6
♣ Q 5 4

*The bidding:*

| WEST | NORTH | EAST | SOUTH |
|------|-------|------|--------|
| 1 ♡ | Pass | Pass | Double |
| Pass | 1 NT | Pass | 3 ◊ |
| Pass | 5 ◊ | Pass | 6 ◊ |
| Pass | Pass | Pass | |

*Opening lead:* Heart king

West leads the king of hearts, and declarer can count eleven tricks: seven diamonds, one club, two spades, and a spade ruff. From the bidding it is highly likely that West has the club king and the heart ace, in which case he can be squeezed. However, one trick must be lost first, and now is the time to lose it. So declarer throws a club on the first trick, and West shifts to a trump. South wins, cashes the king and ace of spades, and ruffs a spade. Then he runs the trumps, arriving at this position:

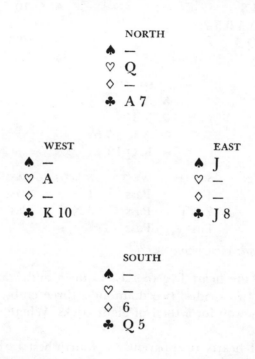

```
                    NORTH
                 ♠ —
                 ♡ Q
                 ◇ —
                 ♣ A 7


     WEST                        EAST
  ♠ —                         ♠ J
  ♡ A                         ♡ —
  ◇ —                         ◇ —
  ♣ K 10                      ♣ J 8


                    SOUTH
                 ♠ —
                 ♡ —
                 ◇ 6
                 ♣ Q 5
```

South leads the last diamond and West gives up the ghost.

Oddly enough, declarer can't make this contract against correct defense if he ruffs the first trick. Try it. It may seem there is plenty of time to lose a trick later. But a competent East will win any later trick and return a club killing dummy's entry. Now the heart queen is marooned, and the squeeze must fail.

### The Suicide Squeeze

**Hand 5**

NORTH
♠ K 9 5 4
♡ 8 4 3
◇ 9 4 2
♣ A J 9

WEST
♠ J 8
♡ A J 9 5 2
◇ Q 3
♣ 8 7 4 2

EAST
♠ Q 10 7 6 2
♡ Q 6
◇ J 10 6
♣ 6 5 3

SOUTH
♠ A 3
♡ K 10 7
◇ A K 8 7 5
♣ K Q 10

*The bidding:*

| SOUTH | WEST | NORTH | EAST |
|-------|------|-------|------|
| 1 ◇ | Pass | 1 ♠ | Pass |
| 2 NT | Pass | 3 NT | Pass |
| Pass | Pass | | |

*Opening lead:* Heart five

West leads the heart five to East's queen and South's king. Declarer counts two spades, two diamonds, three clubs, and the heart he has already won for a total of eight tricks. Where should he look for a ninth?

The five of hearts is apparently a fourth-best card. In this case West may have led from a five-card suit, but he couldn't have more than five, because there is only one smaller card missing, the two. If West started with five hearts, declarer couldn't afford to establish his diamonds. (If he conceded a diamond, the opponents would cash four hearts to set the contract.)

Any time declarer needs exactly one more trick than he has, he should consider the possibility of a squeeze. As West seems to be long in hearts, there is a good chance that East has the length in spades and diamonds. For a squeeze to develop, however, South must first arrange to lose precisely four tricks. So at trick two he gives up a heart. Let's assume West cashes his four heart winners and returns a club. Declarer wins and cashes a second club. This leaves:

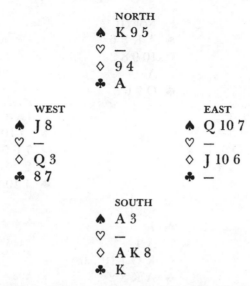

NORTH
♠ K 9 5
♡ —
◇ 9 4
♣ A

WEST
♠ J 8
♡ —
◇ Q 3
♣ 8 7

EAST
♠ Q 10 7
♡ —
◇ J 10 6
♣ —

SOUTH
♠ A 3
♡ —
◇ A K 8
♣ K

Now the last club is led, and East is finished. He has to unguard either the spades or the diamonds, and South must make the rest of the tricks.

Of course, if West started with four hearts instead of five, he could only cash three tricks in the suit and the squeeze would not work. But in this case declarer will have plenty of time later to establish a diamond for his ninth trick.

This particular squeeze is the suicide squeeze. Poor East is squeezed not by the enemy but by his own partner. And on this hand West can do nothing about it. Suppose West wins the second trick and decides not to run his other hearts because he doesn't want to squeeze his partner. Let's say he returns a club. South wins and again establishes diamonds, losing the third round to East. East has no more hearts, and declarer winds up with an overtrick.

\* \*

Hands 1 through 5 are examples of simple squeezes. In each

case, one opponent was squeezed in two suits. Now let's take a look at a double squeeze:

### The Double Squeeze

Hand 6

```
                    NORTH
                    ♠ A K 8 6
                    ♡ 10 9 8 2
                    ◇ A
                    ♣ Q 7 6 3

    WEST                                EAST
    ♠ J 9 5 4                           ♠ Q 10 3 2
    ♡ K Q 4 3                           ♡ 7 6 5
    ◇ 9 8 5 4 3                         ◇ 2
    ♣ —                                 ♣ J 10 9 5 4

                    SOUTH
                    ♠ 7
                    ♡ A J
                    ◇ K Q J 10 7 6
                    ♣ A K 8 2
```

The bidding:

| SOUTH | WEST | NORTH | EAST |
|-------|------|-------|------|
| 1 ◇ | Pass | 1 ♠ | Pass |
| 3 ♣ | Pass | 6 ♣ | Pass |
| 6 NT | Pass | 7 NT | Pass |
| Pass | Pass | | |

Opening lead: Heart king

The bidding is a trifle exuberant, but the final contract is sound. In fact, the grand slam is a lay-down with a normal 3–2 club break.

West leads the king of hearts, which is won by the ace, and a diamond is led to dummy's ace. A club is returned to the ace, and when West discards a heart it looks as though only twelve tricks are available. Declarer doesn't turn a hair, however, because he knows there is an automatic double squeeze. He cashes the other two club honors and all his diamonds. Just before the last diamond is played the position is:

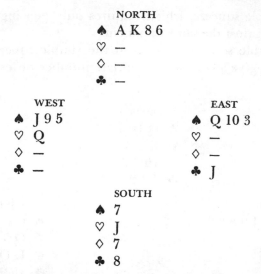

```
                    NORTH
                  ♠ A K 8 6
                  ♡ —
                  ◇ —
                  ♣ —

    WEST                          EAST
  ♠ J 9 5                       ♠ Q 10 3
  ♡ Q                           ♡ —
  ◇ —                           ◇ —
  ♣ —                           ♣ J

                    SOUTH
                  ♠ 7
                  ♡ J
                  ◇ 7
                  ♣ 8
```

Now the last diamond is led, and West must throw a spade in order to keep the heart queen. Dummy discards a spade, and East must also throw a spade in order to keep his club jack. So North wins the last three tricks with the A K 8 of spades.

In effect, what happened was this. West was busy protecting hearts. East was busy protecting clubs. And there was nobody left to mind the spades.

Some people have the idea that a double squeeze requires a great deal of counting. Nonsense! On this hand declarer doesn't count anything except clubs. He knows from the opening lead that the heart jack is a threat against West. And he learns from the play that the club eight is a threat against East. Now he runs all his winners, keeping one eye out for the heart queen and the missing clubs. If West doesn't throw the heart queen away, and if East doesn't throw two clubs away, dummy's spades must automatically win the last three tricks.

Why bother to count them?

Notice that the double squeeze requires *three* ingredients: 1. A threat against West. 2. A threat against East. 3. A general threat (in this case the long spade), which can be guarded by either opponent. To this extent the double squeeze is slightly more complicated than the simple squeeze, which requires only *two* ingredients: two threat cards against the same opponent.

In the double squeeze, just as in the simple squeeze, it is generally vital to give away the appropriate number of losers as soon as possible.

*Hand 7*

NORTH
♠ Q 10 5 4
♡ K 9 3
◇ 10 3 2
♣ 4 3 2

WEST
♠ A K J 9 8 3 2
♡ J 8 7
◇ 8 7 6
♣ —

EAST
♠ 6
♡ Q 5 4 2
◇ K Q J 5 4
♣ 10 9 8

SOUTH
♠ 7
♡ A 10 6
◇ A 9
♣ A K Q J 7 6 5

*The bidding:*

| WEST | NORTH | EAST | SOUTH |
|------|-------|------|-------|
| 4 ♠ | Pass | Pass | 5 ♣ |
| Pass | Pass | Pass | |

*Opening lead:* Spade king

West leads the spade king and shifts to the diamond eight, on which East plays the jack. Declarer pauses to take stock of the situation. He counts ten winners, and the best chance for an eleventh trick seems to be a squeeze. So he examines the available ingredients. The queen of spades is obviously a threat against West. From the play in diamonds it appears that dummy's ten is a threat against East. And the third heart is a general threat against either opponent.

So the requirements for a double squeeze are present, and all that remains is to lose the correct number of tricks—in this case, two.

One trick has already been lost to the spade king, and the best time to lose the second trick is right now. Accordingly South ducks the jack of diamonds. East continues with the king, and declarer wins with the ace and runs all his clubs. Just before the last club is cashed, the situation is:

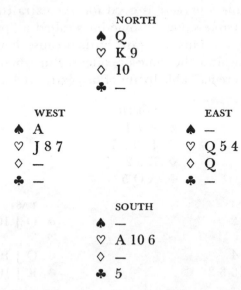

NORTH
♠ Q
♡ K 9
◇ 10
♣ —

WEST
♠ A
♡ J 8 7
◇ —
♣ —

EAST
♠ —
♡ Q 5 4
◇ Q
♣ —

SOUTH
♠ —
♡ A 10 6
◇ —
♣ 5

Watch what happens when the last club is led. West has to keep the spade ace, so he discards a heart. The spade queen now has accomplished its purpose, so declarer throws it away. East has to hold the diamond queen, so he also throws a heart. And declarer happily takes the last three tricks with the king, ace, and ten of hearts.

Again, declarer has no counting or worrying to do. He only has to keep track of two cards, West's ace of spades and East's queen of diamonds. When neither of them appears, South's third heart automatically wins the last trick.

The hardest part of this hand is ducking the second trick. One's instinct is to grab the diamond jack with the ace in order to draw trumps. Now the squeeze must fail against correct defense. It may seem that declarer can afford to win the second trick, draw three rounds of clubs, and then give up a diamond. But this won't work, because East will win and return his other diamond honor, killing one of declarer's threat cards.

### The Triple Squeeze

As a general rule a squeeze is good for *one* extra trick only. The exception is the triple squeeze, sometimes called a "progressive" or "repeating" squeeze. This is a rare bird, because it requires three threat cards, all against the same opponent. But when it does come up, declarer gets a remarkable bonus of *two* extra tricks.

*Hand 8*

|  | NORTH |  |
|---|---|---|
|  | ♠ A 7 4 |  |
|  | ♡ J 10 8 7 |  |
|  | ◇ K 3 2 |  |
|  | ♣ A Q 5 |  |

| WEST |  | EAST |
|---|---|---|
| ♠ 6 3 2 |  | ♠ Q J 10 9 |
| ♡ 4 3 |  | ♡ 5 |
| ◇ 7 6 4 |  | ◇ Q J 10 8 |
| ♣ 8 7 6 3 2 |  | ♣ K J 10 9 |

|  | SOUTH |
|---|---|
|  | ♠ K 8 5 |
|  | ♡ A K Q 9 6 2 |
|  | ◇ A 9 5 |
|  | ♣ 4 |

*The bidding:*

| NORTH | EAST | SOUTH | WEST |
|---|---|---|---|
| 1 ♣ | Pass | 1 ♡ | Pass |
| 2 ♡ | Pass | 4 NT | Pass |
| 5 ♡ | Pass | 5 NT | Pass |
| 6 ◇ | Pass | 7 NT | Pass |
| Pass | Double | Pass | Pass |
| Pass | | | |

*Opening lead:* Club eight

South has his bidding shoes on. A small slam would be a reasonable contract, but seven no-trump is inexcusable. East can hardly believe his ears and he doubles with relish.

A double of a slam often suggests the lead of dummy's suit, and West obediently opens the eight of clubs. Declarer takes stock. He has eleven winners, and if the club finesse works, he will be within one trick of his contract. But South feels sure that this particular club finesse has zero chance of winning. So he goes up with dummy's ace and runs his heart suit. After five rounds of hearts the remaining cards are:

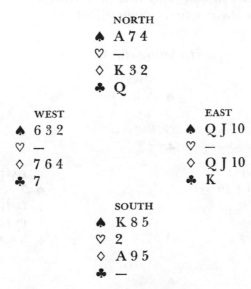

```
                    NORTH
                ♠ A 7 4
                ♡ —
                ◇ K 3 2
                ♣ Q

     WEST                        EAST
 ♠ 6 3 2                     ♠ Q J 10
 ♡ —                         ♡ —
 ◇ 7 6 4                     ◇ Q J 10
 ♣ 7                         ♣ K

                    SOUTH
                ♠ K 8 5
                ♡ 2
                ◇ A 9 5
                ♣ —
```

Declarer leads his last heart. West throws a club, North throws a spade, and East feels the pinch. Let's suppose he lets go a spade. South now cashes the ace, king, and eight of spades, discarding a diamond from dummy. East is pinched again. He probably throws a diamond this time, and declarer wins the last three tricks with the king, ace, and nine of diamonds.

East could do nothing to save himself. Try letting him discard something else. South always winds up with thirteen tricks, even though he starts out with only eleven.

The problem is that East has too much. Declarer has three threat cards: the club queen, the spade eight, and the diamond nine. And

East alone has the burden of protecting all three. So he gets squeezed *twice,* and South gets a bonus of *two* extra tricks.

* *

Up to this point all the squeezes discussed have operated by themselves. Declarer simply had to give up the appropriate number of losers (rectify the count) and then sit back and cash all his winners. If a squeeze was possible, it materialized by itself. Declarer did not have to actively *do* anything.

In the majority of cases this will hold true. Sometimes, however, declarer needs to help matters along slightly.

### Isolating the Menace

*Hand 9*

NORTH
♠ A K 8 6 4
♡ A 6 4 3
◇ K 7
♣ 3 2

WEST
♠ Q J 10 9
♡ J 9 5 2
◇ J 5 4
♣ 9 7

EAST
♠ 7
♡ Q 10 8
◇ Q 10 9 8 6 3
♣ 6 5 4

SOUTH
♠ 5 3 2
♡ K 7
◇ A 2
♣ A K Q J 10 8

*The bidding:*

| NORTH | EAST | SOUTH | WEST |
|-------|------|-------|------|
| 1 ♠ | Pass | 3 ♣ | Pass |
| 3 ♡ | Pass | 4 ♣ | Pass |
| 5 ♣ | Pass | 5 ◇ | Pass |
| 7 ♣ | Pass | Pass | Pass |

*Opening lead:* Spade queen

North-South reach seven clubs, which would be an excellent contract if South had a doubleton spade. As it is, only twelve tricks are available, and the thirteenth must come from a squeeze. Declarer wins the opening lead with the spade ace and examines the possible ingredients. There are only two: the long spade and the long heart. With only two ingredients declarer must try for a simple squeeze, which means that both threats or menaces must be against the same opponent.

Only five spades are missing, so dummy's eight is a threat against the opponent who holds three or more spades. From the opening lead it appears that West is the one who can guard this suit.

Dummy's six of hearts is also a threat card, but it is likely that both opponents have this suit stopped. Therefore, after drawing trumps, declarer plays the king and ace of hearts and ruffs a heart. Now the enemy can no longer cooperate in protecting the suit. Only one opponent can hold four or more hearts, and declarer must hope it is West. He cashes the king and ace of diamonds and runs all the clubs. Just before the last club is cashed, the position is:

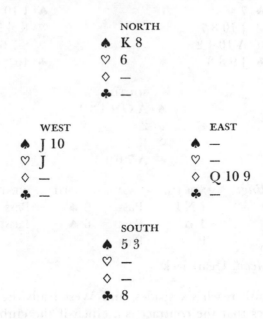

```
                    NORTH
                  ♠ K 8
                  ♡ 6
                  ◇ —
                  ♣ —

        WEST                    EAST
      ♠ J 10                  ♠ —
      ♡ J                     ♡ —
      ◇ —                     ◇ Q 10 9
      ♣ —                     ♣ —

                    SOUTH
                  ♠ 5 3
                  ♡ —
                  ◇ —
                  ♣ 8
```

South leads the last club and West surrenders.

If declarer doesn't ruff a round of hearts, the end position will be the same except that East will have the heart queen left. Now West can safely throw his jack of hearts on the last club and the squeeze will fail.

By ruffing that heart, declarer causes the entire burden of guarding the suit to fall on one opponent's shoulders. In bridge terminology, this maneuver is known as isolating the menace.

### Transferring the Menace

Hand 10

```
                         NORTH
                         ♠ K 8 6 5
                         ♡ A Q 9
                         ◊ Q 9
                         ♣ K Q 5 2

        WEST                                 EAST
        ♠ 7                                  ♠ J 10
        ♡ J 10 8 7                           ♡ K 6 5 4 3
        ◊ A 10 4 2                           ◊ 8 7 6 5 3
        ♣ J 9 8 3                            ♣ 10

                         SOUTH
                         ♠ A Q 9 4 3 2
                         ♡ 2
                         ◊ K J
                         ♣ A 7 6 4
```

The bidding:

| NORTH | EAST | SOUTH | WEST |
|-------|------|-------|------|
| 1 NT  | Pass | 3 ♠   | Pass |
| 4 ♠   | Pass | 6 ♠   | Pass |
| Pass  | Pass |       |      |

Opening lead: Heart jack

North-South reach six spades, and West leads the jack of hearts. Declarer sees that the contract is a cinch if the clubs break 3–2, so he wins the first trick with the ace and draws the outstanding trumps. A diamond is led, and West takes his ace and returns a diamond. Now South cashes the ace and king of clubs and is disappointed when East fails to follow to the second round. This means he has only eleven tricks and must develop a squeeze for the twelfth.

Declarer surveys the threat-card situation and finds only two. The fourth club is a threat against West, and the heart queen is a threat against the player who holds the king. With only two ingredients available he must try for a simple squeeze, which means that both threats must be against the same opponent. Unfortunately, it appears from the opening lead that East is likely to hold the heart king. So, declarer sets out to "transfer the menace," and he leads the queen of hearts from dummy. East must cover with the king (to keep South from discarding his club loser), and declarer ruffs. Now dummy's nine of hearts is a threat against West's ten. South runs his spade suit, and with one trump to go the situation is:

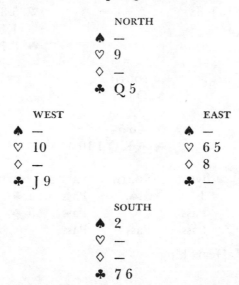

```
                    NORTH
                 ♠  —
                 ♡  9
                 ◇  —
                 ♣  Q 5

     WEST                      EAST
  ♠  —                      ♠  —
  ♡  10                     ♡  6 5
  ◇  —                      ◇  8
  ♣  J 9                    ♣  —

                    SOUTH
                 ♠  2
                 ♡  —
                 ◇  —
                 ♣  7 6
```

Declarer leads that last spade, and West can't find a discard.

### The Vienna Coup

The Vienna Coup is actually an unblocking play in preparation for a squeeze. It was first described in print over one hundred years ago by James Clay of London, the leading English whist authority of his day. He credited its discovery to "the best whist player in Vienna." Originally it was assumed that only a top expert would be capable of such a play. Today, the Vienna Coup is commonplace among good bridge players everywhere.

*Hand 11*

NORTH
♠ A 10 9 8 7
♡ J 7 6
♢ A K Q 3
♣ 4

WEST
♠ 5 3
♡ A K Q 10 9 8
♢ 9 8
♣ 6 5 2

EAST
♠ K J 4 2
♡ 5 3
♢ J 10 4 2
♣ 8 7 3

SOUTH
♠ Q 6
♡ 4 2
♢ 7 6 5
♣ A K Q J 10 9

*The bidding:*

| WEST | NORTH | EAST | SOUTH |
|------|-------|------|-------|
| 3 ♡ | 3 ♠ | Pass | 4 ♣ |
| Pass | 4 ♢ | Pass | 5 ♣ |
| Pass | Pass | Pass | |

*Opening lead:* Heart king

West opens with a pre-emptive bid of three hearts, and South eventually becomes declarer at the reasonable contract of five clubs. West starts out with three top hearts, and declarer ruffs the third round as East discards the spade four.

The contract is a lay-down if the diamonds break 3–3. And if they don't break 3–3, there will be a squeeze if the spade king is in the same hand as the diamond length. Declarer pictures a situation where South has the lead and only four cards are left in everyone's hand:

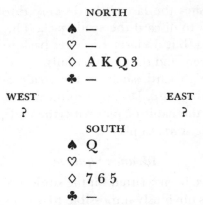

NORTH
♠ —
♡ —
◇ A K Q 3
♣ —

WEST          EAST
?                 ?

SOUTH
♠ Q
♡ —
◇ 7 6 5
♣ —

South cheerfully contemplates the dilemma of any opponent who started with four or more diamonds and the king of spades. Which four cards will the poor guy keep?

But enough daydreaming. Now declarer has to figure out a way to reach this happy four-card ending. Can you see how to get there? Remember, the lead must be in the South hand.

Declarer can never reach this position unless he cashes the spade ace immediately. So, at trick four he leads the spade six to the ace. Now dummy's singleton club is an entry to the South hand. Trumps are run, and the last one squeezes East to a pulp.

If declarer leads even one round of trumps first, it will be too late to get the spade ace out of dummy, because there won't be any convenient re-entry left to the South hand. In this case, the end position will be:

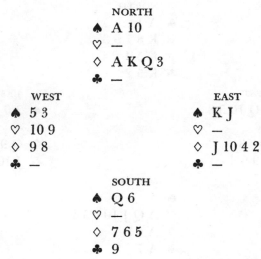

NORTH
♠ A 10
♡ —
◇ A K Q 3
♣ —

WEST                    EAST
♠ 5 3                   ♠ K J
♡ 10 9                  ♡ —
◇ 9 8                   ◇ J 10 4 2
♣ —                    ♣ —

SOUTH
♠ Q 6
♡ —
◇ 7 6 5
♣ 9

When South cashes the last club, dummy throws the spade ten, and East can afford to discard the spade jack. The ace of spades now drops the lone king, but declarer can't get back to his hand to make use of the good queen, and the contract fails.

Unblocking a high card, such as the spade ace in this case, is known as the Vienna coup. Declarer won't find this type of squeeze difficult if he is in the habit of picturing the end position he wishes to achieve before he starts to play.

### Advance Squeezes

Entire books have been written on the subject of advanced squeeze technique, and it is obviously impossible to do more than scratch the surface here. The reader who is beginning to feel out of his depth can skip this section, confident that the majority of squeezes he will meet have already been covered.

### The Compound Squeeze

The compound squeeze resembles the double squeeze, and in both cases three ingredients are involved. Remember that a double squeeze functions with two specific threats (one against each opponent) and one general threat, which can be guarded by either opponent. The compound squeeze functions with only one specific threat and two general threats. A general threat is usually less valuable than a specific threat, and consequently a compound squeeze requires a little more *savoir-faire* on the part of declarer.

*Hand 12*

```
                        NORTH
                        ♠ A J
                        ♡ K 8 7 6 3
                        ◊ K 5 4
                        ♣ K 5 2

        WEST                                    EAST
        ♠ K Q 10 9 8                            ♠ 7 6 5 4 3
        ♡ 2                                     ♡ —
        ◊ J 10 8                                ◊ Q 9 7 3
        ♣ Q 9 6 3                               ♣ J 10 8 4

                        SOUTH
                        ♠ 2
                        ♡ A Q J 10 9 5 4
                        ◊ A 6 2
                        ♣ A 7
```

*The bidding:*

| SOUTH | WEST | NORTH | EAST |
|-------|------|-------|------|
| 1 ♡ | Pass | 3 ♡ | Pass |
| 4 NT | Pass | 5 ◇ | Pass |
| 5 NT | Pass | 6 ♠ | Pass |
| 7 ♡ | Pass | Pass | Pass |

*Opening lead:* Spade king

The contract is seven hearts, and West leads the king of spades. South wins with the ace and counts twelve winners. A squeeze must be found for the thirteenth, so declarer inspects the threat-card situation. The spade jack is clearly a threat against West, and the long diamond and the long club are probably general threats, which can be protected by either opponent.

Declarer's aim is to bring about the conditions for a double squeeze. In order to do this, he must first force West to abandon his guard in one of the minors. So he runs his hearts, and after five rounds the situation is:

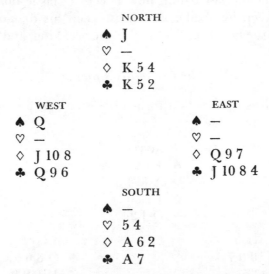

NORTH
♠ J
♡ —
◇ K 5 4
♣ K 5 2

WEST
♠ Q
♡ —
◇ J 10 8
♣ Q 9 6

EAST
♠ —
♡ —
◇ Q 9 7
♣ J 10 8 4

SOUTH
♠ —
♡ 5 4
◇ A 6 2
♣ A 7

The next-to-last heart forces West to relinquish either his diamond stopper or his club stopper. In either case dummy throws a diamond and East a club. At this point East is in full charge of guarding whichever suit West has abandoned. Let's suppose West has discarded a diamond. This means the diamond six is a threat against East alone and the ingredients for a double squeeze are present. Before leading the last trump, however, declarer should cash the king and ace of the suit West has abandoned. This leaves:

NORTH
♠ J
♡ —
♢ —
♣ K 5 2

WEST
♠ Q
♡ —
♢ —
♣ Q 9 6

EAST
♠ —
♡ —
♢ Q
♣ J 10 8

SOUTH
♠ —
♡ 4
♢ 6
♣ A 7

The lead of the last trump now effects a classic double squeeze. West must keep his spade. East must keep his diamond. And declarer makes the last three tricks with the ace, king, and five of clubs.

### The Crisscross Squeeze

The crisscross squeeze is a form of simple squeeze, which at first glance looks impossible.

*Hand 13*

NORTH
♠ J 4 2
♡ A K 4 3
♢ J 10 6
♣ Q J 2

WEST
♠ 10 9 7 3
♡ Q 5
♢ A K Q 9
♣ 9 7 4

EAST
♠ Q 8 6 5
♡ J 10 9 2
♢ 4 2
♣ 6 5 3

SOUTH
♠ A K
♡ 8 7 6
♢ 8 7 5 3
♣ A K 10 8

*The bidding:*

| SOUTH | WEST | NORTH | EAST |
|-------|------|-------|------|
| 1 ♣ | Pass | 1 ♡ | Pass |
| 1 NT | Pass | 3 NT | Pass |
| Pass | Pass | | |

*Opening lead:* Diamond king

Against three no-trump West starts off with four rounds of diamonds. North discards a heart, and East throws two clubs. West shifts to the ten of spades, South wins with the ace and contemplates the situation. There are eight winners available. If one opponent holds the spade queen and at least four hearts, a simple squeeze should operate. But there is something wrong here. Suppose the last four cards are:

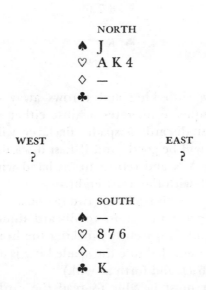

```
              NORTH
           ♠  J
           ♡  A K 4
           ◇  —
           ♣  —

WEST                      EAST
 ?                         ?

              SOUTH
           ♠  —
           ♡  8 7 6
           ◇  —
           ♣  K
```

When South leads his last club, West will be squeezed if he started with the spade queen and long hearts. But if *East* started with the spade queen and the long hearts, the squeeze wouldn't work, because dummy would have to discard first.

Declarer can overcome this problem by saving the king of spades in his hand and throwing dummy's other small heart on the fourth club. After three rounds of clubs the position is:

NORTH
♠ J 4
♡ A K 4
◇ —
♣ —

WEST
♠ 9 7 3
♡ Q 5
◇ —
♣ —

EAST
♠ Q 8
♡ J 10 9
◇ —
♣ —

SOUTH
♠ K
♡ 8 7 6
◇ —
♣ K

South leads the club king and throws away dummy's four of hearts. Now the squeeze operates against either opponent. In the actual case, if East discards a spade, declarer will cash the spade king, and dummy will be good. And if East discards a heart, declarer will cash dummy's A K and return to his hand with the spade king to win the last trick with the heart eight.

The crisscross squeeze is tricky for two reasons:

First, it goes against the grain to discard dummy's other small heart on the last club, apparently blocking the heart suit. (Actually it doesn't block the suit, because the spade king is an extra entry and declarer can cross back and forth at will.)

Second, declarer must be able to read the cards correctly. If he guesses wrong, he may criss when he should cross!

### The Guard Squeeze

This is a squeeze in which one opponent is forced to discard in such a way that his partner is subjected to a finesse.

*Hand 14*

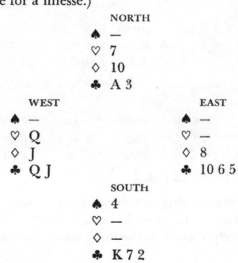

NORTH
♠ 10 8
♡ 7 5 3 2
◊ A 10 5
♣ A 9 8 3

WEST
♠ 3 2
♡ A K Q 10
◊ K Q J 4
♣ Q J 4

EAST
♠ 9 7 6
♡ J 8 4
◊ 8 7 3 2
♣ 10 6 5

SOUTH
♠ A K Q J 5 4
♡ 9 6
◊ 9 6
♣ K 7 2

*The bidding:*

| SOUTH | WEST | NORTH | EAST |
|-------|------|-------|------|
| 1 ♠ | Double | 1 NT | Pass |
| 4 ♠ | Pass | Pass | Pass |

*Opening lead:* Heart king

West cashes two high hearts and then shifts to the king of diamonds. Declarer ducks (to rectify the count), and West continues with the diamond queen, which is won by the ace. A heart is ruffed high, and four rounds of trumps are led. This is then the position: (Notice that declarer was careful to unblock the nine and eight of clubs to prepare for a finesse.)

NORTH
♠ —
♡ 7
◊ 10
♣ A 3

WEST
♠ —
♡ Q
◊ J
♣ Q J

EAST
♠ —
♡ —
◊ 8
♣ 10 6 5

SOUTH
♠ 4
♡ —
◊ —
♣ K 7 2

South leads the last spade, and West must keep the good heart and the good diamond, so he throws the jack of clubs. Now a club to the ace drops the queen, and declarer finesses the seven on the way back.

\* \*

It has been stressed that the majority of squeezes will not operate unless declarer first gives up the appropriate number of losers. There is, however, a class of squeezes called "secondary squeezes" which form the exception to this general rule. In the secondary squeeze (or squeeze without the count), a loser is conceded after the squeeze has operated. Here is an unusual example of a secondary squeeze that bears the picturesque name of "stepping-stone squeeze."

### The Stepping-Stone Squeeze

Hand 15

NORTH
♠ A 10 6 4 3 2
♡ —
◇ 4 3
♣ 8 7 5 3 2

WEST
♠ 9 7
♡ 8 7 2
◇ J 10 9 7 2
♣ J 9 6

EAST
♠ Q J 8 5
♡ 6 4 3
◇ 8 6
♣ A K 10 4

SOUTH
♠ K
♡ A K Q J 10 9 5
◇ A K Q 5
♣ Q

The bidding:

| SOUTH | WEST | NORTH | EAST |
|-------|------|-------|------|
| 2 ♡ | Pass | 2 ♠ | Pass |
| 6 ♡ | Pass | Pass | Pass |

Opening lead: Diamond jack

North-South are playing ace-showing responses over two bids. South bids six hearts with confidence, and West leads the diamond jack. Unfortunately there is something rotten in the State of Denmark. Declarer has twelve tricks all right, but he can't get to dummy to cash the spade ace. He wins the first trick and instinctively runs his seven heart winners. A second diamond honor is cashed and the situation is:

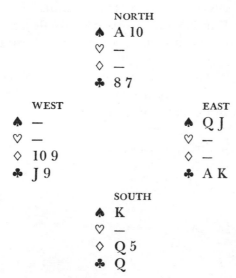

NORTH
♠ A 10
♡ —
◇ —
♣ 8 7

WEST
♠ —
♡ —
◇ 10 9
♣ J 9

EAST
♠ Q J
♡ —
◇ —
♣ A K

SOUTH
♠ K
♡ —
◇ Q 5
♣ Q

South needs three of the last four tricks. He leads the queen of diamonds, and East can't discard a spade because that would allow declarer to score two spade tricks by overtaking the king with dummy's ace. So East throws the club king. South now cashes the spade king and exits with the club queen. East wins, and his remaining spade provides the stepping stone to dummy's ace!

\* \*

Advanced squeezes, such as the last four examples, require accurate card reading and a thorough understanding of end play as well as squeeze technique. The majority of squeezes, however, require very little effort on the part of declarer. In fact most of them operate entirely by themselves if the count is right.

The next time you are playing a hand and find yourself one trick short, don't just give up. Look around for those threat cards. If you find only two, they must both be against the same opponent, in which case there is probably a simple squeeze. If you are lucky enough to find three threat cards, your prospects are even better. If any two of these are against the same opponent, you can try for a simple squeeze. If there is one threat against each opponent and a third general threat that can be guarded by either opponent, look for a double squeeze. With only one threat against a specific opponent and two general threats, you have material for a compound squeeze, (which later boils down to a double squeeze). And if you are fortunate enough to find three threat cards all against the same opponent, you may wind up with a triple squeeze and a bonus of two extra tricks.

Don't worry if you can't remember the names of the various squeezes or the different combination of threats that go with each. The important thing to remember is to give away the appropriate number of losers early (rectify the count). This creates the pressure that operates the squeeze. In most cases all declarer has to do is sit back and cash his winners.

# 9

# *The Gentle Art of Deception*

EVERY GOOD BRIDGE PLAYER has a little larceny somewhere in his soul. This makes a stolen contract much sweeter than one that is earned legitimately.

There is quite an art to deceiving an opponent, and declarer has all the best of it. A *defender* who pulls a hoax runs the risk of fooling his partner. But declarer is a free agent. Who cares if dummy gets fooled?

Deception is basically a matter of pretending to hold a hand that is different from the one you actually hold. Look at the following situation:

NORTH
♠ Q 8
♡ J 3
◇ A K 5
♣ J 7 6 5 4 3

WEST
♠ J 7 4
♡ 9 8 7 6 5
◇ J 9 8 6
♣ K

EAST
♠ A 2
♡ K Q 10 4
◇ 7 4 3
♣ Q 10 9 8

SOUTH
♠ K 10 9 6 5 3
♡ A 2
◇ Q 10 2
♣ A 2

*The bidding:*

| SOUTH | WEST | NORTH | EAST |
|-------|------|-------|------|
| 1 ♠ | Pass | 2 ♣ | Pass |
| 2 ♠ | Pass | 3 ♠ | Pass |
| 4 ♠ | Pass | Pass | Pass |

*Opening lead:* Heart nine

West leads the heart nine, and declarer cannot avoid losing a heart, a club, and the ace of trumps. This means that to make the contract he must guess the location of the spade jack. Life would be much easier if one of the opponents would lead a trump. So declarer decides to play like a man who is anxious to ruff a heart in dummy. He wins the opening lead with the ace and promptly returns a heart. East wins dummy's jack with the queen and will very likely play the ace and another spade to prevent any ruffs. This eliminates the trump guess, and the contract is home.

Of course if East held something like A J x of spades, he wouldn't make the obvious trump return, and declarer would still have to guess the location of the jack himself. But in this case, the very fact that East was reluctant to lead a trump would probably guide declarer to the winning guess.

Try this one:

| | NORTH |
|---|---|
| | ♠ K Q 4 |
| | ♡ K J 8 6 2 |
| | ◇ K J 7 |
| | ♣ 9 4 |

| | SOUTH |
|---|---|
| | ♠ A J 10 8 7 |
| | ♡ 7 3 |
| | ◇ A Q 10 9 |
| | ♣ A K |

*The bidding:*

| NORTH | EAST | SOUTH | WEST |
|---|---|---|---|
| 1 ♡ | Pass | 2 ♠ | Pass |
| 3 ♠ | Pass | 6 ♠ | Pass |
| Pass | Pass | | |

*Opening lead:* Club queen

West leads the club queen, and declarer's only problem is the heart situation. If the A Q of hearts is in the West hand, he can't go wrong. And if they are both in the East hand, he has no chance. But if the heart honors are split, the contract depends on a winning guess.

Declarer can give himself the maximum chance here by pretending to hold a singleton heart. He should win the opening lead with the club ace and immediately lead a heart as though he were trying to steal a trick with dummy's king. If West has the ace he will probably grab it, and the hand is now over. And if West plays low without hesitation, declarer's best bet is to insert dummy's jack.

If declarer postpones the heart guess until the end of the hand, West will be aware of the situation and will automatically play low whether or not he has the ace.

## The Choice of Spot Card

An expert declarer can accomplish a great deal of camouflage through the subtle use of insignificantly small cards. It is important to understand the principle here thoroughly so you don't give away vital information by stopping to think at a crucial moment.

NORTH
♠ 9 4 3
♡ K 7 6 5 2
◇ K Q J
♣ A 10

WEST
♠ A K J 7
♡ —
◇ 10 4 2
♣ 9 7 5 4 3 2

EAST
♠ 10 8 5
♡ 10 9 8
◇ A 7 6 5
♣ J 8 6

SOUTH
♠ Q 6 2
♡ A Q J 4 3
◇ 9 8 3
♣ K Q

*The bidding:*

| SOUTH | WEST | NORTH | EAST |
|-------|------|-------|------|
| 1 ♡   | Pass | 3 ♡   | Pass |
| 4 ♡   | Pass | Pass  | Pass |

*Opening lead:* Spade king

West leads the spade king against four hearts, and East plays the five. Declarer sees a diamond loser and three possible spade losers. The only chance to avoid one of these losers is to persuade West to lead another spade. So South plays the six on the first trick, not the two. This makes East's five look like a signal. West may now think his partner has a doubleton 5 2 or possibly the Q 5 2. In either case he is likely to continue with the spade ace at trick two, and declarer is home. Notice that if South plays the spade two at trick one, West will have no trouble reading East's five as his smallest card, and a shift to any other suit beats the contract.

Now let's make a couple of minor changes in the hand:

NORTH
♠ Q 9 8 3
♡ K 7 6 5 2
◇ K Q
♣ A 10

WEST
♠ A K J 7
♡ —
◇ 10 4 2
♣ 9 7 5 4 3 2

EAST
♠ 5 4
♡ 10 9 8
◇ A 9 7 6 5
♣ J 8 6

SOUTH
♠ 10 6 2
♡ A Q J 4 3
◇ J 8 3
♣ K Q

The bidding is the same and the opening lead is the same. Again East plays the spade five on West's king. Declarer still has a diamond loser and three possible spade losers. But this time he can eliminate one of the spade losers later himself by leading toward dummy's queen. He definitely does *not* want West to continue the suit, because of the possibility of a ruff. An inexperienced declarer might drop the ten on the first trick, trying to pretend he had a singleton. This won't fool West a bit, because he knows his partner wouldn't play the five holding the 6 5 4 2. The right card for South to play this time is the two. Now, from West's point of view, East could hold the 10 6 5, in which case a shift would be in order.

The principle here is that declarer should play his lowest spot card if he wants an opponent to stop leading a suit, and he should play a higher card if he wants the suit continued. This is easy to remember since it is exactly the same as the "come on" signal by defender.

*Warning:* Don't overdo the size of the spot card when you are anxious for a continuation.

NORTH
◊ 4 2

WEST
◊ A K 3

EAST
◊ 10 9 6

SOUTH
◊ Q J 8 7 5

South is playing three no-trump, having concealed a five-card diamond suit in the auction. West leads the king, and East contributes the six. Declarer wants West to lead another diamond, and the proper card to play is the seven, not the eight. If he plays the seven, West may think his partner has played the six from something like Q J 6 5, and he will lead another diamond. But if South plays the eight, West will wonder what has become of the seven spot. If East held both the six and the seven and wanted a continuation, he would signal with the seven, not the six. (For example, with Q J 7 6 5 it would be automatic for East to play the seven on partner's king, not the six.) West will now suspect that it is South who is signaling for a continuation, not East, and he may shift to some other suit.

NORTH
♠ 6 3
♡ 8 6 5
◊ K Q J 10 2
♣ 8 6 3

WEST
♠ 9 4
♡ J 4 3 2
◊ 9 6 4
♣ 10 7 5 4

EAST
♠ K J 10 8 7
♡ K Q 9
◊ A 8 5
♣ 9 2

SOUTH
♠ A Q 5 2
♡ A 10 7
◊ 7 3
♣ A K Q J

| The bidding: | EAST | SOUTH | WEST | NORTH |
|---|---|---|---|---|
| | 1 ♠ | Double | Pass | 2 ◊ |
| | Pass | 2 NT | Pass | 3 NT |
| | Pass | Pass | Pass | |

*Opening lead:* Spade nine

Against three no-trump West leads the spade nine, East plays the ten, and South wins with the queen. Declarer realizes that in order to make the contract he will have to win two diamond tricks. Let's suppose he leads the diamond three at trick two. West will play the four, his lowest card, to show partner that he was dealt an odd number of diamonds. Dummy wins with the king as East ducks. Now declarer leads the queen from dummy, and East takes his ace, having no difficulty figuring out that West started with three diamonds and South with two. So declarer makes only one diamond trick, and the contract fails.

Now see what happens if declarer leads the seven originally, instead of the three. Again West plays his lowest card, the four, and dummy's king wins. But his time when the queen is led, East is in a quandary. He doesn't know that the four was partner's lowest card. West could be playing high-low with a doubleton 4 3, in which case East must duck again. Rather than risk giving declarer three more diamond tricks, East will probably hold off with his ace once more, and South is now home.

Let's alter the South and West cards slightly:

```
                    NORTH
                ♠ 6 3
                ♡ 8 6 5
                ◇ K Q J 10 2
                ♣ 8 6 3

    WEST                            EAST
♠ 9 4                           ♠ K J 10 8 7
♡ J 4 3 2                       ♡ K Q 9
◇ 6 4                           ◇ A 8 5
♣ J 10 7 5 4                    ♣ 9 2

                    SOUTH
                ♠ A Q 5 2
                ♡ A 10 7
                ◇ 9 7 3
                ♣ A K Q
```

The bidding and the opening lead are the same, and South again wins the first trick with the spade queen. This time, however, South wants East to think that declarer has a doubleton diamond and that West is the one with three. His best bet is to start the suit by leading the three. West will play the six, and dummy's king will win. When the queen is led from dummy, East has a problem. West could be playing the six from the 9 7 6, in which case East should win this trick. It is true that he will probably duck again rather than risk giving declarer three more diamond tricks. But at least he has a chance of going wrong. Note that if South leads the seven or the nine originally, East can tell immediately that his partner cannot have three diamonds, so there is no chance of his going wrong.

It will frequently occur that an opponent has to decide whether his partner has a doubleton in a suit and declarer has three, or vice versa. If he is forced to make this decision after seeing only one of partner's cards and only one of declarer's cards, he can be fooled. And generally the way to fool him is for declarer to lead small himself from a three-card holding and high from a doubleton.

### The Choice of Honor Cards

It is a general principle that declarer should win a trick with the higher of equal honor cards.

NORTH
◇ 5

WEST
◇ J 9 7 2

EAST
◇ Q 10 6 4 3

SOUTH
◇ A K 8

Against a four-spade contract West leads the two of diamonds. East plays the queen, and declarer instinctively wins with the ace, leaving both opponents in the dark as to the location of the king. If declarer wins with the king, instead, he will not fool anyone as to the location of the ace. East knows that West would not lead away from an ace in a suit contract. And West knows that East would have played the ace on dummy's singleton if he had it.

Here's a hand that demonstrates the advantage of winning with the higher honor:

```
                          NORTH
                       ♠ A 10 5
                       ♡ 7 4 2
                       ◇ K Q 4
                       ♣ Q J 10 9

        WEST                              EAST
     ♠ Q                              ♠ K 8 7 4 3 2
     ♡ A 10 8 6 3                     ♡ J 9
     ◇ J 10 7 2                       ◇ 6 5 3
     ♣ K 3 2                          ♣ 5 4

                          SOUTH
                       ♠ J 9 6
                       ♡ K Q 5
                       ◇ A 9 8
                       ♣ A 8 7 6
```

| *The bidding:* | SOUTH | WEST | NORTH | EAST |
|---|---|---|---|---|
| | 1 ♣ | Pass | 1 ◇ | Pass |
| | 1 NT | Pass | 3 NT | Pass |
| | Pass | Pass | | |

*Opening lead:* Heart six

West leads the heart six against three no-trump, East plays the jack, and South wins with the king, leaving both opponents uncertain as to the whereabouts of the queen. Dummy is entered with a diamond, and the club queen is led for a finesse. West wins the second round of clubs with the king and tries to analyze the situation. From his point of view it looks as though declarer started with the club ace, the diamond ace, the heart king, and possibly the spade king, which gives him nine tricks ready to run. West is likely to think that the only chance for the defense is to cash four heart tricks immediately.

In this case he will probably lay down the heart ace, expecting East to unblock with the queen. Unfortunately for the defense, this sets up a ninth trick for declarer. With any return except a heart, South can never make more than eight tricks.

If South had won the first trick with the heart queen instead of the king, West would have had no trouble defeating this contract. He would have known that declarer started with the K Q of hearts as well as the two minor aces. South couldn't have the spade king as well, because this would give him 16 points. West now realizes that declarer can never make nine tricks if left to his own devices. There is no reason to make a risky heart lead, and with any other return the contract must eventually fail.

\* \*

In bridge almost every principle has its exceptions. Here is an unusual situation where declarer does best to win with the *lower* of equal honors:

NORTH
♠ 7 5
♡ 8 4 3
♢ A 9
♣ A Q J 8 4 2

WEST
♠ Q 10 8 4 2
♡ A 10 6
♢ 4 3 2
♣ 5 3

EAST
♠ J 6 3
♡ K J 5 2
♢ 10 8 7 6
♣ K 6

SOUTH
♠ A K 9
♡ Q 9 7
♢ K Q J 5
♣ 10 9 7

*The bidding:*

| SOUTH | WEST | NORTH | EAST |
|-------|------|-------|------|
| 1 ♢ | Pass | 2 ♣ | Pass |
| 2 NT | Pass | 3 NT | Pass |
| Pass | Pass | | |

*Opening lead:* Spade four

West opens the spade four, and East plays the jack. Declarer has no intention of holding up because he is much more worried about hearts than spades. It is just a question of whether he should win with the ace or the king. The better play is the king. Now the club is finessed, and when East wins the king he is likely to return a spade in the hope that West started with A Q x x x. If the first trick is won with the ace, East will wonder why declarer didn't make a normal holdup play in spades, which he would do if he held A x x. East may now find the heart shift, which beats the contract.

### Throwing a Smoke Screen over the Weak Suit

Frequently declarer will have one very weak suit. He is naturally anxious to conceal this weakness from his opponents, and there are several ways to do so.

It is a psychological fact that defenders are reluctant to lead a suit that declarer is apparently trying to establish. As a result, declarer can sometimes cause the opponents to go astray by brazenly attacking his own weak spot.

NORTH
♠ J 7
♡ A J 10 9
◊ K Q J 5
♣ 8 5 4

WEST
♠ K 9 4 2
♡ 8 7
◊ 10 9 8 7
♣ K Q 3

EAST
♠ A 10 8 3
♡ 6 5 4 3
◊ 4
♣ A 7 6 2

SOUTH
♠ Q 6 5
♡ K Q 2
◊ A 6 3 2
♣ J 10 9

*The bidding:*

| | NORTH | EAST | SOUTH | WEST |
|---|---|---|---|---|
| | 1 ♡ | Pass | 2 NT | Pass |
| | 3 NT | Pass | Pass | Pass |

*Opening lead:* Diamond ten

North and South both stretched a point in the bidding, and the final contract of three no-trump can charitably be called "inferior." West leads the diamond ten, and declarer sees no legitimate play for nine tricks. If he cashes his eight red winners the enemy will surely save the A K of spades and the A K Q of clubs to score the last five tricks. Rather than concede defeat South decides to try a diversion. He wins the diamond lead in dummy and promptly leads a club to the jack, which loses to West's queen. The opponents can hardly imagine that declarer is wide open in clubs, and looking at dummy they will probably launch a vigorous attack on the spade suit. South wins the third round of spades with the queen, and a hopeless contract is suddenly home.

Here is another example of the same principle, this time at the slam level:

NORTH
♠ A Q 6 5
♡ 8 7 3
◇ Q 3 2
♣ A 7 5

WEST
♠ 10 7 3
♡ A 10 2
◇ 5 4
♣ K Q 10 8 6

EAST
♠ J 9 8 4
♡ K 9 6 4
◇ 7
♣ J 4 3 2

SOUTH
♠ K 2
♡ Q J 5
◇ A K J 10 9 8 6
♣ 9

*The bidding:*

| SOUTH | WEST | NORTH | EAST |
|-------|------|-------|------|
| 1 ◇ | Pass | 1 ♠ | Pass |
| 3 ◇ | Pass | 6 ◇ | Pass |
| Pass | Pass | | |

*Opening lead:* Club king

Against six diamonds West leads the club king, and the ace wins the first trick. Again there is no legitimate way to make twelve tricks, and declarer's best bet is to lead a heart immediately. East plays small and the queen loses to the ace. West will probably return the queen of clubs. (It is pretty difficult for him to picture the king of hearts in his partner's hand.) South ruffs and cashes all but one of his trumps. This leaves:

NORTH
♠ A Q 6 5
♡ —
◇ —
♣ 7

WEST
♠ 10 7
♡ 10 2
◇ —
♣ 10

EAST
♠ J 9 8 4
♡ K
◇ —
♣ —

SOUTH
♠ K 2
♡ J 5
◇ 6
♣ —

South leads the last diamond, discarding the club from dummy, and East tosses in the sponge.

\* \*

Sometimes declarer can hide his "Achilles heel" by simulating weakness in some other suit. Here is an example from a team game:

NORTH
♠ 6 4
♡ K Q J 10
◇ Q J 10 9
♣ Q 7 2

WEST
♠ K 10 7 5 2
♡ 5 3 2
◇ K 7
♣ J 10 3

EAST
♠ J 9 3
♡ 9 8 4
◇ 5 4 2
♣ A K 9 8

SOUTH
♠ A Q 8
♡ A 7 6
◇ A 8 6 3
♣ 6 5 4

| *The bidding:* | SOUTH | WEST | NORTH | EAST |
|---|---|---|---|---|
| | 1 ◇ | Pass | 1 ♡ | Pass |
| | 1 NT | Pass | 2 NT | Pass |
| | 3 NT | Pass | Pass | Pass |

*Opening lead:* Spade five

The bidding was the same at both tables, and both Wests led the five of spades. At the first table, declarer took East's jack with the queen and entered dummy with a heart in order to take a diamond finesse. West won the diamond king and stopped to think. He knew from the first trick that South had the A Q of spades. It also appeared that declarer had four heart tricks and at least three diamond tricks for a total of nine winners. The only chance for the defense seemed to lie in the club suit. Accordingly, West shifted to the jack of clubs, with gratifying results. The contract was down one.

At the second table, declarer was more subtle. He won the opening lead with the spade *ace* instead of the queen. This left West under the impression that he had hit his partner with Q J x or possibly Q J x x in spades. When he later won the diamond king he happily led another spade, firmly convinced that he was about to set the contract. To his horror South won with the queen and claimed nine tricks.

* *

NORTH
♠ A Q J 10
♡ K Q 3
◇ Q 4 2
♣ Q 4 2

WEST
♠ K 8 5 3
♡ 9 8 7
◇ K 6 3
♣ J 6 3

EAST
♠ 9 6 4 2
♡ 2
◇ A J 9 5
♣ 10 9 7 5

SOUTH
♠ 7
♡ A J 10 6 5 4
◇ 10 8 7
♣ A K 8

| *The bidding:* | NORTH | EAST | SOUTH | WEST |
|---|---|---|---|---|
| | 1 NT | Pass | 3 ♡ | Pass |
| | 4 ♡ | Pass | 6 ♡ | Pass |
| | Pass | Pass | | |

*Opening lead:* Heart nine

South overbids to reach a poor heart slam, and he's lucky not to get an opening diamond lead. This gives him a legitimate play for twelve tricks, provided East has the spade king. He wins the opening lead in his hand and plays a spade to the ace. Now he leads the spade queen for a ruffing finesse. If East covers with the king, declarer will ruff, draw the outstanding trumps, and eventually discard two of his diamond losers on the good J 10 of spades.

When East plays a small spade on the queen, South's instinct is to throw away one of his diamond losers. If West takes the spade king and does not return a diamond, declarer will still make his contract. However, West sees that declarer is desperately trying to get rid of diamonds, and he will almost surely return a diamond, defeating the contract by two tricks.

South can give himself a much beter chance here by discarding the eight of clubs on the spade queen instead of a diamond. West wins the king and will probably assume that declarer is trying to get rid of *clubs*, not *diamonds*. Now he will shift to a club, and the contract is home. (Two diamonds eventually go on the good spades, and the other one goes on the club queen.)

South was wise to take the ruffing finesse in spades before drawing trumps. A second trump lead would have given East an opportunity to signal for a diamond shift.

\* \*

Here is a slight variation on the same theme:

NORTH
♠ K J 10 5 4
♡ 10 6
◊ Q 5 2
♣ Q J 6

WEST
♠ 3 2
♡ K 9
◊ J 10 8 7
♣ 10 8 5 4 3

EAST
♠ 7
♡ 5 4 3 2
◊ K 9 6 4 3
♣ A 9 2

SOUTH
♠ A Q 9 8 6
♡ A Q J 8 7
◊ A
♣ K 7

*The bidding:*

| SOUTH | WEST | NORTH | EAST |
|-------|------|-------|------|
| 1 ♠ | Pass | 2 ♠ | Pass |
| 3 ♡ | Pass | 4 ♠ | Pass |
| 6 ♠ | Pass | Pass | Pass |

*Opening lead:* Diamond jack

West opens the jack of diamonds against six spades. There is no problem if the king of hearts is on side, and South may be able to steal the contract even if the heart king is wrong. (If West doesn't shift to a club when he takes the heart king, declarer can eventually throw away dummy's clubs on the good hearts.)

South starts his deceptive tactics at trick one by covering the jack of diamonds with dummy's queen. East plays the king and the singleton ace wins. Dummy is entered with a spade, and the heart ten is finessed at trick three. West wins the king and is naturally under the impression that declarer has another diamond left. (A player with a singleton ace wouldn't have wasted the queen from dummy at trick one.) So West tries to cash his diamond ten, and that is the end of the defense.

Again, South did well to try the heart finesse as early as possible. A second trump lead would have allowed East to make a revealing discard.

Here is an old chestnut that still works against most defenders:

NORTH
♠ 6 5
♡ Q 7 2
◇ Q J 10 8 5
♣ 5 3 2

WEST
♠ K J 9 3 2
♡ 6 5
◇ 7 6 4 3
♣ Q 4

EAST
♠ Q 10 7 4
♡ A J 10 4
◇ 2
♣ J 10 8 7

SOUTH
♠ A 8
♡ K 9 8 3
◇ A K 9
♣ A K 9 6

*The bidding:*

| SOUTH | WEST | NORTH | EAST |
|-------|------|-------|------|
| 2 NT  | Pass | 3 NT  | Pass |
| Pass  | Pass |       |      |

*Opening lead:* Spade three

With any lead but a spade declarer would have no trouble developing a heart for his ninth trick. The spade lead is awkward, however, because it puts the defense in position to grab at least four spade tricks in addition to the heart ace.

South considers a hold up play, but there appears to be no advantage here, so he wins the first trick with the ace. (Ducking one round would only serve to emphasize his spade weakness.)

Now declarer decides to introduce a distraction in order to take the enemy's mind off the spade situation. He cashes the A K of diamonds and abruptly switches to the king of hearts. East, who was expecting more diamond leads, eyes the heart king with suspicion. He wonders why South doesn't cash the rest of those diamonds, and suddenly it hits him that South *can't* cash his diamonds because he started with A K alone and has no entry to dummy. If East takes the heart king with his ace, dummy's queen will be an entry to the "marooned" diamonds. A defender is usually reluctant to do anything that declarer apparently wants him to do. (Remember, East doesn't know his partner has four good spades at this point. West could have led the three from something like J 9 8 3.) So East will probably duck the heart king to kill the dummy. To his chagrin, South produces the nine of diamonds and claims his contract.

This ruse will not work against expert defenders. When the A K of diamonds are led, West should echo (play high-low) to tell his partner he was dealt an even number of diamonds. East will then realize that declarer can't have a doubleton A K, and he will smell a rat. In practice, however, most defenders will fail to echo with the West holding, and most Easts will fall into declarer's trap.

### Swindle in the Trump Suit

The trump suit offers declarer many opportunities to get away with murder. Some situations are quite automatic. Suppose, for example, the North-South trump holding is as follows:

NORTH
J 6 4

WEST                                    EAST
?                                       ?

SOUTH
A K 9 7 5 3 2

South is declarer and has no information about the opponents' distribution. His best play is to lead the jack from dummy. Naturally he does not plan to finesse. If East plays small without undue distress, declarer will go up with the ace and hope the suite is divided 2–1.

But if East has all three outstanding trumps, he might cover the jack with the queen.

NORTH
J 6 4

WEST                                    EAST
—                                       Q 10 8

SOUTH
A K 9 7 5 3 2

Now declarer finesses against the ten next round and avoids a normal trump loser.

Of course East should not cover. And he probably won't. But it costs declarer nothing to lead the jack just in case.

Here is a similar situation:

NORTH
Q 9 5 4

WEST                                    EAST
A                                       K 8

SOUTH
J 10 7 6 3 2

Again this is the trump suit, and South does best to lead the queen from dummy. If East is asleep at the switch he may cover with the king!

Let's try a complete deal:

NORTH
♠ J 6 5 2
♡ A K 10 9
◇ J 5
♣ A K 8

WEST
♠ Q
♡ 5 3
◇ 10 9 8 7 6
♣ 9 7 6 5 4

EAST
♠ K 10 4
♡ J 7 6
◇ A K Q 4
♣ Q J 10

SOUTH
♠ A 9 8 7 3
♡ Q 8 4 2
◇ 3 2
♣ 3 2

*North-South vulnerable*

*The bidding:*

| EAST | SOUTH | WEST | NORTH |
|------|-------|------|-------|
| 1 NT | Pass | 2 ◇ | Double |
| 3 ◇ | 3 ♠ | Pass | 4 ♠ |
| Pass | Pass | Pass | |

*Opening lead:* Diamond ten

East opens the bidding with one no-trump, and South eventually becomes declarer at four spades. The diamond ten is led, and East cashes two diamond honors and then shifts to the queen of clubs, which is won by dummy's ace.

As the cards lie, East-West have two natural trump tricks, and the contract should be defeated. But declarer may steal the game if he leads the spade jack from dummy. East doesn't know the situation and he's apt to cover the jack with the king, crashing his partner's queen and handing South an impossible game. (Don't blame East too severely for covering this time. It would be wrong not to cover if declarer's hand were: ♠ A Q 9 8 7 ♡ 8 4 3 2 ◇ 3 2 ♣ 5 3.)

Note that leading the spade jack can only lose if East has a singleton queen or king. On the bidding this is hardly possible.

\* \*

The most satisfactory of all trump swindles is to bring home a small slam missing the A K of trumps:

NORTH
♠ A
♡ 10 6
◊ A K Q 10 6 5
♣ A K 3 2

WEST
♠ K Q 10 9
♡ K 4 2
◊ 7 4
♣ 10 8 7 6

EAST
♠ 8 7 6 5 4 3 2
♡ A 3
◊ 9 8
♣ J 4

SOUTH
♠ J
♡ Q J 9 8 7 5
◊ J 3 2
♣ Q 9 5

*East-West vulnerable*

*The bidding:*

| SOUTH | WEST | NORTH | EAST |
|-------|------|-------|------|
| 2 ♡ | Pass | 6 ♡ | Pass |
| Pass | Pass | | |

*Opening lead:* Spade king

North-South are playing weak two-bids, and this one is a real cream puff. North can't be criticized for bidding six hearts, and West leads the spade king, which is won by dummy's ace.

Prospects are bleak, but declarer does have a chance against average defenders if he keeps his head. He leads the heart ten, on which East plays the three and South the five. West hesitates slightly at this point and then ducks. He quite properly plans to win the second round of trumps so that he can cash the spade queen when dummy is no longer able to ruff.

But declarer next crosses to the club queen and leads a heart from his hand. West suddenly realizes that his previous hesitation has given away his trump holding, and he fears he may lose his king altogether if he doesn't take it. After some agonizing he rises with the king, and we will leave East's comments to the reader's imagination.

This ruse wouldn't have worked if West had been a top-notch player, because he would have ducked the first heart smoothly with no telltale hesitation. When trumps are next led from the closed hand, he wonders why declarer doesn't repeat the apparently successful trump finesse. West now realizes that declarer is playing like a man who is missing the A K of trumps, and the jig is up.

As a final example of highway robbery, watch declarer bring home twelve tricks on this hand:

NORTH
♠ K Q 6 4
♡ Q 7 6
♢ 5 2
♣ K Q 6 3

WEST
♠ A 8 3 2
♡ 5 4
♢ J 10 9 7 6
♣ 7 2

EAST
♠ 10 9 7 5
♡ 10 3
♢ 8 4 3
♣ A J 10 5

SOUTH
♠ J
♡ A K J 9 8 2
♢ A K Q
♣ 9 8 4

*The bidding:*

| SOUTH | WEST | NORTH | EAST |
|-------|------|-------|------|
| 1 ♡ | Pass | 1 ♠ | Pass |
| 3 ♡ | Pass | 5 ♡ | Pass |
| 6 ♡ | Pass | Pass | Pass |

*Opening lead:* Diamond jack

You may think that the auction leaves a little something to be desired. (Blackwood, for example.) However the bidding is given as it actually occurred, and declarer wound up with twelve tricks, so it is hard to quarrel with success. South won the opening lead with the ace of diamonds and led a heart to the queen. A low spade from dummy lost to the ace, and West returned a trump as East began to feel sick. Declarer still had absolutely no play for twelve tricks. However, he ran all his red winners and with one heart left the position was this:

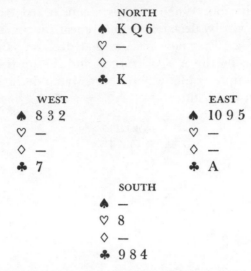

NORTH
♠ K Q 6
♡ —
◇ —
♣ K

WEST
♠ 8 3 2
♡ —
◇ —
♣ 7

EAST
♠ 10 9 5
♡ —
◇ —
♣ A

SOUTH
♠ —
♡ 8
◇ —
♣ 9 8 4

South led the last heart, throwing the king of clubs from dummy, and East felt even sicker. He couldn't imagine that declarer had no spades left. (Who would deliberately abandon two good tricks in dummy?) So he prayed that West had the club nine as he discarded the ace, clinging grimly to his spade stopper. Declarer took the last three tricks with the 9 8 4 of clubs!

They say that wild bidders are often the best at stealing tricks, because they get so much practice playing impossible contracts. There is no reason why good bidders shouldn't be just as proficient when they occasionally get overboard.

So the next time partner puts you in a ridiculous contract, keep your head and all may not be lost. When dummy appears, smile confidently. It is very important to exude the same air of assurance that you would if the contract were a lay-down. (Remember, the opponents probably don't know what a pickle you are in.)

Now think of some kind of defensive error that would allow you to make the contract. This is not too hard, as there are hundreds of outlandish errors defenders can make. Next comes the difficult part, which is to dream up a situation where that outlandish play would actually be the correct defense. Proceed to play the dummy as though this situation really existed. With enough ingenuity and proper timing you will occasionally trap even the best of defenders.

Anyhow, it's worth a try!

# 10

## *What Are the Odds?*

PEOPLE GENERALLY ASSUME that bridge mathematics are very complicated. This is not true. At the table, practically all you need to know is how to count up to thirteen. Away from the table a little grade-school arithmetic can make you the local authority on percentage plays and other apparently advanced mathematical problems.

First look at the following table. This gives the expected distribution of the cards in the two hidden hands. For example, if you are missing five cards of a suit, they will divide 3–2 about 68 percent of the time. About 28 times out of 100 they will break 4–1 and the chances of one opponent holding all five cards are only about 4 percent.

This is hardly startling information. An experienced bridge player may not know these exact figures. But he is quite aware that five cards

> usually break 3–2
> occasionally break 4–1
> rarely break 5–0

This is close enough for practical purposes.

Don't try to memorize this table. Do notice, however, the following: If only two cards are missing, it is almost a tossup as to whether they will divide 1–1 or 2–0. In all other cases the missing cards *prob-*

| | Table Showing Distribution of Cards in the Two Unknown Hands | |
| --- | --- | --- |
| Cards missing | Division | Probability, expressed as percent |
| 2 | 1–1 | 52.00% |
| | 2–0 | 48.00 |
| 3 | 2–1 | 78.00 |
| | 3–0 | 22.00 |
| 4 | 3–1 | 49.74 |
| | 2–2 | 40.70 |
| | 4–0 | 9.57 |
| 5 | 3–2 | 67.83 |
| | 4–1 | 28.26 |
| | 5–0 | 3.91 |
| 6 | 4–2 | 48.45 |
| | 3–3 | 35.53 |
| | 5–1 | 14.53 |
| | 6–0 | 1.49 |
| 7 | 4–3 | 62.17 |
| | 5–2 | 30.52 |
| | 6–1 | 6.78 |
| | 7–0 | 0.52 |
| 8 | 5–3 | 47.12 |
| | 4–4 | 32.72 |
| | 6–2 | 17.14 |
| | 7–1 | 2.86 |
| | 8–0 | 0.16 |

*ably will not break exactly in half.* Thus, four cards probably will divide 3–1, not 2–2. Five cards, however, can be expected to break 3–2, which is not exactly in half. Six cards probably will not break exactly 3–3. A 4–2 division is more likely. But seven cards can be expected to break 4–3. Etc.

Of what use is all this? Try the following example:

NORTH
♠ 5 3
♡ 8 5
◇ 6 3
♣ A J 6 5 4 3 2

SOUTH
♠ A K Q J 10
♡ A Q
◇ A K Q J 10
♣ 2

*The bidding:*

| SOUTH | WEST | NORTH | EAST |
|-------|------|-------|------|
| 2 ♠ | Pass | 2 NT | Pass |
| 3 ◇ | Pass | 4 ♣ | Pass |
| 4 ◇ | Pass | 4 ♠ | Pass |
| 4 NT | Pass | 5 ◇ | Pass |
| 7 ♠ | Pass | Pass | Pass |

*Opening lead:* Club king

South is understandably awed by this beauty and contracts for a grand slam in spades. He wins the club lead in dummy and is faced with the immediate problem of what to do with the heart queen. There are two possible solutions:

    1. He can take a heart finesse.

    2. He can play three rounds of diamonds, discarding a heart from the north hand. Then he can cash the heart ace and trump the heart queen in dummy.

Which method offers the better chance of success?

Solution 1 depends on finding the heart king in the East hand, which is a 50 percent proposition. Solution 2 needs a 3–3 break in diamonds to succeed. This can be expected to occur only about 36 percent of the time (see table). 

A 50 percent chance is clearly better than a 36 percent chance, so the heart finesse is the better play.

Of course, declarer doesn't have a table like this available when he is actually playing bridge. And he doesn't need it. He is simply aware of the fact that six cards probably will *not* break 3–3. So he correctly takes the heart finesse, which is an even-money shot.

Don't get the idea that studying a table of probabilities is a short cut to learning how to play the dummy. Let me tell you a story about Percival and Harry. (The names have been changed for obvious reasons.) Percival is a mathematician who has recently taken up bridge. He can quote percentages for every possible suit distribution and feels quite superior to Harry, who has never looked at a probability table, although he is an experienced bridge player. At a recent duplicate tournament, Percival and Harry, playing with different partners, both encountered the following South hand:

NORTH
♠ 6 5 2
♡ A K Q 7
◇ Q J 10 9
♣ Q 8

SOUTH
♠ A Q J
♡ 6 5 3
◇ K 3 2
♣ A K J 10

*The bidding:*

| SOUTH | WEST | NORTH | EAST |
|-------|------|-------|------|
| 1 ♣ | Pass | 1 ♡ | Pass |
| 2 NT | Pass | 6 NT | Pass |
| Pass | Pass | | |

*Opening lead:* Diamond eight

In both cases the final contract was six no-trump, and East won the opening lead with the diamond ace and returned a spade. With only eleven winners, Percival saw two possibilities of making his twelfth trick. The spade finesse represented a 50 percent chance. And he knew there was only a 35.53 percent chance of finding the hearts 3–3. So he put in the spade queen at trick two and went down one when West produced the king. To his dismay, it turned out that the hearts had been 3–3 all the time.

After the tournament Percival hurried over to Harry's table to see how his rival had fared on this hand. When he learned that Harry had gone up with the spade ace at trick two and made the slam, Percival was extremely annoyed and accused Harry of knowing nothing about percentage plays. Harry in turn accused Percival of knowing nothing about bridge.

Who made the correct play, Harry or Percival? Why?

Harry's play of rising with the spade ace at trick two was correct. Percival went wrong because he could only see two possibilities; the spade finesse or the 3–3 heart break. There are actually three chances to make this slam:

1. East may have the spade king.
2. The hearts may break 3–3.
3. The spade king may be in the same hand as the heart length.

Percival limited himself to possibility number 1 when he took the spade finesse. By playing the spade ace at trick two, Harry was able to combine chances number 2 and number 3. Thus Harry's play succeeds any time the hearts are 3–3. And it also succeeds almost half the time that the hearts are not 3–3. Suppose the entire deal is this:

```
                         NORTH
                       ♠ 6 5 2
                       ♡ A K Q 7
                       ◇ Q J 10 9
                       ♣ Q 8
       WEST                                EAST
     ♠ K 9 7                             ♠ 10 8 4 3
     ♡ J 8 4 2                           ♡ 10 9
     ◇ 8 7 6                             ◇ A 5 4
     ♣ 9 4 2                             ♣ 7 6 5 3
                         SOUTH
                       ♠ A Q J
                       ♡ 6 5 3
                       ◇ K 3 2
                       ♣ A K J 10
```

After winning the spade ace at trick two, declarer cashes all his diamonds and clubs, reducing everyone to four cards. West can't keep the spade king and all four hearts, so declarer must make the rest of the tricks.

In other words, a knowledge of percentages does not make up for a lack of bridge ability. But it does increase one's perspective to have a general idea of how to solve different problems. Furthermore it's fun! So let's try a few.

In bridge columns you often read that such and such a contract has a 43 percent chance of success, or a 92 percent chance, etc. How do they calculate these odds? Let's start with a hand that combines the chances of a 3–3 break and a finesse.

*Example 1*

NORTH
♠ A K Q 7 6 5 2
♡ K
◇ 6 4
♣ 9 8 4

SOUTH
♠ —
♡ A Q J 10
◇ A Q J 9 8
♣ A K Q J

South becomes declarer at seven no-trump and receives a heart lead. He wins the first trick in dummy and cashes the A K Q of spades, throwing diamonds from his hand. If the spades break 3–3, he is home, and if not he finesses East for the diamond king. What are his chances?

The spades will divide 3–3 about 36 percent of the time. This means they will not break 3–3 about 64 percent of the time. But half of the time that the spades don't break declarer will still succeed because East has the diamond king. So declarer's total chance of success is 36 percent plus half of 64 percent, which comes to 68 percent.

Notice that it would be wrong to simply add 50 percent for the diamond finesse to the 36 percent for the spade break, which would give you a total of 86 percent. It's true that the diamond finesse is a 50 percent proposition, but in this case declarer does not get the benefit of the full 50 percent. Whenever the spades are 3–3, it does no good to find that East has the diamond king. Declarer only profits from the diamond finesse when the spades do not break 3–3.

Let's alter the North-South cards slightly to make the calculation a little different.

*Example 2*

NORTH

♠ A K J 10 9 8 7
♡ K
◇ 6 4
♣ 9 8 4

SOUTH

♠ —
♡ A Q J 10
◇ A K J 9 8
♣ A K Q J

Again the contract is seven no-trump, and West leads a heart. Declarer wins in dummy and cashes the A K of spades. If the queen does not drop, he finesses East for the diamond queen. He will succeed if the spade queen drops singleton or doubleton, or if the diamond finesse works.

First figure the chance of someone having a singleton queen of spades. With six cards missing, the chance of a 5–1 break is about 15 percent (see table). Only ⅙ of this time will the singleton be the queen. So the chances of dropping a singleton queen are ⅙ of 15 percent, or about 2½ percent.

Now figure the chance of someone's having a doubleton queen of spades. A 4–2 break occurs about 48 percent of the time, and the queen has two chances out of six of being in the hand with the doubleton. Thus the queen will drop doubleton about 16 percent of the time.

The total chance of dropping either a singleton or a doubleton queen is 2½ percent plus 16 percent, or 18½ percent. This means the queen will *not* fall 81½ percent of the time, in which case declarer has to depend on the diamond finesse. This should work half of the 81½ percent, or 40¾ percent. So the total chance of making the contract is 18½ percent plus 40¾ percent, or about 59¼ percent.

\* \*

The next question is how you can determine what chance of success makes it worth while to bid a small slam or a grand slam.

To calculate this, it is necessary to weigh what you stand to gain against what you stand to lose. For example, suppose you are playing rubber bridge with both sides vulnerable. If you bid six spades and make it, you will score 1430, which is 750 better than the 680 you would have scored had you not bid the slam. However, if the slam fails, you will score −100, which is 750 worse than the 650 you would have scored if you had stayed out of slam and made eleven tricks. As you stand to gain or lose exactly the same amount, the chances of success required to bid the small slam are about 50 percent.

To bid a grand slam you require a greater possibility of success, because if you go down one you lose the small slam bonus as well as the game you would have scored had you bid only six. If you bid seven spades (both vulnerable) and make it, you will score 2210. This is 750 better than the 1460 you would have scored had you stopped at six spades but made seven. And if you bid seven spades and go down one you will score −100, which is 1530 worse than the 1430 you would have scored for stopping at six. So, you stand to lose about twice as much as you stand to gain, and you should not bid seven unless you expect to make it twice as often as not. The fraction is actually

$$\frac{1530}{1530 + 750}$$

which is about 67 percent.

These percentages of 50 percent for a small slam and 67 percent for a grand slam vary slightly with the form of scoring used, the vulnerability, and whether the contract is a major, a minor, or no-trump. (The only material deviation is at International Match Point scoring, where about 57 percent chance of success is sufficient to make a grand slam worthwhile.) These percentages do not take into account the effect of being doubled or going down more than one, etc. But for practical purposes, any time you have better than an even chance to take twelve tricks, it's worth bidding a small slam. And it's worth bidding a grand slam if you expect to make it at least two times out of three.

So, Example 1 above was a reasonable grand slam. Example 2 was inferior.

Now let's get back to that table of probabilities. Where did it come from? Is this something that only a mathematician can construct?

Not at all. A twelve-year-old can construct this table once he pictures what he is trying to do.

A simple way to visualize the problem here is to imagine a round wooden tray with twenty-six holes in it. Now mentally draw a line down the middle of the tray so there are thirteen holes on either side of the line. Assume that the tray is constructed in such a manner that a marble falling on it has an equal chance of coming to rest in any one of the twenty-six holes.

The thirteen holes on the left of the line represent West's thirteen cards, and the thirteen holes on the right represent East's. Let's start with the case where only two cards of a suit are missing and drop two imaginary marbles to represent the two missing cards.

What are the chances of West getting both marbles? When you drop the first marble it has 13 chances out of 26 of going to West. Thus West's chance of getting the first marble is $^{13}/_{26}$, or one-half. When you drop the second marble, there are only 12 holes left on the West side, because one is already filled up by the first marble. And there are only 25 holes left on the entire tray. So the chance of West getting the second marble is only $^{12}/_{25}$. Since West's chance of getting the first marble is one-half, and his chance of getting the second is $^{12}/_{25}$, his chance of getting them both is one-half of $^{12}/_{25}$, which is $^{6}/_{25}$, or 24 percent.

Obviously, if West's chances of getting both marbles are 24 percent, East's chances of getting both are also 24 percent. Thus the total chance of either opponent getting both marbles (or cards) is 48 percent.

If a 2–0 split is 48 percent, the quickest way to find the chance of a 1–1 split is to subtract 48 percent from 100 percent, leaving 52 percent (see table).

Now use three marbles to find the percentages when three cards of a suit are missing. Dropping one marble at a time, we see that the chance of West having all three is $^{13}/_{26} \times {}^{12}/_{25} \times {}^{11}/_{24}$, or 11 percent. East also will have 11 percent chance of getting all three, so the total chance of a 3–0 split is 22 percent. This leaves 78 percent for a 2–1 break.

The more cards that are missing the more marbles you have to use and the more multiplication that is involved.

For the case of a 3–1 split you need four marbles. Imagine that West is going to get a singleton and East the other three. By dropping marbles one at a time, you get $^{13}/_{26} \times {}^{13}/_{25} \times {}^{12}/_{24} \times {}^{11}/_{23}$. This result must be multiplied by four, as there are four possible singletons that West could hold. And the final result must be doubled to take into account the times that East has the singleton and West the other three. This gives 49.74 percent.

There is no reason why anyone should give himself a headache by actually doing all this multiplication and division. It's much quicker to just look at a probability table. But it's a good idea to realize how you could figure out such percentages if you actually needed to.

* *

So far we have said very little about the chance of one particular opponent holding a specific card or cards. With no information to guide you, a straight finesse is clearly a 50 percent chance. Of course, if you are missing a particular queen, for example, and you know that West started with four cards in this suit and East with only two, the odds become four to two that West has the queen.

Now, suppose you need one out of two finesses to make your contract. What are your chances? Let's assume you must take a spade finesse and a heart finesse. Four things can happen:

1. Both finesses work.
2. Only the spade finesse works.
3. Only the heart finesse works.
4. Both finesses fail.

In the first three cases you will make your contract. Only in the last case will you go down. Thus your chances of success are theoretically three out of four, or 75 percent. This is good enough for all practical purposes. Actually, the true percentage is always slightly greater or smaller than 75 percent, depending on whether the two finesses are both taken into the same hand or into different hands.

Here is a familiar combination:

NORTH
A J 10

SOUTH
x x x

In order to make two tricks here, South takes two finesses into the East hand. He will only fail if East has both the king and the queen. Using the wooden tray and two marbles to represent the king and queen, you find that the exact chance of East holding them both is 24 percent. This means declarer's actual chance of success is 76 percent. In a case where two finesses have to be taken into different hands, the chance of at least one finesse succeeding is only 74 percent.

Here is a problem which is apt to stump even the most experienced bridge player. Suppose you are in a small slam and find you must take three finesses, of which you can only afford to lose one. What are your chances of success? In other words, what are the chances of at least two out of three finesses succeeding? If you enjoy problems, stop and think about it for a minute.

Here's the solution. Let's call the finesses A, B, and C. There are now eight possibilities which can exist:

1. Finesses A, B, and C all succeed.
2. Only finesses A and B succeed.
3. Only finesses A and C succeed.
4. Only finesses B and C succeed.
5. Only finesse A succeeds.
6. Only finesse B succeeds.
7. Only finesse C succeeds.
8. None succeeds.

Of these eight situations the first four lead to success, and the last four to failure. Thus the chances of at least two out of three finesses succeeding are four out of eight or 50 percent.

\* \*

Many card combinations lend themselves to different lines of play, and the exact chance of success of each line is easy to compute. However, these mathematical results frequently fail to take into consideration the frailties of human nature. For example, suppose you, South, are playing a no-trump contract and need three tricks from the following combination. How do you proceed?

NORTH

A x x x

SOUTH

Q 10 9 8

There are three lines of play worth considering:

1. Most textbooks recommend taking two finesses through West. You will succeed if West has either the king or the jack or both,

which we have seen is a 76 percent chance. In fact, if you start by leading the ten (or nine or eight) you will also succeed if West is void. (With five cards missing, the chance of a particular opponent having a void is half of 3.91 percent, which is about 2 percent.) So your total chance of success with this line of play is about 78 percent.

2. An alternative line of play is to lead a small card from dummy immediately, with the intention of finessing the ten if East plays low. If this loses to West's jack, you finesse West for the king next time. This line wins any time East has the jack (50 percent) or any time West has both the king and the jack (24 percent), and your total chances are theoretically 74 percent. However, there is a considerable chance East may assist you here. Suppose the cards are:

NORTH
A x x x

| WEST | | EAST |
|------|---|------|
| J x x | | K x |

SOUTH
Q 10 9 8

When you lead a small card from dummy, East will almost surely rise with the king, solving all your problems. East will hold K x about 10 percent of the time. If you assume he will always go up with the king from K x in this position, your chances of success using line 2 are actually 84 percent, not 74 percent.

(There is actually more to this situation than meets the eye. We did not discuss what happens if East plays the king the first round. You are not home free yet because East may have started with K J x x or a singleton king. K J x x is three times as likely as a singleton king so you should continue by playing the ace next.

(A more important consideration is what to do if West takes the ten with the king. In most games you are safe in assuming that West doesn't have the jack and you now lead to the ace to protect yourself against J x x x in the East hand. But an expert West is capable of winning the ten with the king holding K J x x. Against such a top flight defender you have to play the queen next to protect yourself against this larceny. This means you will lose when West really started with a singleton king and the 84% is reduced to about 81%. And if East is good enough to duck occasionally with the K x the chances are even further reduced. Nevertheless it is safe to say that against all but the most expert defenders line #2 has close to

84% chance of success.)

3. It is also possible to start by cashing the ace and then leading toward your hand. This line has the least chance of success. You will fail automatically if East is void (2 percent) or if he has a small singleton (8 percent) or a small doubleton (10 percent). And when East holds K x x or J x x (20 percent), you will be on a guess as to what to play from your hand. Presumably you will guess right 10 percent and wrong 10 percent. Your total chance of failure is 30 percent, and line 3 has a 70 percent chance of success.

Thus Number 1 has the greatest theoretical chance of success. But in practice, Number 2 is the winning line.

### Restricted Choice

Now we come to an area that is apt to prove more of a stumbling block to the mathematically inclined than to the average player. Suppose you need only one trick from the following combination:

NORTH
### K 10 9

SOUTH
### x x x

Assume you start by leading a small card from the South hand to the nine and East wins with the jack. When you regain the lead, you play from the South hand again and West follows small. Should you finesse the ten or go up with the king, or is it just an even-money guess?

It is correct to put in the ten. In fact, the ten is approximately twice as good a play as the king. To understand this, it is helpful to consider all the material situations. There are three vital honors missing: the ace, the queen, and the jack. If all three are in the East hand, it doesn't matter what South plays, because he is doomed either way. And if West has at least two of the missing honors, it doesn't matter either, because South will always succeed in making one trick. The only material cases are where East was dealt exactly two of the missing honors. He can have started with the A J, the A Q, or the Q J. Only if East started with the Q J is it correct to go up with the king. Taking two finesses (playing the nine the first time and the ten the next) will work if East started with either A J or A Q. Thus it is twice as good a play. Ninety percent of the readers will accept this straightforward explanation and are ready to go on to the next subject. Unfortunately, the mathematically inclined reader who is not an experienced bridge player has spotted what appears to be a snag.

"Hold on a minute," cries Percival. "Once East wins the first trick with the jack, it is proved that he can't have started with the A Q. He must have started with either the A J or the Q J. As these are two equal possibilities, it must be a 50–50 proposition as to whether to play the ten the second time or the king!"

Percival has just opened up Pandora's box, and the troubles are about to begin. The readers who were satisfied one paragraph ago are no longer happy. Even Harry (who knows from long experience that the ten is the winning play) is perplexed by the logic of Percival's argument.

Percival is partially right. It's true that once East has shown up with the jack, the only two material cases left are those where East started with the A J or the Q J. And it's true that these two cases are of equal frequency. But it's not true that the play of the king will succeed as often as the play of the ten. The ten is still twice as good a play.

To solve this apparent dilemma it's necessary to understand what is called "the principle of restricted choice," which is based on the fact that in bridge certain cards are equal to each other. For example, in this case the queen and the jack are equal cards. If East holds them both, he knows that they are equal. Thus he can choose to win the first trick with either the queen or the jack. Theoretically he'll win with the jack half the time and with the queen the other half. However, if he started with the A J he has no choice. He must win the first trick with the jack.

Translated into mathematical terms, you can say that if East's chances of holding the Q J are $x$ percent, his chances of playing the jack the first time from this combination are $\frac{1}{2} x$ percent. His chances of holding the A J are also $x$ percent. But with this holding he must win with the jack all $x$ percent of the time. Since $x$ percent is twice as great a chance as $\frac{1}{2} x$ percent, it's twice as good to finesse the ten on the second round.

For those who don't care for explanations containing $x$'s and $\frac{1}{2} x$'s, let's try something more colorful. Here is another example of the same principle:

NORTH

x x x

SOUTH

A K 10 9 x x

Declarer needs six tricks with this combination, and he starts by leading the ace, on which West drops the queen. If this is a singleton, South must take a second-round finesse against J x x in the East hand. And if West started with Q J doubleton, declarer must lay down the king next. Which should he do?

With four cards missing, the chances of one opponent's holding the singleton queen are so close to the chances of his holding the doubleton Q J that for practical purposes we can say they are equal (singleton Q 6.22 percent; doubleton Q J 6.68 percent). But the second-round finesse is about twice as good a play. Why?

Again the queen and the jack are equal cards. So declarer should not object to removing these two cards and replacing them with two identical face cards. By combining the letters in "queen" and "jack," we will christen these new face cards "quacks."

Declarer again leads the ace, on which West drops a quack. Did West start with a doubleton quack-quack, or did he start with a singleton quack? There is only one chance that West started with the doubleton quack-quack. But there are two chances that West started with a singleton quack, because there are now two quacks in the deck. So the second round finesse is twice as good a play.

\* \*

Do the odds ever change as a hand progresses? Look at the play in six hearts on the following example:

NORTH

♠ 9 6 2

♡ J 7 5

◇ 7 5

♣ K J 7 3 2

SOUTH

♠ A 7

♡ A K 8 6 4 3

◇ A Q 2

♣ A 5

| *The bidding:* | SOUTH | WEST | NORTH | EAST |
|---|---|---|---|---|
| | 1 ♡ | Pass | 2 ♡ | Pass |
| | 6 ♡ | Pass | Pass | Pass |

*Opening lead:* Spade queen

South wins the first trick with the spade ace, cashes the A K of hearts and is pleased to find the outstanding trumps divided 2–2. He continues with the club ace and a club to the king. Both opponents follow but the club queen does not appear.

The moment of decision has now arrived. If the clubs are 3–3 declarer can make the slam by ruffing a club. And if the diamond king is on side he can succeed by taking a diamond finesse. Unfortunately, there is no way to combine these chances. Thus if he ruffs a club and the suit does not break 3–3 he is automatically down regardless of the location of the diamond king. And if he finesses the diamond and loses he is automatically down regardless of the club division. Should South play for the 3–3 break or the finesse?

The diamond finesse is clearly a 50–50 proposition, and the question is what are the chances of a 3–3 club break at this point. Originally they were about 36 out of 100 (see table) but they have improved considerably. It is now possible to eliminate the 5–1 and the 6–0 breaks since both opponents have already followed to two rounds of clubs. The fact that the club queen has not appeared is also significant and it eliminates the possibility that anyone started with a doubleton queen. When six cards break 4–2 the queen has two chances out of six of being in the hand with the doubleton. The original chance of a 4–2 break was about 48 percent (see table). After eliminating ⅔ or one-third of this the figure reduces to 32 percent. So the odds are now approximately 36 to 32 in favor of the clubs breaking 3–3. This is slightly better than the even money shot offered by the diamond finesse and the club ruff is the better play.

By the way, if dummy's clubs had been K 7 4 3 2 instead of K J 7 3 2 the appearance or non-appearance of the club queen would not be particularly significant. All the missing clubs would then be "equal cards" and declarer should not attach undue importance to any particular one. In this case the odds would be about 48 to 36 in favor of a 4–2 club break and the diamond finesse would be the better play.

\* \*

Here's a problem that requires ingenuity:

NORTH
♠ 9 8 6 2
♡ K Q
◇ K J 4 2
♣ Q 5 3

SOUTH
♠ A K Q 5 4
♡ A 5 4
◇ 7 6
♣ J 8 2

*The bidding:*

| WEST | NORTH | EAST | SOUTH |
|------|-------|------|-------|
| Pass | Pass | Pass | 1 ♠ |
| Pass | 3 ♠ | Pass | 4 ♠ |
| Pass | Pass | Pass | |

*Opening lead:* Heart three

After three passes you bid one spade. North raises to three, and you carry on to game. You win the heart lead in dummy and draw three rounds of trumps. West, who started with a singleton spade, discards two hearts. You now lead a diamond toward dummy, and West plays small. Do you play the jack or the king? Why? Approximately what are the odds in favor of your choice?

*Answer:* If the A Q of diamonds are in the same hand, it doesn't matter what you do. If East has them both, you're dead. And if West has them both, you can't fail. So you assume they are in opposite hands, and the question is who has which?

The clue here lies in the location of the ace and king of clubs. We know that West cannot have both club honors because in that case he would surely have led the club king in preference to a heart. This means they are either divided or both in the East hand. If the club honors are divided, the diamond ace can be anywhere. But if East has both club honors, he cannot also have the diamond ace or he would have opened the bidding in third seat. So the diamond ace has more chance of being in the West hand, and the correct play is the king from dummy.

To figure out the odds here requires a little organization. Consider just the ace of diamonds and the ace and king of clubs. There are eight ways these three cards can theoretically be distributed:

East could have

1. ◇ A ♣ A K
2. ◇ A ♣ A
3. ◇ A ♣ K
4. ♣ A ♣ K
5. ◇ A
6. ♣ A
7. ♣ K
8. none

Bridgewise, Numbers 1, 5, and 8 can be eliminated for the reasons just discussed. This leaves five possible situations. In three of them West has the diamond ace (Numbers 4, 6, and 7). And in two of them East has it (Numbers 2 and 3). So the odds are approximately three to two in favor of going up with dummy's king.

\* \*

This chapter has dealt with different types of problems that require what are called "bridge mathematics." Most of these are fun rather than practical. However, an interest in this area does broaden a player's general perspective on bridge.

If by any chance this whole chapter has seemed as clear as mud, don't worry about it. The ability to do problems like these may make a player shine at the cocktail party after the game. But it rarely helps him at the table.

# PART III  ♠ ♡ ◇ ♣  PROBLEM HANDS

HERE ARE FORTY-ONE PROBLEMS arranged, as far as possible, in order of difficulty. In all cases you are South, and your object is to make the contract. Do not concern yourself with overtricks.

Unless otherwise stated, all the bidding is standard. Thus if an opponent opens with one no-trump, you can count on his having 16–18 points, and so on.

Try not to read the answer until you have spent several minutes working on the solution. The more time expended here, the more you will get out of these problems.

By the way, if the average bridge player were to meet these hands in actual play, he would probably get every one wrong. (A problem isn't a problem if the average player gets it right.) So don't be discouraged when you miss. In bridge as in real life, people profit most from their mistakes.

If you want to keep score, you may rate yourself according to the following scale:

> 0 to 5 right . . . . Well, at least you're honest.
> 6 to 15 right . . . . Average.
> 16 to 25 right . . . . Above average.
> 26 to 35 right . . . . Very good.
> 36 to 40 right . . . . Will your partner believe this?
> 41 right . . . . . . . . When is YOUR book coming out?

## THE CURSE OF SCOTLAND

```
                    NORTH
                ♠ K
                ♡ 6 5 3
                ◊ J 9 2
                ♣ 8 7 6 4 3 2
                    SOUTH
                ♠ A 8 4 3
                ♡ A K 9
                ◊ A Q 10 4
                ♣ A J
```

*South dealer. Both vulnerable*

*The bidding:*

| SOUTH | WEST | NORTH | EAST |
|-------|------|-------|------|
| 2 NT  | Pass | 3 NT  | Pass |
| Pass  | Pass |       |      |

*Opening lead:* Spade queen

West leads the spade queen, and the king wins the first trick. Which card should you lead from dummy at trick two, and why?

*Answer:* You have nine tricks, provided the diamond king is on side. Since dummy has no more entries, the time to finesse is now, and the right card to lead is the diamond nine. This allows you to remain in dummy for two subsequent finesses should they prove necessary. Suppose the complete hand is this:

```
                    DUMMY
                ♠ K
                ♡ 6 5 3
                ◊ J 9 2
                ♣ 8 7 6 4 3 2

  WEST                              EAST
♠ Q J 10 9 5                      ♠ 7 6 2
♡ 8 7 4                           ♡ Q J 10 2
◊ 5 3                             ◊ K 8 7 6
♣ Q 10 9                          ♣ K 5

                    YOU
                ♠ A 8 4 3
                ♡ A K 9
                ◊ A Q 10 4
                ♣ A J
```

Notice that it would be a mistake to start with the diamond jack. This would hold the trick, and you'd next lead another diamond to the ten, which would also win. But now there'd be no way to get back to dummy for a third finesse, and the contract would fail. It would do no good to drop the ten under the jack on the first round. In this case, when you continue with the nine, East will cover with the king, promoting his eight spot.

Look how easy life is if you start with the nine. This wins, and you continue with the jack. When East plays small, you can get under the jack with the ten, leaving yourself in dummy for that vital third finesse.

This diamond combination is approximately the same as one discussed in Chapter 1. Some readers probably got the answer to the problem from the title, even if they failed to recognize the combination. Among card players, the nine of diamonds has long been known as the "curse of Scotland," although the origin of the term is uncertain.

There's a legend that the Duke of Cumberland, son of George II, wrote the order for the massacre at the battle of Culloden (1746) on the back of a nine of diamonds. This victory by "Butcher Cumberland," as he subsequently became known, destroyed the Scottish insurrection led by the young pretender, Charles Edward Stuart (Bonnie Prince Charlie) and put an end to attempts of the Stuart family to regain the throne of England. A monumental cairn and several green mounds can be seen today on the heath of Culloden where over a thousand of the slain lie buried. And the nine of diamonds has been known ever since as the "curse of Scotland."

## TWO BITES AT THE CHERRY

NORTH
♠ 8 6 4 2
♡ A 4 3
◇ K Q J
♣ 4 3 2

SOUTH
♠ A K 5
♡ K Q J
◇ A 10 9 8
♣ A K J

*South dealer. Both vulnerable*

*The bidding:*

| SOUTH | WEST | NORTH | EAST |
|-------|------|-------|------|
| 3 NT | Pass | 6 NT | Pass |
| Pass | Pass | | |

*Opening lead:* Heart ten

Your opening bid promises about 25 points, and partner places the contract at six no-trump. The heart ten is led. How do you play?

*Answer:* There are eleven tricks on top, and the twelfth can come from one of two sources: a successful club finesse or a 3–3 spade break. The question of which suit to test first is very important. For example, suppose declarer tries the club finesse first. If this loses, it is too late to make the contract, even if the spades divide 3–3.

The proper play is to test the spades first, and declarer should start by playing a small spade from both hands. In this way he retains control of the suit. Later he will cash the A K of spades, and if the suit breaks 3–3, dummy's eight will provide the twelfth trick. And if the spades do not break, he will fall back on the club finesse.

Here is the entire hand:

NORTH
♠ 8 6 4 2
♡ A 4 3
◇ K Q J
♣ 4 3 2

WEST
♠ Q 10 7
♡ 10 9 8 7
◇ 5 4 2
♣ Q 9 6

EAST
♠ J 9 3
♡ 6 5 2
◇ 7 6 3
♣ 10 8 7 5

SOUTH
♠ A K 5
♡ K Q J
◇ A 10 9 8
♣ A K J

## BAREFOOT THROUGH LONDON

NORTH
♠ K 10 6
♡ A K J
◇ A Q 6 2
♣ 7 6 2

SOUTH
♠ A J 9 8 7 5
♡ 8 7
◇ 3
♣ A 8 4 3

*North dealer. Neither vulnerable*

*The bidding:*

| NORTH | EAST | SOUTH | WEST |
|-------|------|-------|------|
| 1 NT  | Pass | 4 ♠   | Pass |
| Pass  | Pass |       |      |

*Opening lead:* Diamond ten

West leads the diamond ten. How do you play four spades?

*Answer:* This one looks easy, but many players go wrong. They win the first trick with the diamond ace and immediately lead the king and ace of spades in an effort to extract the trumps. They wind up losing three clubs and one spade whenever the East-West cards are divided something like this:

NORTH
♠ K 10 6
♡ A K J
◇ A Q 6 2
♣ 7 6 2

WEST
♠ Q 3 2
♡ 10 4 2
◇ 10 9 8
♣ K J 9 5

EAST
♠ 4
♡ Q 9 6 5 3
◇ K J 7 5 4
♣ Q 10

SOUTH
♠ A J 9 8 7 5
♡ 8 7
◇ 3
♣ A 8 4 3

Before touching a card, declarer should reason as follows: There is a possible trump loser here, and to ensure the contract it is necessary to lose only two club tricks. The fourth club will automatically be good if the suit breaks 3–3. Otherwise a club will have to be ruffed in dummy.

Proper play is to take the diamond ace and immediately lead the ace and another club. Win any return, and lead still another club. If the suit has broken 3–3, all is well and trumps can be drawn. Otherwise you ruff the fourth club in dummy and then tackle the spades.

Don't worry about an opponent's ruffing the second or third round of clubs. What do you care if he ruffs your losing club? (West would have to be void in clubs to ruff the ace, and that possibility is so remote it can be ignored.)

And don't be distracted by the presence of the heart jack and the diamond queen. Those are just red herrings to trap the unwary.

By the way, if you don't recognize the title, see Chapter 4.

## THE EXTRA EDGE

NORTH
♠ A Q 8 5
♡ A K 8
◇ 6 4 2
♣ 6 4 3

SOUTH
♠ 6 4 2
♡ 7 6 3 2
◇ A K Q
♣ A K 7

*South dealer. Neither vulnerable*

*The bidding:*

| SOUTH | WEST | NORTH | EAST |
|-------|------|-------|------|
| 1 NT | Pass | 3 NT | Pass |
| Pass | Pass | | |

*Opening lead:* Heart queen

West leads the heart queen against three no-trump, and you win with dummy's ace. With eight tricks in view you decide to attack the spade suit in an effort to develop that ninth trick. (A 3–3 heart break will also produce a ninth trick, but there is no rush to test the hearts.) The question here is what is the best way to start the spades?

*Answer:* It may seem normal to enter your hand with a diamond in order to take a spade finesse. You will legitimately make a second spade trick any time West has the king or any time the suit breaks 3–3. To give yourself a little extra edge however, you should postpone the spade finesse. Instead, lead a small spade from dummy at trick two. This protects against the remote possibility that East has a singleton king, and at the same time it gives East a good chance to go wrong with a doubleton king. Here is a possible layout:

NORTH

♠ A Q 8 5
♡ A K 8
◇ 6 4 2
♣ 6 4 3

WEST

♠ J 10 7 3
♡ Q J 10 9
◇ J 9
♣ Q 10 8

EAST

♠ K 9
♡ 5 4
◇ 10 8 7 5 3
♣ J 9 5 2

SOUTH

♠ 6 4 2
♡ 7 6 3 2
◇ A K Q
♣ A K 7

East will probably defeat you if he calmly plays the spade nine at trick two and returns a heart. You will eventually take a spade finesse, losing to the king, and proper defense will now hold you to eight tricks. But how many players do you know that would play the nine when you lead that small spade from dummy at trick two? Most of the time East will go up with his doubleton king and hand you the contract.

## THE CASE OF THE PHONY INSURANCE RACKET

NORTH
♠ 7 6
♡ K Q 10 4 2
◇ K Q 5
♣ K J 6

SOUTH
♠ A K J 10 9 8
♡ A
◇ J 7 6
♣ A Q 10

*North dealer. Neither vulnerable*

*The bidding:*

| NORTH | EAST | SOUTH | WEST |
|-------|------|-------|------|
| 1 ♡ | Pass | 2 ♠ | Pass |
| 2 NT | Pass | 6 ♠ | Pass |
| Pass | Pass | | |

*Opening lead:* Diamond ace

After partner opens the bidding, it is difficult to stay out of a slam with this hand. You make a jump shift of two spades, and when partner rebids two no-trump, you decide to take the bull by the horns and say six spades.

West chooses to lead the diamond ace, which is annoying, as there would be some possibility of disposing of all your diamond losers without that lead. At trick two West shifts to a club, and the whole hand hinges on avoiding a trump loser. Do you cash the ace and king of trumps in hopes that the queen will fall? Do you win the club in dummy and take an immediate trump finesse? Or do you cash one high trump first and then go to dummy for a finesse? Don't read on until you decide which line to adopt and why.

*Answer:* It is wrong to cash the ace and king of trumps. With five cards missing the queen probably will not fall. It's just a question of whether to finesse immediately or whether to cash one high trump and then finesse on the second round.

The average declarer cashes one high trump first with this combination and then goes to dummy for a finesse. He is lured by the idea of taking out insurance against the singleton queen of spades in West's hand. He forgets, however, that he will have to pay off every time West has a small singleton.

Suppose the trump situation is this:

DUMMY

7 6

| WEST | EAST |
|------|------|
| 4 | Q 5 3 2 |

YOU

A K J 10 9 8

Now, if you cash the ace first, there will be only one trump left in dummy to finesse with, and you won't be able to pick up East's queen. By finessing immediately you are able to take two finesses and make your contract.

There are four small singletons West could hold and only one singleton queen, so the chances of his holding a small singleton are four times as likely as the singleton queen.

Be suspicious of an insurance policy that protects you from one danger by exposing you to another, which is four times as great.

## CHERCHEZ LA FEMME

NORTH
♠ 8 7 5
♡ Q J 4 2
◇ A J 2
♣ 6 3 2

SOUTH
♠ 9 2
♡ A K 10 9 8
◇ K 10 3
♣ A K J

*South dealer. East-West vulnerable*

*The bidding:*

| SOUTH | WEST | NORTH | EAST |
|-------|------|-------|------|
| 1 ♡ | Pass | 2 ♡ | Pass |
| 4 ♡ | Pass | Pass | Pass |

*Opening lead:* Spade king

West leads the king and ace of spades and continues with a third spade to East's queen, which you ruff. You now cash two rounds of trumps and both opponents follow. What is your plan for the rest of the hand?

*Answer:* It is impossible to go down with correct play. Simply cash the ace and king of clubs and lead the club jack. Whoever wins the queen will be forced to solve all your problems for you by either leading a diamond or giving you a ruff and a discard.

Why rack your brains looking for a queen when you can force an opponent to do the job for you with 100 percent efficiency?

## THE CASE OF THE DOG THAT DIDN'T BARK
## IN THE NIGHT

NORTH
♠ A Q
♡ K 9 5
◇ K J 9 4 3
♣ 9 3 2

SOUTH
♠ K J 10
♡ A J 10 8 3
◇ 8
♣ Q 8 7 5

*East dealer. Neither vulnerable*

*The bidding:*

| EAST | SOUTH | WEST | NORTH |
|------|--------|------|-------|
| 1 ◇ | Double | Pass | 2 NT |
| Pass | 3 ♡ | Pass | 4 ♡ |
| Pass | Pass | Pass | |

*Opening lead:* Diamond two

West leads the diamond two, you play small from dummy, and East wins with the queen. East cashes the A K of clubs and leads the club jack, which you win with the queen as West follows suit. Everything now hinges on finding the queen of trumps. Who has it?

*Answer:* There's a famous Sherlock Holmes story in which an important clue to the whereabouts of the missing race horse, Silver Blaze, turns out to be the fact that the stable dog didn't bark the night the horse was stolen. This causes Holmes to reject the theory that a stranger had broken into the stable. Instead he realized it was someone the dog knew well, and this led him to the eventual solution, namely that the horse's trainer was the guilty one. Similar reasoning here should lead declarer to the whereabouts of the missing queen.

Let's start by reconstructing East's hand. He can't have the diamond ten or he surely would have played it on the first trick instead of the queen. This gives West three diamonds, including the ten. (He would not lead the two with a doubleton.) Thus East started with A Q x x of diamonds and A K J of clubs. This leaves him with six cards in the majors, and they must be divided 3–3 or 4–2. (He would not have bid a four-card minor suit ahead of a five- or six-card major.) So East's distribution is either 4–3–3–3 or 4–4–3–2.

With the heart queen he would have a balanced hand of 16 points and a perfect opening bid of one no-trump. Why didn't he bid one no-trump? Because he didn't have the heart queen. West has it!

Don't forget to weigh negative evidence, whether it is a dog that doesn't bark in the night or an opponent who doesn't bid one no-trump.

## BLIND SPOT

NORTH
♠ A 9 6 5
♡ —
◇ A Q 10 8 6 5 2
♣ A J

SOUTH
♠ K 8 3 2
♡ A K 7
◇ K J 9 7
♣ 8 6

*South dealer. Both vulnerable*

*The bidding:*

| SOUTH | WEST | NORTH | EAST |
|-------|------|-------|------|
| 1 ◇ | Pass | 7 ◇ | Pass |
| Pass | Pass | | |

*Opening lead:* Club king

You open one diamond, West passes, and North's face lights up with a mischievous smile as he raises to seven diamonds. West leads the club king, which you win with the ace. How do you hope to make thirteen tricks?

*Answer:* The grand slam will succeed with a normal 3–2 spade break. Draw the outstanding trumps and throw two of dummy's spades on the A K of hearts. Now cash the two high spades and ruff a spade in dummy. If the suit breaks 3–2, dummy's club jack can be discarded on your fourth spade and the contract is home.

Here is the whole hand:

NORTH
♠ A 9 6 5
♡ —
♢ A Q 10 8 6 5 2
♣ A J

WEST
♠ J 7 4
♡ J 9 6 5 2
♢ 4
♣ K Q 10 2

EAST
♠ Q 10
♡ Q 10 8 4 3
♢ 3
♣ 9 7 5 4 3

SOUTH
♠ K 8 3 2
♡ A K 7
♢ K J 9 7
♣ 8 6

Declarer is apt to have a blind spot here and discard dummy's club jack on one of the high hearts. Now there is no way to avoid a spade loser, and the contract must fail.

## ONE MAN'S MEAT

NORTH
♠ K Q 6
♡ Q 10
◇ K J 10 9 4
♣ A 7 5

SOUTH
♠ A J 8 7
♡ K 9
◇ A 8 2
♣ K J 8 2

*South dealer. Both vulnerable*

*The bidding:*

| SOUTH | WEST | NORTH | EAST |
|-------|------|-------|------|
| 1 NT | Pass | 4 NT | Pass |
| Pass | Pass | | |

*Opening lead:* Heart five

It often happens that a hand should be played in different ways depending on the level of the contract. For example, if South were in *three* no-trump here and received a heart lead to East's ace and a heart continuation, he wouldn't dream of taking a finesse. Nine tricks are there for the asking, and it would be foolish to jeopardize the contract.

However, if the contract were *six* no-trump, South would have no choice but to try for five diamond tricks. His proper play would be to cash the diamond ace and then finesse West for the queen. (Naturally he would not consider a club finesse at six no-trump, because even if it succeeded it would do him virtually no good.)

Now suppose you are declarer at *four* no-trump with these cards. (You open one no-trump, partner invites a slam by bidding four no-trump, and you refuse because your no-trump was a minimum.)

Again West leads a heart to the ace, and a heart is returned. You cash four rounds of spades; East-West each follow three times, and each discard a heart on the fourth round. How do you continue to give yourself the maximum chance to make ten tricks?

*Answer:* Four no-trump will succeed if you can locate either the club queen or the diamond queen. But if you finesse for one queen and lose, the opponents will defeat you with heart leads before you can try for the other queen. The object here is to combine your chances in the two suits. First cash the A K of the suit where you have the most cards. (In this case, diamonds.) There is some chance that the diamond queen may drop, in which case you are home. If it doesn't drop, cash the club ace and finesse East for the club queen.

## DANGER FROM THE FAR EAST

NORTH
♠ 6 4
♡ A 7
◇ K Q 8 5
♣ A 8 7 3 2

SOUTH
♠ K 8
♡ 2
◇ A J 10 9 4 3 2
♣ K 10 5

*West dealer. Both vulnerable*

*The bidding:*

| WEST | NORTH | EAST | SOUTH |
|------|-------|------|-------|
| 1 ♡ | Pass | 2 ♡ | 3 ◇ |
| 3 ♡ | 5 ◇ | Pass | Pass |
| Pass | | | |

*Opening lead:* Heart king

West opens one heart, and North, who has no convenient bid at this point, passes. East raises to two hearts, and you naturally overcall three diamonds. West competes with three hearts, and North comes to life with a jump to five diamonds. This becomes the final contract, and the opening lead is the heart king. What is your plan for the hand and how do you proceed?

*Answer:* You have three possible losers: one club and two spades. Or, viewing things the other way, you have ten sure tricks: seven diamonds, two clubs, and one heart. Let's look at the entire deal and then see how it would be played by four different declarers: a beginner, an intermediate, an advanced player, and an expert.

NORTH
♠ 6 4
♡ A 7
◇ K Q 8 5
♣ A 8 7 3 2

WEST
♠ A Q 9 2
♡ K Q 9 8 5 4
◇ 7
♣ 9 4

EAST
♠ J 10 7 5 3
♡ J 10 6 3
◇ 6
♣ Q J 6

SOUTH
♠ K 8
♡ 2
◇ A J 10 9 4 3 2
♣ K 10 5

The beginner wins the first trick with the heart ace and draws the outstanding trump. From then on he wanders around rather aimlessly, making no real effort to develop that vital eleventh trick. He may at some point lead a spade toward his king in the vague hope that East holds the ace. Of course, on the bidding, this is impossible, and the beginner winds up with the same ten tricks he started with.

The intermediate player is slightly more sophisticated in his approach. At least he has a plan in mind. After winning the first trick and drawing trump he intends to develop extra tricks from the long club suit. So, he leads the ace, the king, and a small club. As the suit breaks 3–2, both dummy's remaining clubs are now good and can be used for spade discards. Unfortunately, however, East wins the third club and returns the spade jack. The enemy cash two spades, and the intermediate declarer also winds up with the same ten tricks he started with.

The advanced player also plans to develop clubs. However, he is cagier than the intermediate declarer, and he intends to establish the suit without letting East into the lead. (East is the dangerous opponent, the only one who can attack spades.) Accordingly, after winning the first trick with the heart ace and drawing trumps, he leads a small club from dummy toward his hand. If East plays small, he plans to put in the ten and lose the trick to West, who can't attack the spade weakness. Unfortunately, East happens to have both the queen and jack of clubs, and he splits his honors. This foils declarer's scheme as East can no longer be prevented from gaining the lead for the fatal spade switch. This declarer deserved a better fate. He tried much harder than the others and would normally make this hand with his line of play. However, he too winds up with the same ten tricks he started with.

The expert, like the intermediate and advanced declarers, also plans to establish the club suit. But he makes 100 percent sure that East never gets in with a club honor. How? By simply ducking the opening lead of the heart king! This gives the enemy a heart trick that they don't deserve. However, it means declarer will not lose a club trick since the third club is now discarded on the heart ace. After drawing trumps, the club suit is easily established by playing the king and ace and then ruffing a club.

In effect, the expert gave West a heart trick instead of giving East a club trick. The difference is that he makes at least eleven tricks. In fact, if West doesn't grab his spade ace at trick two, the expert declarer will make twelve tricks!

## THE PLAY'S THE THING

NORTH
♠ J 6 5
♡ 5 3 2
◇ K 7 6
♣ Q 8 6 2

SOUTH
♠ A Q
♡ A Q J 10 7 6
◇ A 3 2
♣ A 5

*South dealer. Neither vulnerable*

*The bidding:*

| SOUTH | WEST | NORTH | EAST |
|-------|------|-------|------|
| 1 ♡   | Pass | 1 NT  | Pass |
| 4 ♡   | Pass | Pass  | Pass |

*Opening lead:* Diamond queen

West leads the diamond queen against four hearts. What's the best way to play this one?

*Answer:* You have four possible losers—a spade, a heart, a diamond, and a club. There are various methods to dispose of one of these losers, and the question is which method offers the best chance.

For example, you could win the diamond in dummy and take a heart finesse. If this loses, however, you are in bad shape, because there are no more entries to dummy, and you are likely to lose three more tricks for down one. And even if the heart finesse wins you are not out of the woods. East could have K x x of hearts, and as there is no way to repeat the finesse, you still may lose a trick in each suit.

Here is the complete deal:

NORTH
♠ J 6 5
♡ 5 3 2
◊ K 7 6
♣ Q 8 6 2

WEST
♠ K 9 8 4
♡ 9
◊ Q J 10 4
♣ 10 7 4 3

EAST
♠ 10 7 3 2
♡ K 8 4
◊ 9 8 5
♣ K J 9

SOUTH
♠ A Q
♡ A Q J 10 7 6
◊ A 3 2
♣ A 5

A slightly better plan is to win the diamond king and take a spade finesse. At least if this wins you are home.

Even better is to win the diamond in the South hand and lead the ace and another club. If West has the club king, you can probably throw a loser on dummy's queen. And even if the club king is off side, you still have the diamond king as an entry to try the spade finesse later.

By far the surest way to play the hand, however, involves no finessing at all. Win the diamond lead in your hand, and lead the ace and queen of spades. The queen loses to the king, but dummy's jack is now available as a parking place for one of your losers. And the diamond king is still in dummy as an entry to the parking place.

Barring very unusual distribution this last line of play will succeed regardless of the location of the three missing kings.

## AN ACUTE CASE OF FINESSITIS

NORTH
♠ Q 8 4 2
♡ 9 6 4 3
♢ A Q 6
♣ 8 2

SOUTH
♠ J 5 3
♡ A K Q J 10
♢ 8 2
♣ A K Q

*South dealer. Both vulnerable*

*The bidding:*

| SOUTH | WEST | NORTH | EAST |
|-------|------|-------|------|
| 1 ♡ | Pass | 2 ♡ | Pass |
| 4 ♡ | Pass | Pass | Pass |

*Opening lead:* Club jack

West leads the club jack against four hearts. You win and play two rounds of trumps, both opponents following. How do you continue?

*Answer:* Cash the other two club honors, throwing the six of diamonds from dummy. Now take the diamond ace and lead the diamond queen. Whoever wins the king must either lead a minor suit or a spade. If he leads a minor, you ruff in dummy and discard a spade from your hand. If he leads a spade, one of your three spade losers is automatically eliminated. In all cases you wind up losing one diamond and two spades, and there is nothing the opponents can do to defeat the contract. Here is the complete deal:

NORTH
♠ Q 8 4 2
♡ 9 6 4 3
◇ A Q 6
♣ 8 2

WEST
♠ A 10 6
♡ 5 2
◇ J 7 4 3
♣ J 10 9 6

EAST
♠ K 9 7
♡ 8 7
◇ K 10 9 8
♣ 7 5 4 3

SOUTH
♠ J 5 3
♡ A K Q J 10
◇ 5 2
♣ A K Q

Although the *opponents* can do nothing to set this contract, it is easy enough for declarer to defeat himself by taking a diamond finesse. If this loses, as in the diagram, East will make the safe return of a diamond, and declarer will have to tackle the spade suit himself. As the cards lie he will lose three spade tricks as well as the diamond king for down one.

## EARLY DECISION

NORTH
♠ J 10
♡ 9 8 3
◇ A K 8 6 2
♣ J 3 2

SOUTH
♠ Q
♡ A 10 2
◇ 7 4
♣ A K Q 10 9 5 4

*South dealer. Both vulnerable*

*The bidding:*

| SOUTH | WEST | NORTH | EAST |
|-------|------|-------|------|
| 1 ♣ | Pass | 1 ◇ | Pass |
| 3 ♣ | Pass | 4 ♣ | Pass |
| 5 ♣ | Pass | Pass | Pass |

*Opening lead:* Diamond queen

West leads the diamond queen against your contract of five clubs. How do you play this one?

*Answer:* Ten tricks are easy, and the eleventh can only come from the diamond suit. To give yourself the maximum chance to establish an extra diamond, you must duck the opening lead. Here is the entire deal:

NORTH
♠ J 10
♡ 9 8 3
◇ A K 8 6 2
♣ J 3 2

WEST
♠ A 9 8 4
♡ Q 7 6 4
◇ Q J 10 9
♣ 6

EAST
♠ K 7 6 5 3 2
♡ K J 5
◇ 5 3
♣ 8 7

SOUTH
♠ Q
♡ A 10 2
◇ 7 4
♣ A K Q 10 9 5 4

When the diamond queen holds, let's assume West continues with the jack. You win with the ace and ruff a small diamond with a high club. Now draw trumps, ending in dummy. The king and eight of diamonds take care of your two heart losers, and the contract is home.

If you win the opening lead, it is impossible to establish the diamonds (unless the suit breaks 3–3), because there are not enough entries to dummy. By ducking the first diamond, you guarantee the contract whether the diamonds break 3–3 or 4–2.

## NEVER SAY DIE

NORTH
♠ A Q J
♡ K 8 6 4
◇ K 8 6
♣ K 6 2

SOUTH
♠ K 10 5
♡ A J 10 9 2
◇ A 9 5
♣ A 10

*North dealer. East-West vulnerable*

*The bidding:*

| NORTH | EAST | SOUTH | WEST |
|-------|------|-------|------|
| 1 NT | Pass | 3 ♡ | Pass |
| 4 ♡ | Pass | 6 ♡ | Pass |
| Pass | Pass | | |

*Opening lead:* Diamond queen

West leads the diamond queen against six hearts, and there appears to be an obvious diamond loser and a possible trump loser. You win the first trick with the diamond ace and hopefully cash the king and ace of hearts. To your annoyance West discards a diamond on the second heart. Is there still a chance to make this hand against correct defense? If so what is the chance and how do you capitalize on it?

*Answer:* Things look black, but you're not down yet. You still have a chance if East has no more than two diamonds. What you hope for is something like this:

NORTH
♠ A Q J
♡ K 8 6 4
◇ K 8 6
♣ K 6 2

WEST
♠ 7 6 4
♡ 7
◇ Q J 10 7 4
♣ Q 8 4 3

EAST
♠ 9 8 3 2
♡ Q 5 3
◇ 3 2
♣ J 9 7 5

SOUTH
♠ K 10 5
♡ A J 10 9 2
◇ A 9 5
♣ A 10

Cash the ace and king of clubs and ruff dummy's small club. Now cash the three spades and the diamond king. The position will be:

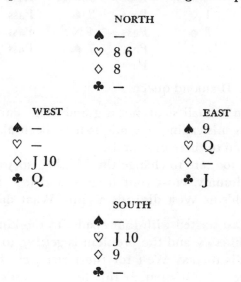

NORTH
♠ —
♡ 8 6
◇ 8
♣ —

WEST
♠ —
♡ —
◇ J 10
♣ Q

EAST
♠ 9
♡ Q
◇ —
♣ J

SOUTH
♠ —
♡ J 10
◇ 9
♣ —

The stage is now set, and you lead a heart. East must win with the queen and return a black card, giving you a ruff and a sluff and the contract.

## DESPERATE MEASURES

NORTH
♠ 7 6 2
♡ A 10
◇ A K 9 8 7
♣ J 10 9

SOUTH
♠ A Q J 10 9 8
♡ K Q 8
◇ 6
♣ A K Q

*North dealer. North-South vulnerable*

*The bidding:*

| NORTH | EAST | SOUTH | WEST |
|-------|------|-------|------|
| 1 ◇ | Pass | 2 ♠ | Pass |
| 3 ♠ | Pass | 4 NT | Pass |
| 5 ♡ | Pass | 7 ♠ | Pass |
| Pass | Pass | | |

*Opening lead:* Diamond queen

You belong in a small slam, not a grand slam. Partner's rebid of three spades was misleading. He might have been able to slow you down with a rebid of three diamonds.

However, it's too late to change the bidding, so you win the diamond lead in dummy, cross your fingers, and lead a spade to the queen. This holds as West discards a club. What do you do next?

*Answer:* As East started with four spades to the king, you need to take two more finesses, and the problem is getting to dummy twice. The only hope is to play West for the heart jack. Lead the heart eight and finesse dummy's ten. If this loses to East's jack, you will be down two. But if it wins, you now have sufficient entries to make the grand slam.

Here is the entire deal:

NORTH
♠ 7 6 2
♡ A 10
◇ A K 9 8 7
♣ J 10 9

WEST
♠ —
♡ J 5 3 2
◇ Q J 10 5 4
♣ 8 6 4 3

EAST
♠ K 5 4 3
♡ 9 7 6 4
◇ 3 2
♣ 7 5 2

SOUTH
♠ A Q J 10 9 8
♡ K Q 8
◇ 6
♣ A K Q

Yes, West can ruin you by going up with the heart jack when you lead the eight. But how many defenders are that good?

## TIT FOR TAT

NORTH
♠ 8 6 2
♡ Q 10 9 6 3 2
◇ K 5 4
♣ 6

SOUTH
♠ K 9 5
♡ A K J 4
◇ A 8 7 6
♣ A 10

*South dealer. North-South vulnerable*

*The bidding:*

| SOUTH | WEST | NORTH | EAST |
|-------|------|-------|------|
| 1 ♡ | 1 ♠ | 2 ♡ | Pass |
| 3 NT | Pass | 4 ♡ | Pass |
| Pass | Pass | | |

*Opening lead:* Club king

You bid one heart, West overcalls one spade, and partner gives a single raise to two hearts. With nineteen high-card points you do not intend to settle for less than game. However, there is some chance that North has raised with only three hearts, and to allow for this you bid three no-trump. On this sequence partner will usually correct to four hearts if he has four-card support. With *six* trumps North is only too happy to say four hearts, and East leads the club king.

Oddly enough three no-trump from the South position is a laydown, and four hearts is going to require luck as well as skill. How do you proceed?

*Answer:* You appear to have three spade losers and one diamond loser. Of course, it is possible that East has the spade ace, which would eliminate one of the losers in that suit. But in view of the bidding this is unlikely.

There is also a chance that the diamond suit will break 3–3, in which case one of dummy's spades can be discarded on South's fourth diamond. The difficulty here is that in the process of establishing the fourth diamond you may have to give East the lead. In this case he will quickly shift to a spade, and the enemy may grab four tricks before you can make use of South's long diamond. Here is the whole hand:

```
                        NORTH
                    ♠  8 6 2
                    ♡  Q 10 9 6 3 2
                    ◇  K 5 4
                    ♣  6

    WEST                                    EAST
♠  A Q 10 4 3                           ♠  J 7
♡  8 7                                  ♡  5
◇  J 3 2                                ◇  Q 10 9
♣  K Q 9                                ♣  J 8 7 5 4 3 2

                        SOUTH
                    ♠  K 9 5
                    ♡  A K J 4
                    ◇  A 8 7 6
                    ♣  A 10
```

The solution is to let West hold the club king. Suppose he shifts to a heart. After trumps are extracted you discard a diamond from dummy on the club ace. Now cash the king and ace of diamonds and ruff the third round in dummy. When the suit breaks 3–3, South's fourth diamond takes care of one of dummy's spades, and the contract is home.

It seems odd to give the opponents a club trick that they don't deserve. But in so doing you avoid a diamond loser, so the exchange is apparently even. The advantage is that East *might* win the diamond trick, but he can't possibly win the club.

## A NEEDLESS RISK

NORTH
♠ 6 5 3 2
♡ Q 4
◊ Q 10
♣ A Q J 10 9

SOUTH
♠ A K Q J
♡ A 6
◊ A J 3
♣ 8 7 6 4

*North dealer. East-West vulnerable*

*The bidding:*

| NORTH | EAST | SOUTH | WEST |
|-------|------|-------|------|
| Pass | Pass | 1 ♣ | Pass |
| 3 ♣ | Pass | 3 ♠ | Pass |
| 5 ♣ | Pass | 6 ♣ | Pass |
| Pass | Pass | | |

*Opening lead:* Heart jack

North should have bid four spades over three spades. However, the final contract of six clubs is not unreasonable, and West leads the heart jack. You hopefully cover with the queen, East plays the king, and you win with the ace. What do you do next?

*Answer:* The correct play at trick two is a club to the ace. Now lead the diamond queen for a finesse. If East has the diamond king, you get rid of dummy's other heart on South's third diamond. You then turn your attention back to clubs, conceding a trick to the king. When the opponents' trumps are extracted, you claim the balance.

Here is the complete deal:

NORTH
♠ 6 5 3 2
♡ Q 4
◇ Q 10
♣ A Q J 10 9

WEST
♠ 9 7 4
♡ J 10 9 5
◇ 9 8 6 5 4
♣ 2

EAST
♠ 10 8
♡ K 8 7 3 2
◇ K 7 2
♣ K 5 3

SOUTH
♠ A K Q J
♡ A 6
◇ A J 3
♣ 8 7 6 4

After the first trick the contract cannot be made if West has the diamond king. You will eventually have to take a diamond finesse, and if it loses, West will cash a heart for the setting trick.

The club finesse, however, is a needless risk. If it loses, you are automatically down. And if it wins, you are virtually no better off than you were before.

## TO PLACE AN ACE

NORTH
♠ J 10 7 6
♡ 9 6 4 2
◇ J 4 3
♣ A 9

SOUTH
♠ A 9 8 5 4 3
♡ K J
◇ K 6
♣ K 8 7

*West dealer. Neither vulnerable*

*The bidding:*

| WEST | NORTH | EAST | SOUTH |
|------|-------|------|-------|
| Pass | Pass | Pass | 1 ♠ |
| Pass | 2 ♠ | Pass | 4 ♠ |
| Pass | Pass | Pass | |

*Opening lead:* Club queen

You open in fourth position with a spade. Partner gives you a rather thin raise to two spades, and you push a bit with four spades. West leads the club queen, and when dummy appears you see there are rough waters ahead. You win the first trick with the club ace and lead the spade jack. East covers with the queen, and you win with the ace as West contributes the two. You now cash the club king and ruff a club. Then you lead a spade in the hopes that West will be endplayed. Unfortunately, West discards a club as East wins with the spade king and returns a small heart. Do you play the heart jack or the king and why?

*Answer:* If the ace and queen of hearts are both in the same hand, it naturally doesn't matter what you do. Only if they are divided is it important. It may seem a matter of guesswork, but it isn't. The right play at this point is clearly the heart jack. Here's the reason: In order to make this hand, you must hold yourself to one diamond loser. As you'll have to play diamonds yourself, it means you'll have to find the diamond ace in East's hand. If East has the diamond ace in addition to the king-queen of spades, he can't possibly have the heart ace or he would have opened the bidding. Your only hope is that East has the heart queen, so you put in the jack.

If making a contract depends upon finding a particular card in a certain hand, assume that it is there and act accordingly!

## THINK NOW, PLAY LATER

NORTH
♠ J 9 8 4 2
♡ A 10 2
◇ Q 8 7
♣ 6 3

SOUTH
♠ A 5
♡ Q 4
◇ 3
♣ A K Q J 10 5 4 2

*South dealer. Neither vulnerable*

*The bidding:*

| SOUTH | WEST | NORTH | EAST |
|-------|------|-------|------|
| 1 ♣ | Pass | 1 ♠ | Double |
| 5 ♣ | Pass | Pass | Pass |

*Opening lead:* Heart three

You open one club, partner responds one spade, East doubles for take-out, and you close the proceedings with a jump to five clubs. The heart three is led, dummy plays the two, and East wins with the king. Can you see any chance to make eleven tricks? How?

*Answer:* Virtually the only chance to make this contract is to find West with the heart jack. To capitalize on this possibility, however, you must throw the heart queen under East's king at trick one. Later you will be able to lead the heart four to dummy's ten. If the finesse succeeds, dummy's heart ace will provide the eleventh trick.

Here is the complete deal:

NORTH
♠ J 9 8 4 2
♡ A 10 2
◇ Q 8 7
♣ 6 3

WEST
♠ 7 6 3
♡ J 9 6 3
◇ K 9 6 5
♣ 8 7

EAST
♠ K Q 10
♡ K 8 7 5
◇ A J 10 4 2
♣ 9

SOUTH
♠ A 5
♡ Q 4
◇ 3
♣ A K Q J 10 5 4 2

If declarer is not thinking at trick one, he will drop the heart four instead of the queen. Now he can never score two heart tricks, and the contract must fail.

## EENY, MEENY, MINEY, MO

NORTH
♠ J 7 6
♡ A K Q
◇ 9 7 2
♣ A 8 7 2

SOUTH
♠ Q 10 9 8 5
♡ 6 2
◇ A J 8
♣ K Q 5

*North dealer. Neither vulnerable*

*The bidding:*

| NORTH | EAST | SOUTH | WEST |
|-------|------|-------|------|
| 1 ♣ | Pass | 1 ♠ | Pass |
| 1 NT | Pass | 3 ♣ | Pass |
| 3 ♠ | Pass | 4 ♠ | Pass |
| Pass | Pass | | |

*Opening lead:* Club jack

West leads the club jack, and East plays the three, as you win in your hand with the king. There is no reason to delay pulling trumps, so you lead a spade at trick two. West takes the king and continues with the club ten. East follows with the four, and you win the queen and lead another trump. This time West takes the ace and leads the six of clubs.

You now have the ace-eight of clubs left in dummy and the five in your hand. The only club spot unaccounted for is the nine. Should you finesse the eight in dummy, or should you go up with the ace? Why?

*Answer:* It may seem that this is a matter of guessing the whereabouts of the club nine. Actually there is no guess involved at all.

The correct play is to finesse the eight, because this guarantees the contract regardless of the location of the nine. Suppose the eight loses to the nine. No harm is done, because after drawing the last trump you throw one of your losing diamonds on the club ace and the other on the heart queen. East-West make in all two spades and one club.

However, if you go up with dummy's ace of clubs, you run the risk of being defeated if the cards are like this:

NORTH
♠ J 7 6
♡ A K Q
♢ 9 7 2
♣ A 8 7 2

WEST
♠ A K
♡ 9 7 5 3
♢ Q 10 3
♣ J 10 9 6

EAST
♠ 4 3 2
♡ J 10 8 4
♢ K 6 5 4
♣ 4 3

SOUTH
♠ Q 10 9 8 5
♡ 6 2
♢ A J 8
♣ K Q 5

East ruffs the club ace, and you lose a diamond for down one.

## MAXIMUM SECURITY

NORTH
♠ 3
♡ 8 6 4
◇ A J 7 5
♣ K Q 10 3 2

SOUTH
♠ A 5
♡ A Q
◇ K 3 2
♣ A J 9 8 7 6

*South dealer. Both vulnerable*

*The bidding:*

| SOUTH | WEST | NORTH | EAST |
|-------|------|-------|------|
| 1 ♣ | Pass | 3 ♣ | Pass |
| 6 ♣ | Pass | Pass | Pass |

*Opening lead:* Spade king

You open one club, partner raises to three clubs, and without further ado you bid six clubs. West leads the spade king, which you win with the ace. You draw the opponents' trumps in one round and then ruff your losing spade in dummy. How do you proceed?

*Answer:* You can count eleven tricks, so all you need is one extra trick from either diamonds or hearts. The chances of getting the extra trick from this diamond suit are excellent, provided you don't mind losing one trick in the process—which, of course you don't. Cash the ace and king of diamonds first and then lead a diamond toward the jack. This line of play will produce three diamond tricks any time that

1. West has the queen.

2. The diamonds break 3–3.
3. East has the singleton queen.
4. East has the doubleton queen.

And if all these possibilities fail, you can still try the heart finesse as a last resort. Here is the complete hand:

NORTH
♠ 3
♡ 8 6 4
♢ A J 7 5
♣ K Q 10 3 2

WEST
♠ K Q J 6
♡ K 10 3 2
♢ 10 9 8 6
♣ 4

EAST
♠ 10 9 8 7 4 2
♡ J 9 7 5
♢ Q 4
♣ 5

SOUTH
♠ A 5
♡ A Q
♢ K 3 2
♣ A J 9 8 7 6

## CLUBBED TO DEATH

NORTH
♠ Q 9 5
♡ A Q 9
◇ 10 9 7 6
♣ A J 9

SOUTH
♠ A J 10 8 7
♡ K J 10
◇ 8 5 3 2
♣ 7

*East dealer. Neither vulnerable*

*The bidding:*

| EAST | SOUTH | WEST | NORTH |
|------|-------|------|-------|
| 1 ♣ | 1 ♠ | Pass | 2 NT |
| Pass | 3 ♠ | Pass | 4 ♠ |
| Pass | Pass | Pass | |

*Opening lead:* Club two

You become declarer at four spades after East has opened the bidding with one club. West leads the club two, dummy plays the ace, and East contributes the eight. How do you handle this one?

*Answer:* With a normal break in diamonds you will lose three tricks in the suit. This means you can probably make the contract if you can handle the trumps without loss. But care is required. The player whose lifelong convictions require him to draw trumps first and worry later is in trouble. Here is the complete deal:

NORTH
♠ Q 9 5
♡ A Q 9
◇ 10 9 7 6
♣ A J 9

WEST
♠ 6 4 3
♡ 8 7 6 5 3
◇ J 4
♣ 10 6 2

EAST
♠ K 2
♡ 4 2
◇ A K Q
♣ K Q 8 5 4 3

SOUTH
♠ A J 10 8 7
♡ K J 10
◇ 8 5 3 2
♣ 7

Suppose declarer wins the first trick with the club ace, extracts the opponents trumps in three rounds, and then turns his attention to the diamond suit. East takes the first diamond with the queen and returns the club king, which South ruffs. Another diamond is conceded to the king, and East leads the club queen forcing South to ruff with his last trump. Now declarer can't establish his fourth diamond without being literally clubbed to death by East, and the contract must fail.

South can protect himself against this onslaught of clubs by establishing the fourth diamond before dummy's trumps are gone. Win the first trick with the club ace and lead a diamond immediately. East takes the queen and continues with the club king, which you ruff. A second diamond is conceded to the king and you ruff East's return of the club queen and lead a third diamond. Dummy is now out of clubs, so if East returns a club you can ruff in the North hand, draw three rounds of trumps, and claim the balance.

## TIMING WILL TELL

NORTH
♠ K J 8 7 4
♡ K 9 6
◇ A 10
♣ 8 3 2

SOUTH
♠ A Q 10 3 2
♡ A 5 4
◇ J 5
♣ A Q 5

*South dealer. Both vulnerable*

*The bidding:*

| SOUTH | WEST | NORTH | EAST |
|-------|------|-------|------|
| 1 ♠   | Pass | 3 ♠   | Pass |
| 4 ♣   | Pass | 4 ♠   | Pass |
| Pass  | Pass |       |      |

*Opening lead:* Diamond king

You open one spade, and when partner jumps to three spades, you make a slam try with four clubs. North's hand is a minimum for his previous bidding, and his club holding is particularly unfavorable, so he signs off with four spades. (If North held ♠ K 8 7 5 4 ♡ K 9 8 6 ◇ A 10 ♣ K 8, he would be happy to cooperate in the slam effort and show his ace by bidding four diamonds over four clubs. Then you would reach an excellent contract of six spades.) In the actual case, when North denies interest by simply returning to the agreed trump suit, you give up hopes of a slam and settle for four spades.

West leads the diamond king, and when dummy appears you see that even four spades is going to require care, because there is a diamond loser, a heart loser, and two possible club losers. How do you proceed?

*Answer:* West appears to have the diamond queen, in which case an end play can be arranged. Proper timing is essential, however. Here is the whole hand:

NORTH
♠ K J 8 7 4
♡ K 9 6
◇ A 10
♣ 8 3 2

WEST
♠ 9 5
♡ J 8 3
◇ K Q 9 8
♣ K 9 7 6

EAST
♠ 6
♡ Q 10 7 2
◇ 7 6 4 3 2
♣ J 10 4

SOUTH
♠ A Q 10 3 2
♡ A 5 4
◇ J 5
♣ A Q 5

Win the first trick with the diamond ace, draw the trumps, and play the ace, king, and another heart. Best defense is for East to win and return the club jack. You rise with the club ace, spurning the finesse, and lead the diamond jack. West takes the queen, and whatever he returns the defenders get only one more trick regardless of the location of the club king.

## TEST THAT LINE

NORTH
♠ Q 3
♡ A Q 9 4 2
◇ 5 3
♣ 10 6 5 2

SOUTH
♠ A K J 10 9 8 4
♡ —
◇ A K 8 6 2
♣ A

*South dealer. North-South vulnerable*

*The bidding:*

| SOUTH | WEST | NORTH | EAST |
|-------|------|-------|------|
| 2 ♠ | Pass | 3 ♡ | Pass |
| 3 ♠ | Pass | 4 ♠ | Pass |
| 6 ♠ | Pass | Pass | Pass |

*Opening lead:* Diamond queen

You open with a strong two-bid, and when North makes a positive response and then supports spades, you confidently jump to slam. West leads the queen of diamonds, which you win with the ace as East follows suit with the four. How do you continue?

*Answer:* This looks like a cinch. One's instinct is to cash the diamond king and then ruff a diamond with the spade queen. Before actually doing this, however, it is important to picture what will happen to you, depending on how the diamond suit breaks.

1. Suppose the diamonds break 3–3. When you ruff the third diamond with the spade queen, your problems are over. You simply draw trumps and claim thirteen tricks.

2. If the diamonds break 4–2 you are still O.K. You eventually

concede one diamond trick to the opponents and wind up making six.

3. If the diamonds break 5–1, however, you are in trouble. Someone is probably going to ruff the diamond king at trick two. Now you will be able to trump one diamond safely with the spade queen and throw one on the heart ace. But you will still have a losing diamond left at the end, and the contract will be down one.

It is good you thought of this before actually playing to trick two. Because now it's not too late to test an alternative line of play. So you mentally lead a *small* diamond at trick two and see what happens. Of course, you will lose this trick. But now you can ruff one diamond loser with the spade queen and throw one on the heart ace. After drawing trumps you are left with the diamond king, which is good, and the slam is home regardless of how the diamonds are divided. Here is the entire deal:

NORTH
♠ Q 3
♡ A Q 9 4 2
◇ 5 3
♣ 10 6 5 2

WEST
♠ 2
♡ J 8 6
◇ Q J 10 9 7
♣ K J 9 4

EAST
♠ 7 6 5
♡ K 10 7 5 3
◇ 4
♣ Q 8 7 3

SOUTH
♠ A K J 10 9 8 4
♡ —
◇ A K 8 6 2
♣ A

Anyone can make this slam if the diamonds are 3–3 or 4–2. But only the careful declarer leads a small diamond at trick two and succeeds even when the diamonds are 5–1.

## RED CHOICE

NORTH
♠ A Q 10
♡ A K 7
◇ J 10 8 7 2
♣ K J

SOUTH
♠ K J 9 7
♡ J 10 9 8 6
◇ A 9
♣ A Q

*South dealer. Neither vulnerable*

*The bidding:*

| SOUTH | WEST | NORTH | EAST |
|-------|------|-------|------|
| 1 ♡ | Pass | 2 ◇ | Pass |
| 2 NT | Pass | 6 NT | Pass |
| Pass | Pass | | |

*Opening lead:* Club ten

Your rebid of two no-trump shows 15 or 16 points, so North quite properly bids the slam. What's the best way to play this contract after the lead of the club ten?

*Answer:* You have nine top winners and must develop three more tricks either from hearts or diamonds. The question is which red suit should you attack first?

If you start on hearts, you will make five tricks in the suit if West has Q x or Q x x or if either opponent has a singleton queen. (Simply cash one high honor and then finesse West for the queen.) However, if the heart finesse loses, you are finished. It is too late to develop the diamonds regardless of how favorably they are divided.

To give yourself the maximum chance, you should play on the diamonds first. Now you will succeed if East has a singleton dia-

mond honor or a doubleton diamond honor or if he has both diamond honors. And if all this fails, you still retain the play for five
heart tricks.

Win the club ten in dummy and lead the diamond two. If East
plays an honor, you win with the ace and lead the nine to knock out
the other honor for an easy twelve tricks.

If East plays small you finesse the nine. If the nine holds, your
problems are over. With two diamond tricks in the bag you switch
your attention to hearts. It's easy to make *four* hearts, which brings
you to twelve tricks.

If the diamond nine loses, you may still drop a doubleton honor
when you cash the ace. In this case dummy's three remaining diamonds are good, which again brings you to twelve tricks. And if
the diamonds are not divided favorably, you can still play for five
heart tricks.

In other words, by starting on diamonds you make the slam if
either red suit behaves. By starting on hearts you only succeed if the
hearts behave.

The entire deal is:

NORTH
♠ A Q 10
♡ A K 7
◇ J 10 8 7 2
♣ K J

WEST
♠ 6 3 2
♡ 5 4
◇ Q 5 4 3
♣ 10 9 8 7

EAST
♠ 8 5 4
♡ Q 3 2
◇ K 6
♣ 6 5 4 3 2

SOUTH
♠ K J 9 7
♡ J 10 9 8 6
◇ A 9
♣ A Q

## AN UNUSUAL CURE FOR HEART ATTACK

NORTH
♠ 9 7
♡ Q 6
◇ A J 9 6 2
♣ 9 6 3 2

SOUTH
♠ A K Q 5 2
♡ 10
◇ K Q 10
♣ A Q 8 5

*West dealer. Both vulnerable*

*The bidding:*

| WEST | NORTH | EAST | SOUTH |
|------|-------|------|-------|
| Pass | Pass | Pass | 1 ♠ |
| Pass | 1 NT | Pass | 3 ♣ |
| Pass | 4 ♣ | Pass | 4 ♠ |
| Pass | Pass | Pass | |

*Opening lead:* Heart nine

You open fourth hand and eventually become declarer at four spades. The heart nine is led, and East wins the jack and returns the king. At this point you pause to take stock. It appears that East has the A K J of hearts, and as he did not open in third position, he is unlikely to hold the club king. How can you make this contract with a normal 4–2 trump break and the club king in the West hand?

*Answer:* It looks as though it should be a cinch to take four spades, five diamonds, and one club for a total of ten tricks. But there is a serious danger of losing control here. Assume the opponents' cards are divided something like this:

NORTH
♠ 9 7
♡ Q 6
♢ A J 9 6 2
♣ 9 6 3 2

WEST
♠ 8 3
♡ 9 8 7 5 4
♢ 5 4 3
♣ K J 7

EAST
♠ J 10 6 4
♡ A K J 3 2
♢ 8 7
♣ 10 4

SOUTH
♠ A K Q 5 2
♡ 10
♢ K Q 10
♣ A Q 8 5

Suppose you ruff the heart king, cash the A K Q of trumps, and start on diamonds. East ruffs the third round, cutting you off from dummy, and you must lose at least two more tricks for down one.

Now suppose you *don't* ruff the heart king but discard a club instead. East shifts to a club and you must lose at least one club and one spade in addition to the two hearts already lost. Down one again!

The solution is to ruff the heart king and lead a *small* trump from your hand. East wins but can't attack hearts, because there is still a trump in dummy. Suppose he returns a club. You take the ace, cash the A K Q of spades, and run all the diamonds for an easy ten tricks.

## QUICK THINKING

NORTH
♠ K Q 5
♡ J 9 6 5 2
◇ A 8 3
♣ Q J

SOUTH
♠ A 10 6 4 3 2
♡ K 3
◇ —
♣ A K 7 5 3

*East dealer. Both vulnerable*

*The bidding:*

| EAST | SOUTH | WEST | NORTH |
|------|-------|------|-------|
| 1 ♡ | 1 ♠ | Pass | 3 ♠ |
| Pass | 6 ♠ | Pass | Pass |
| Pass | | | |

*Opening lead:* Heart four

East opens the bidding with one heart, and you make a conservative overcall of one spade. When partner jumps to three spades, you become bullish and try six. This ends the auction, and West leads the four of hearts.

What are your plans for the hand?

*Answer:* If you think to yourself, "There is no rush to make any plans until I see what happens at trick one," you are a dead duck.

You know West's four of hearts is a singleton. East is going to play the ace on this trick, and when you follow with the three, East will also know the four is a singleton. He will return a heart, West will ruff your king, and it will be too late to make any plans, because you are down already.

Here is the complete hand:

<pre>
                        NORTH
                     ♠ K Q 5
                     ♡ J 9 6 5 2
                     ◊ A 8 3
                     ♣ Q J

      WEST                              EAST
   ♠ 9 8                             ♠ J 7
   ♡ 4                               ♡ A Q 10 8 7
   ◊ 10 9 7 5 4 2                    ◊ K Q J 6
   ♣ 9 6 4 2                         ♣ 10 8

                        SOUTH
                     ♠ A 10 6 4 3 2
                     ♡ K 3
                     ◊ —
                     ♣ A K 7 5 3
</pre>

You can probably avert this disaster if you think the situation out before playing from dummy to the first trick. Now when East plays his heart ace, you will smoothly drop the king. East will almost surely assume his partner started with the doubleton ♡ 4 3. Rather than establish dummy's heart jack he will probably shift to the diamond king. Off goes the heart three on dummy's ace of diamonds, and you have stolen the slam.

## AN HONOR WITHOUT PROFIT

NORTH
♠ A
♡ A K 7
◇ A K Q J 10 9 3
♣ A 2

SOUTH
♠ K Q J 10 4 3
♡ J 10 9
◇ 7 2
♣ Q J

*South dealer. Neither vulnerable*

*The bidding:*

| SOUTH | WEST | NORTH | EAST |
|-------|------|-------|------|
| 3 ♠ | Pass | 4 NT | Pass |
| 5 ♣ | Pass | 5 NT | Pass |
| 6 ◇ | Pass | Pass | Pass |

*Opening lead:* Spade nine

You open the bidding with three spades and are somewhat surprised to find yourself declarer at six diamonds. The spade ace wins the first trick, and you pause to take stock. Dummy has a heart loser and a club loser, which could be thrown on your good spades if there were any way to get into the South hand. The first thought that occurs to you is that one opponent may have a singleton eight of diamonds, in which case the diamond seven will be an entry. There doesn't seem to be any harm in testing this, so you lead the ace of diamonds, and West discards a club. How do you continue in order to ensure twelve tricks?

*Answer:* The only foolproof way to make the contract is to cash two more high diamonds and then play the diamond three. East must win, and whatever he returns will automatically create an entry to the South hand.

You have heard of prophets without honor in their own land. For a while this looked like a case of honors without profit in your own hand.

## MORTON'S FORK

NORTH
♠ A Q 8 7
♡ 5 4
◇ Q 3 2
♣ A 9 7 3

WEST
♠ 2
♡ K 10 9 8 3
◇ A J 8
♣ K Q 10 2

EAST
♠ —
♡ Q 7 6
◇ 10 9 6 5 4
♣ J 8 6 5 4

SOUTH
♠ K J 10 9 6 5 4 3
♡ A J 2
◇ K 7
♣ —

*West dealer. Both vulnerable*

*The bidding:*

| WEST | NORTH | EAST | SOUTH |
|------|-------|------|-------|
| 1 ♡ | Double | 2 ♡ | 6 ♠ |
| Pass | Pass | Pass | |

*Opening lead:* Club king

West opens one heart, partner doubles for take-out, and East raises to two hearts. Thoughts of a grand slam flit through your head, but you eventually decide that it is virtually impossible to conduct the necessary investigation and you settle for a modest six spades.

West leads the club king, and when dummy appears you find that even six spades requires a little care. How do you play to be sure of making the contract regardless of how the opponents defend?

*Answer:* There is no rush to take a discard on the club ace, so ruff the opening lead in your hand and draw the outstanding trump.

Now lead the seven of diamonds from your hand toward dummy. If West rises with his ace, you will eventually discard one heart on the club ace and another on the diamond queen to make the slam. If West ducks, you win with the diamond queen in dummy and discard the diamond king on the club ace, avoiding a diamond loser. You now give up one heart trick and again make your slam.

Notice that the time was not ripe for a discard on the club ace at trick one. In fact, if you win the first trick with the club ace, you can't make the hand against proper defense.

The term "Morton's fork coup" has recently been applied to declarer's play on this type of hand. Archbishop Morton, Chancellor under Henry VII, was famous for his method of extracting "contributions" to the king's purse. A person who lived extravagantly was forced to make a large contribution, because it was obvious that he could afford it. Someone who lived modestly was forced to make a large contribution because it was clear that he must have saved a lot of money on living expenses. Which ever way he turned he was said to be "caught on Morton's fork."

On this hand East-West appear to have two defensive tricks—the diamond ace and one heart. But when South leads that low diamond, West is in a dilemma. If he plays his ace, he loses a trick. And if he doesn't play his ace, he loses a trick. Whichever way he turns he is caught on Morton's fork.

## QUICK, WATSON, THE SCISSORS!

NORTH
♠ 6 3
♡ A Q 5 4
◇ Q 7 6
♣ A K J 10

SOUTH
♠ 8
♡ 7
◇ K J 10 9 4 3 2
♣ 6 5 4 2

*West dealer. Neither vulnerable*

*The bidding:*

| WEST | NORTH | EAST | SOUTH |
|------|-------|------|-------|
| 1 ♠ | Double | 4 ♠ | 5 ◇ |
| Pass | Pass | Pass | |

*Opening lead:* Club queen

West opens one spade, your partner doubles, and East bids four spades. You try five diamonds, which becomes the final contract. West leads the club queen, which you win in dummy as East follows suit. What do you do now, and why?

*Answer:* That club queen looks ominous. Why didn't West lead a spade? It looks as though the scoundrel has a singleton club. When he gets in with the trump ace, he plans to put East in with a spade in order to ruff a club, and that will be the end of a perfectly good contract!

Forewarned is forearmed, however, and now that you suspect what West is up to, the problem is how to cut the enemy's communications.

At trick two, lead the heart ace from dummy and follow with the heart queen. If East covers with the king, of course, you have to ruff and start on trumps. But if West has the heart king as you hope, throw your singleton spade on the heart queen, deliberately giving the enemy a heart trick instead of a spade trick. The only difference is that East can never get the lead to give his partner the fatal club ruff, and you make five diamonds.

Here's the complete hand:

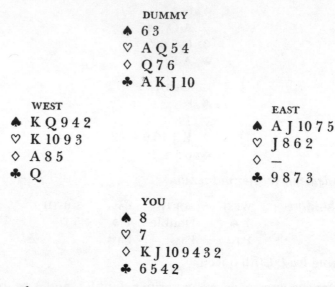

DUMMY
♠ 6 3
♡ A Q 5 4
◊ Q 7 6
♣ A K J 10

WEST
♠ K Q 9 4 2
♡ K 10 9 3
◊ A 8 5
♣ Q

EAST
♠ A J 10 7 5
♡ J 8 6 2
◊ —
♣ 9 8 7 3

YOU
♠ 8
♡ 7
◊ K J 10 9 4 3 2
♣ 6 5 4 2

Cutting the opponents' communications like this was originally called by Culbertson "the coup without a name." Today it is known by the more appropriate title of the "scissors coup."

## A SUSPICIOUS CASE OF INDIGESTION

NORTH
♠ Q 6
♡ 6 5 4 2
◇ A K Q 5 2
♣ 8 3

SOUTH
♠ A J 10 9
♡ A 3
◇ 9 8 7 6
♣ A K 7

*South dealer. Both vulnerable*

*The bidding:*

| SOUTH | WEST | NORTH | EAST |
|-------|------|-------|------|
| 1 NT | Pass | 3 NT | Pass |
| Pass | Pass | | |

*Opening lead:* Heart queen

West leads the heart queen against your contract of three no-trump. East plays the king, and you let him hold the first trick. East returns the heart eight to your ace as West follows with the seven. You now cash the ace and king of diamonds. Both opponents follow the first round, but West discards a spade on the second round, revealing that East started with J 10 3 of diamonds.

All right. Your problem is to be sure of taking nine tricks regardless of how the rest of the cards are divided or how the opponents defend.

Warning! This is not a misprint. If you don't see the problem, look again. On this hand most players don't see the problem until it is too late.

*Answer:* When the diamonds break 3–1, most players breezily assume they have nine cold tricks: five diamonds, one spade, one heart, and two clubs. So they cash the A K Q of diamonds and then the awful truth hits them. The fourth round of diamonds has to be won in declarer's hand, and there is no way to return to dummy to cash the fifth diamond.

Here's the complete hand :

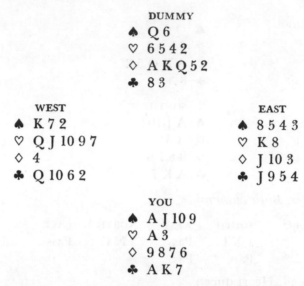

DUMMY
♠ Q 6
♡ 6 5 4 2
♢ A K Q 5 2
♣ 8 3

WEST
♠ K 7 2
♡ Q J 10 9 7
♢ 4
♣ Q 10 6 2

EAST
♠ 8 5 4 3
♡ K 8
♢ J 10 3
♣ J 9 5 4

YOU
♠ A J 10 9
♡ A 3
♢ 9 8 7 6
♣ A K 7

The diamond suit contains what is called an internal block. Although you have five diamond tricks, you can't cash them.

If you cashed the A K Q of diamonds after winning the heart ace, you can no longer make three no-trump. Whatever you do, West will eventually get in with his spade king and defeat you with three more heart tricks.

What can be done about this diamond block? You instinctively realize that your fourth diamond is a terrible nuisance to you. If you could tear it up into little pieces and throw it away you could happily run five diamond tricks and make the contract. Unfortunately, the opponents might object to this maneuver.

There's a story of a player in a somewhat similar position who actually ate a card that was in his way. He slipped it inside his ham sandwich when no one was looking. This solution is a bit drastic. In the first place it's unethical. In the second place you probably wouldn't get away with it. And in the third place it would surely lead to indigestion.

Fortunately there is an easier solution. After cashing the ace and king of diamonds and discovering the 3–1 break, lead a heart from dummy and throw one of your two remaining diamonds on it. West can't have enough hearts left to set you, and when you regain the lead, the diamond suit will no longer be blocked, so you will peacefully run nine tricks.

## THE CASE OF THE QUEEN THAT WASN'T MISSING

NORTH
♠ K 4 2
♡ A K J 10
◇ 3 2
♣ K 8 7 4

WEST
♠ 6
♡ 9 5 3 2
◇ Q J 10 9 4
♣ Q 3 2

EAST
♠ Q J 10
♡ 8 7
◇ K 8 7 6
♣ J 10 9 5

SOUTH
♠ A 9 8 7 5 3
♡ Q 6 4
◇ A 5
♣ A 6

*North dealer. Both vulnerable*

*The bidding:*

| NORTH | EAST | SOUTH | WEST |
|-------|------|-------|------|
| 1 ♡ | Pass | 1 ♠ | Pass |
| 2 ♠ | Pass | 6 ♠ | Pass |
| Pass | Pass | | |

*Opening lead:* Diamond queen

You win the opening lead with the diamond ace and naturally lead trumps immediately. If the spades break 2–2, you will be able to throw the losing diamond on the fourth heart and make all thirteen tricks. Unfortunately West shows out on the second round of trumps. Now your natural inclination is to lead three rounds of hearts, winding up in the dummy. If East has to follow three times you can still throw the losing diamond on the fourth heart and make twelve tricks. As the cards lie, however, East will ruff the third heart and cash his diamond king for down one. Can you see any chance to steal this slam with the cards divided as they are in the diagram?

*Answer:* There is a deceptive maneuver available here that may cause East to go wrong. After playing the two high spades don't cash three rounds of hearts, ending up in dummy. Instead lead the ace and king of hearts, concealing the queen. Now lead the heart jack from dummy as though you were trying to ruff out the queen. From East's point of view the situation could be something like this:

NORTH
♠ K 4 2
♡ A K J 10
◊ 3 2
♣ K 8 7 4

WEST
♠ 6
♡ Q 9 5 3 2
◊ Q J 10 9 4
♣ 3 2

EAST
♠ Q J 10
♡ 8 7
◊ K 8 7 6
♣ J 10 9 5

SOUTH
♠ A 9 8 7 5 3
♡ 6 4
◊ A 5
♣ A Q 6

He will be afraid to ruff your "losing heart," which would give you the contract if the cards actually were like this. Assuming his partner has the heart queen, East will probably discard instead, and your queen will win. Now back to dummy with the club king, and the losing diamond goes off on the fourth heart.

Note that against expert defense this maneuver won't work. West will expose your plot by playing high-low on the first two heart leads to indicate that he was dealt an even number of cards in the suit. East will now know that you were dealt an odd number of hearts, and he may smell a rat.

In practice many good players will neglect to echo with the West holding, and declarer can frequently steal the contract.

# THE DIAMONDS WERE INSURED

NORTH
♠ 8 6 4 2
♡ —
◇ K 9 7
♣ A K Q J 10 7

SOUTH
♠ A J 9
♡ J 10 3
◇ A Q 10 8 3
♣ 6 4

*South dealer. Both vulnerable*

*The bidding:*

| SOUTH | WEST | NORTH | EAST |
|-------|------|-------|------|
| 1 ◇ | Pass | 2 ♣ | Pass |
| 2 ◇ | Pass | 6 ◇ | Pass |
| Pass | Pass | | |

*Opening lead:* Heart king

North's bidding is not particularly scientific, but it is very effective. West leads the heart king, which you ruff in dummy with the trump seven. What do you do next?

*Answer:* With a normal 3–2 trump break it is easy to take all thirteen tricks (one heart ruff, five diamonds, six clubs, and the spade ace). But as long as you have only bid a small slam, you can afford to take out insurance against a 4–1 trump break. At trick two lead the nine of diamonds, planning to play the three from your hand if East follows small. This guarantees the contract any time the trumps are 4–1 or 3–2. Here is the complete hand:

NORTH
♠ 8 6 4 2
♡ —
◇ K 9 7
♣ A K Q J 10 7

WEST
♠ K 10 5 3
♡ K Q 9
◇ J 6 5 4
♣ 9 3

EAST
♠ Q 7
♡ A 8 7 6 5 4 2
◇ 2
♣ 8 5 2

SOUTH
♠ A J 9
♡ J 10 3
◇ A Q 10 8 3
♣ 6 4

West wins the second trick with the jack of diamonds. But the diamond king is still in dummy to deal with a heart return, and whatever West leads, you draw the remaining trumps and claim the balance.

If declarer does not make this safety play in diamonds, he will go down as the cards lie. Try it.

The occasional loss of a 20-point overtrick is a very tiny premium to pay to ensure a small slam.

## RESISTING TEMPTATION

NORTH
♠ A 8 6 5 2
♡ A 5
◇ Q 9
♣ A 8 3 2

SOUTH
♠ K Q 10 3
♡ 7 6
◇ J 10 8 7 5 3 2
♣ —

*West dealer. Both vulnerable*

*The bidding:*

| | WEST | NORTH | EAST | SOUTH |
|---|---|---|---|---|
| | 1 ♡ | Double | 2 ♡ | 3 ◇ |
| | 3 ♡ | Pass | Pass | 3 ♠ |
| | Pass | 4 ♠ | Pass | Pass |
| | Pass | | | |

*Opening lead:* Heart king

West deals and opens one heart, North doubles, East raises to two hearts, and you eventually become declarer at four spades. The lead is the heart king, which you win with dummy's ace. How do you plan the play from here?

*Answer:* You naturally intend to establish the diamond suit, and you should hope to lose only two diamonds and one heart. It is tempting to discard South's other heart on the ace of clubs. But those who succumb to this temptation will be defeated. Here is the complete deal:

NORTH
♠ A 8 6 5 2
♡ A 5
◇ Q 9
♣ A 8 3 2

WEST
♠ 9
♡ K Q 10 8 2
◇ A 6
♣ K J 9 7 4

EAST
♠ J 7 4
♡ J 9 4 3
◇ K 4
♣ Q 10 6 5

SOUTH
♠ K Q 10 3
♡ 7 6
◇ J 10 8 7 5 3 2
♣ —

Suppose you win the opening lead with the heart ace, cash the club ace, discarding the other heart, lead a trump to the king, and play a diamond to the queen. West wins with the king and returns a heart, forcing you to ruff with the spade three. You lead a second diamond to West's ace, and he returns a club, forcing you to ruff with the spade ten. Now the diamonds are established, but you have only the lone spade queen left, and East still has the J 7 of trumps. So you can never enjoy any of those good diamonds, and the contract must fail. The same thing happens whether you draw all the trumps or none of the trumps before starting on diamonds. You simply do not have enough spades in the South hand to draw three rounds of trumps and also ruff twice.

The solution is not to allow the opponents to force you to ruff twice. And the way to do this is to keep the club ace in dummy to protect yourself against one of the ruffs. When East takes his diamond king, he will cash one heart, and then the best he can do is return a club to dummy's ace. West wins the second diamond and forces you once with a club. You can afford one ruff, and the diamonds are now established, so you draw the remaining trumps, ending in your hand, and claim the balance.

It is true that leaving the club ace in dummy gives up the chance of an overtrick, which would materialize if the trumps were 2–2. But it is worth giving up a possible overtrick to keep yourself from losing control when the trumps are 3–1.

Take full credit if you resisted the temptation to discard a heart on dummy's club ace.

## THE CRYSTAL BALL

NORTH
♠ J
♡ Q 9
◇ K 8 3 2
♣ A Q 10 9 5 2

SOUTH
♠ A 9 6
♡ A K J 10 8
◇ 6 5
♣ J 8 7

*East dealer. Both vulnerable*

*The bidding:*

| EAST | SOUTH | WEST | NORTH |
|------|-------|------|-------|
| 1 ♠ | 2 ♡ | Pass | 4 ♡ |
| Pass | Pass | Pass | |

*Opening lead:* Spade two

North's jump is unusual with only two hearts, but the final contract is reasonable. West leads the spade two, and East covers dummy's jack with the king. How should South proceed?

*Answer:* The successful declarer must be good at looking into the future. Before playing from his hand to trick one, he tries to picture the entire sequence of plays. Suppose he wins the spade ace and ruffs a spade. There is not enough transportation to ruff the other spade, so he mentally draws the trumps and finesses the club. It doesn't take a crystal ball to predict that East will win the club king and return a spade to West's queen. Now a diamond lead through dummy's king defeats the contract. Here is a probable layout:

NORTH
♠ J
♡ Q 9
◇ K 8 3 2
♣ A Q 10 9 5 2

WEST
♠ Q 4 3 2
♡ 7 6 5 4
◇ 10 9 4
♣ 6 3

EAST
♠ K 10 8 7 5
♡ 3 2
◇ A Q J 7
♣ K 4

SOUTH
♠ A 9 6
♡ A K J 10 8
◇ 6 5
♣ J 8 7

A declarer who is in the habit of looking ahead like this will naturally try to prevent any such foreseeable disaster. On this hand it is easy to change the course of events simply by ducking the first trick. Now the contract can't be defeated with normal distribution. When the spade king holds, East will probably return a heart (but it doesn't matter what he does). Declarer draws trumps and finesses the club. East wins the king but can't get his partner in for a diamond lead, because South still has the spade ace. The defense can only make three tricks, and the contract is home.

## TRANSPORTATION TROUBLE

NORTH
♠ 9
♡ A J 9 6 5 4
◇ A K
♣ J 8 3 2

SOUTH
♠ A Q 3
♡ 2
◇ Q J 10 9 8 7
♣ Q 7 5

*North dealer. East-West vulnerable*

*The bidding:*

| NORTH | EAST | SOUTH | WEST |
|-------|------|-------|------|
| 1 ♡ | Pass | 2 ◇ | Pass |
| 2 ♡ | Pass | 2 NT | Pass |
| 3 ♣ | Pass | 3 NT | Pass |
| Pass | Pass | | |

*Opening lead:* Spade five

West leads the spade five against three no-trump, and East plays the king on dummy's nine. What's the most practical way to make this contract?

*Answer:* You actually have nine tricks—six diamonds, two spades, and the heart ace. The diamond suit is blocked, however, which makes the transportation very tricky. Suppose you win the first trick with the spade ace and cash the A K of diamonds. Now you have to get back to your hand, which is easier said than done. The opponents may realize by this time that you are planning to run the diamond suit, and once they put their minds to keeping you out of your hand, you're in trouble.

Here is the complete deal:

NORTH
♠ 9
♡ A J 9 6 5 4
◇ A K
♣ J 8 3 2

WEST
♠ J 8 7 5 2
♡ K Q 10 8
◇ 4 2
♣ A 9

EAST
♠ K 10 6 4
♡ 7 3
◇ 6 5 3
♣ K 10 6 4

SOUTH
♠ A Q 3
♡ 2
◇ Q J 10 9 8 7
♣ Q 7 5

There is a very practical solution to this transportation problem: Let East hold the first trick with the spade king. He will almost certainly return a second spade, and now you can discard the A K of diamonds on the A Q of spades. With the diamond suit unblocked you run nine tricks with ease.

## WITH THE DOWN SIDE UP

NORTH
♠ Q 6 4 2
♡ Q J 10
◇ K Q 5
♣ A Q 2

SOUTH
♠ 5
♡ A K 9 5 3
◇ A J 10 3 2
♣ J 4

*North dealer. Neither vulnerable*

*The bidding:*

| NORTH | EAST | SOUTH | WEST |
|-------|------|-------|------|
| 1 NT  | Pass | 3 ♡   | Pass |
| 4 ♡   | Pass | 6 ♡   | Pass |
| Pass  | Pass |       |      |

*Opening lead:* Spade jack

Against six hearts West leads the spade jack, and when this holds the trick, he continues with the ten, which you ruff. (East contributes the seven, then the three.) What is your plan for the hand?

*Answer:* The most obvious plan is to draw the trumps, cash the diamonds, and try the club finesse. This method will succeed about 50 percent of the time.

A better plan, however, is to aim for a dummy reversal. After ruffing the second spade, cash the queen and jack of hearts. If everyone follows you ruff a third spade with the heart ace, return to dummy with the diamond king, and ruff the last spade with the heart king. Now go over to the club ace and draw the one outstanding trump with dummy's heart ten. As you have no more hearts in your hand, you shed a club on this trick and claim the balance.

Of course, if one opponent fails to follow to the second round of trumps you have to abandon the dummy reversal idea, because dummy's trumps are not long enough to handle a 4–1 break. In this case you revert to the obvious method of drawing all the trumps, and you sink or swim with the club finesse.

Here is the complete deal:

NORTH
♠ Q 6 4 2
♡ Q J 10
◇ K Q 5
♣ A Q 2

WEST
♠ J 10 9 8
♡ 8 7 4
◇ 8 4
♣ 9 7 6 5

EAST
♠ A K 7 3
♡ 6 2
◇ 9 7 6
♣ K 10 8 3

SOUTH
♠ 5
♡ A K 9 5 3
◇ A J 10 3 2
♣ J 4

A dummy reversal (see Chapter 7) often seems like an upside-down way to play a hand. But it is clearly the superior plan here, because it eliminates the risk of the club finesse.

## THE GENTLEMAN FROM VIENNA

NORTH
♠ 6 2
♡ A Q 9 8
◇ A Q 9
♣ 10 9 8 7

SOUTH
♠ A K J 8 7 5 3
♡ 2
◇ J 2
♣ 6 5 4

*West dealer. Both vulnerable*

*The bidding:*

| WEST | NORTH | EAST | SOUTH |
|------|-------|------|-------|
| Pass | 1 ♣ | Pass | 1 ♠ |
| Pass | 1 NT | Pass | 4 ♠ |
| Pass | Pass | Pass | |

*Opening lead:* Club king

West deals and passes, North opens one club, and you eventually become declarer at four spades. West cashes the A K Q of clubs and continues with the club jack, which you ruff.

(East, who had two clubs originally, discards the five and three of hearts on the third and fourth club.) At trick five you lay down the spade ace and are pleasantly surprised when East follows suit with the queen. The question is what do you play next?

*Answer:* Those who decide to cash a second high trump next may go to the back of the class.

Those who elected to take a heart or a diamond finesse next may be seated just behind those who cashed the second high trump.

Go to the head of the class if you lead the two of diamonds to the ace. Here is the entire hand:

NORTH
♠ 6 2
♡ A Q 9 8
◊ A Q 9
♣ 10 9 8 7

WEST
♠ Q
♡ 7 6 4
◊ 8 7 6 4 3
♣ A K Q J

EAST
♠ 10 9 4
♡ K J 10 5 3
◊ K 10 5
♣ 3 2

SOUTH
♠ A K J 8 7 5 3
♡ 2
◊ J 2
♣ 6 5 4

Declarer knows from the bidding that East has both red kings. (West has already shown up with the A K Q J of clubs and the spade queen. He would have opened the bidding with even a button to spare.)

This means that any heart or diamond finesse is doomed to fail. It also means that a squeeze against East is bound to succeed, provided declarer doesn't block himself.

After cashing the diamond ace, return to your hand with dummy's second spade and run the trumps. With only three cards left the position will be:

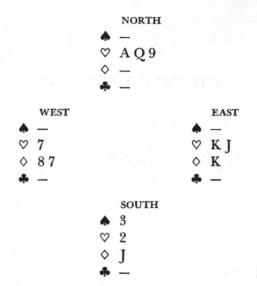

NORTH
♠ —
♡ A Q 9
◇ —
♣ —

WEST
♠ —
♡ 7
◇ 8 7
♣ —

EAST
♠ —
♡ K J
◇ K
♣ —

SOUTH
♠ 3
♡ 2
◇ J
♣ —

When the final spade is cashed, East is squeezed, and declarer makes the last two tricks without a finesse.

Notice that this three-card ending (with the lead in the South hand) can never be reached if declarer forgets to unblock the diamond ace before dummy's last trump has disappeared.

This play was credited over one hundred years ago to the best whist player in Vienna, and it has been known ever since as the Vienna coup.

## THE DEVIL'S BEDPOSTS

NORTH
♠ A 3
♡ A 7 6 3 2
◇ A K Q 8
♣ 3 2

WEST
♠ 10 6
♡ 4
◇ J 9 6 5
♣ K J 9 8 6 5

EAST
♠ K Q 9 8 7 4 2
♡ —
◇ 10 3 2
♣ Q 10 7

SOUTH
♠ J 5
♡ K Q J 10 9 8 5
◇ 7 4
♣ A 4

*East dealer. Both vulnerable*

*The bidding:*

| EAST | SOUTH | WEST | NORTH |
|------|-------|------|-------|
| 3 ♠ | 4 ♡ | Pass | 7 ♡ |
| Pass | Pass | Pass | |

*Opening lead:* Spade ten

You become declarer at a grand slam in hearts after East has opened the bidding with three spades. There are only twelve tricks in view, but if you read Chapter 8 you should expect to make the contract with ease. The question this time is which card do you expect will win the last trick?

*Answer:* If you play your cards in the correct order, you should expect to win the last trick with the four of clubs.

Win the spade ace in dummy and cash all seven hearts, throwing a spade and a club from dummy. West must save his diamond stopper, so he has to discard five clubs. Now take the diamond honors, and just before the queen is cashed the situation becomes:

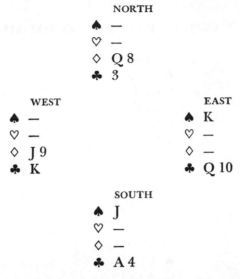

NORTH
♠ —
♡ —
◇ Q 8
♣ 3

WEST
♠ —
♡ —
◇ J 9
♣ K

EAST
♠ K
♡ —
◇ —
♣ Q 10

SOUTH
♠ J
♡ —
◇ —
♣ A 4

When you lead the diamond queen, East must keep the spade king, so he throws a club. You discard your spade and win the last two tricks with the ace and four of clubs.

As you expected, this hand turned out to be a double squeeze. West had to protect diamonds, East had to protect spades, and there was no one left to protect clubs.

The clue in the title probably didn't help many readers. Devil's Bedposts is an old English term for the four of clubs.

## YOU CAN'T GET THERE FROM HERE

NORTH
♠ A 7 5 4 3 2
♡ K 4 3 2
◇ A 6 4
♣ —

WEST
♠ Q 9 6
♡ 6
◇ 5
♣ J 10 8 6 5 4 3 2

EAST
♠ K J 10
♡ —
◇ K Q J 10 9
♣ A K Q 9 7

SOUTH
♠ 8
♡ A Q J 10 9 8 7 5
◇ 8 7 3 2
♣ —

*East dealer. East-West vulnerable*

*The bidding:*

| EAST | SOUTH | WEST | NORTH |
|------|-------|------|-------|
| 1 ◇ | 4 ♡ | Pass | 6 ♡ |
| Pass | Pass | Pass | |

*Opening lead:* Diamond five

Everyone chuckles at the story of the motorist who stops to ask directions from a local farmer. After scratching his head for a while the farmer comes up with that marvelous reply, "You can't get there from here."

Study declarer's predicament in six hearts after West leads the diamond five. You are likely to have quite a bit of sympathy for the farmer's point of view. How can the contract be made as the cards lie?

*Answer:* The diamond lead is obviously a singleton, and the only real hope is to find the spades divided 3–3. But the entry problem is a dilly. Suppose you win the first trick with the diamond ace, cash the spade ace, ruff a spade, return to the heart king, and ruff another spade. Dummy's spades are all good at this point but there is no way to get back there to use them, and declarer must lose two diamonds for down one.

The solution is to win the first trick with the diamond ace, cash the spade ace, and ruff a spade. Now lead the five of hearts, and when West plays the six let him hold the trick! West can't return a diamond, and if he leads a spade, you ruff, establishing the suit. Now the heart king is an entry to the good spades. And if West returns a club, you trump in dummy, establish the spades with one more ruff, and again return to the heart king to cash the good spades.

## DISTRACTED BY A QUEEN

NORTH
♠ 7 6 5 2
♡ K 7 5 3
◇ 7 6
♣ K J 4

SOUTH
♠ A K 3
♡ A 6
◇ 5 2
♣ A 10 9 8 6 5

*East dealer. North-South vulnerable*

*The bidding:*

| EAST | SOUTH | WEST | NORTH |
|------|-------|------|-------|
| 3 ◇ | 4 ♣ | Pass | 5 ♣ |
| Pass | Pass | Pass | |

*Opening lead:* Diamond three

You become declarer at five clubs after East has opened the bidding with a pre-empt of three diamonds. The diamond three is led, and East wins with the ace and returns the queen. West overtakes the queen with the king and exits with the spade queen, which you take with the ace. After analyzing the whole hand carefully, you naturally attack the trump suit first. How?

*Answer:* The real problem here is to avoid a spade loser. This can only be done if one opponent has at least five hearts and at least four spades. East does not have room for nine cards in the majors, as he is already marked with six diamonds. So you have to hope that West has five hearts and four spades. From the lead it is clear that West started with three diamonds. If he has nine or more cards in the majors, he can have at most one club. The situation to hope for is something like this:

NORTH
♠ 7 6 5 2
♡ K 7 5 3
♢ 7 6
♣ K J 4

WEST
♠ Q J 9 8
♡ Q J 8 4 2
♢ K 8 3
♣ 2

EAST
♠ 10 4
♡ 10 9
♢ A Q J 10 9 4
♣ Q 7 3

SOUTH
♠ A K 3
♡ A 6
♢ 5 2
♣ A 10 9 8 6 5

At trick four lead a club to the king. Return the jack, and if the queen does not appear, play low from your hand. Now run the trumps. With only one club left, the position will be:

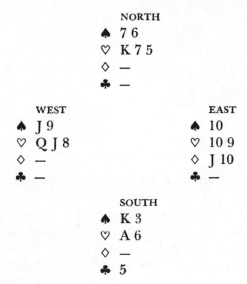

NORTH
♠ 7 6
♡ K 7 5
♢ —
♣ —

WEST
♠ J 9
♡ Q J 8
♢ —
♣ —

EAST
♠ 10
♡ 10 9
♢ J 10
♣ —

SOUTH
♠ K 3
♡ A 6
♢ —
♣ 5

When you lead the last trump, West is squeezed, and the remaining tricks are yours.

Most players are distracted here by the problem of looking for the club queen. Thoughts pop into their heads such as "Shall I play the trumps to be 2–2 (eight ever, nine never)?" or "East has six diamonds. Isn't he likely to be short in clubs?" All this conjecture is useless, because it does no good to find the club queen and then lose a spade trick. Once you realize that West has to have five hearts and four spades to make the hand, you have no choice but to play East for the club length.